Night Comes

Night Comes

Death, Imagination, and the Last Things

Dale C. Allison Jr.

William B. Eerdmans Publishing Company
Grand Rapids, Michigan / Cambridge, U.K.

Published 2016 by
WM. B. EERDMANS PUBLISHING CO.
2140 Oak Industrial Drive N.E., Grand Rapids, Michigan 49505 /
P.O. Box 163, Cambridge CB3 9PU U.K.

Printed in the United States of America

22 21 20 19 18 17 16   7 6 5 4 3 2 1

Library of Congress Cataloging-in-Publication Data

Names: Allison, Dale C., Jr., 1955- author.
Title: Night comes : death, imagination, and the last things / Dale C. Allison Jr.
Description: Grand Rapids, Michigan : Eerdmans Publishing Company, 2016. |
          Includes bibliographical references.
Identifiers: LCCN 2015046672 | ISBN 9780802871183 (pbk. : alk. paper)
Subjects: LCSH: Eschatology.
Classification: LCC BT823 .A45 2016 | DDC 236 — dc23
LC record available at http://lccn.loc.gov/2015046672

www.eerdmans.com

For Bill Vineyard

A brother is born to share adversity.

Proverbs 17:17

Contents

Preface

THE FOLLOWING CHAPTERS served as the basis for the Stone Lectures, given at Princeton Theological Seminary in October of 2014. When, two years earlier, I received and accepted the invitation to deliver those lectures, I was teaching at Pittsburgh Theological Seminary. By the time I gave them, I was on the faculty at Princeton. So one important goal of the lecture series—to bring an outsider to campus—was thwarted. Whether the other goals were met isn't mine to say. I can, however, attest to having had a most enjoyable time, for which I thank especially President Craig Barnes, Dean Jim Kay, Clifton Black, Dennis Olson, Leong Seow, and all those who attended the lectures.

Eschatological subjects have long fascinated me. My honors thesis in college was on the eschatology of Jesus. It grew into my M.A. thesis, which grew into my Ph.D. thesis, which grew into my first book. And that wasn't the end of it. I've continued throughout my academic career to write about eschatological subjects. This book, however, is different. It doesn't consistently aspire, as have most of my previous books and articles, to persuade through the arguments of an evenhanded historian. It's rather, in large measure, a personal theological exploration. It's an attempt to move from reconstructing the past to pondering the future.

The following pages—which retain the informal style of the original lectures—are, I should emphasize, severely circumscribed. *Night Comes* is a miscellany, a book of thoughts. It's partial and incomplete at every turn. My purpose isn't to offer a full or balanced treatment of any topic but rather to share some scattered observations and suggestions on subjects that continue to absorb and vex me.

In addition to the discussions that followed each Stone lecture, I've profited immensely from the comments of those who've read all or a part of the manuscript—my children, Emily, Andrew, and John; my ever-supportive wife, Kristine, who persuaded me that I needed to add the chapter on heaven; my former administrative assistant at Pittsburgh Seminary, Kathy Anderson, whose help with a million things I much miss; my former colleagues at Pittsburgh, John Burgess and Ron Tappy, with whom I've had several quite rewarding and very enjoyable discussions about the last things; Ph.D. students Joel Estes, Tucker Ferda, and Nathan Johnson; my longtime friend, theologian Chris Kettler; and fellow New Testament scholars Joel Marcus and Michael Thate. Above all, however, I wish to thank Bob Harrington, with whom I've discussed just about everything under the sun since the 1960s. Even though he'll disagree with all of my religious premises as well as with all of my theological proposals, his observations and critical questions over the years inform this book from beginning to end.

Finally, I dedicate this book to Bill Vineyard, whose faithful friendship, help in hard times past, passion for Kierkegaard, and work for the down and out mean so much to me.

CHAPTER 1

Death and Fear

···

Death is the most fearful thing of all.

ARISTOTLE

The weariest and most loathed worldly life,
That age, ache, penury and imprisonment
Can lay on nature, is a paradise,
To what we fear of death.

CLAUDIO, IN *MEASURE FOR MEASURE*

I do not understand those men who tell me that the prospect
of the yonder side of death has never tormented them, that the
thought of their own annihilation never disquiets them.

MARTIN GARDNER

···

WHEN MY DAUGHTER was seventeen, she asked me one evening, "Dad, what do Jews believe about hell?"

I said: "Well, Emily, in one rabbinic text, some are thrown into the fire of Gehenna, suffer for twelve months, and then cease to be; but the worst of the wicked are there for eternity."

Emily was aghast: "That's hideous, Dad."

I agreed: "How could God let anyone suffer without end?"

To which she responded: "No, the other one. How dreadful not to exist." For my teenage daughter, suffering forever seemed preferable to perishing utterly.

Not everyone feels the same way. On the day that he graduated from college, my younger son told me that lately he'd been thinking about death, and that what bothered him most wasn't going out of existence but rather the everlasting loss of his most cherished memories. I asked him to distill his thoughts in an email. He sent me this:

> I am not first and foremost afraid of this ego or self being extinguished when my body wears out. . . . No, what saddens and terrifies me is that my experiences and memories—the things that I learned, felt, valued, sensed, and loved—will not be remembered after I die. For example, one of my dearest memories is of me lying on a hilltop one summer night as I watched a heat lightning storm play across a star-filled sky, and a beautiful girl slept upon my shoulder. . . . Truly frightening is the prospect that no one at all will remember this, that it will be lost, never to be appreciated ever again by me or anyone else after I'm dead. It is not my death as a self, then, that chiefly frightens me, but that . . . no one will be able to know what I've known, feel what I've felt, and love what I've loved.

For my son, personal extinction generated anxiety not because his ego might be erased but because his memories might be expunged. The museum of his mind will be closed: no more visitors.

There are additional reasons, of course, why one might shrink from death.[1] One is the doctrine of hell. Matthew 10:28 admonishes: "Do not fear those who kill the body but cannot kill the soul; rather fear him who can destroy both soul and body in Gehenna." What if one sincerely fears the possibility of post-mortem punishment? I can't illustrate the circumstance by quoting one of my children, because my wife and I didn't teach them to fear hell. We didn't believe that such would dissuade them from vice or move them to virtue. Historically, however, some have indeed dreaded death because they've dreaded hell. John Bunyan was, at one point in his life, tormented by the possibility that he'd blasphemed against the Holy Spirit, a sin which would, he supposed, put him forever beyond forgiveness. He confessed:

> Then would I be with a very great trembling, insomuch that sometimes I could, for whole days together, feel my very body, as well as my mind, to shake and totter under the sense of the dreadful judgment of God, that should fall on those that have sinned that most fearful and unpardonable sin. I felt also such a clogging and heat at my stomach, by reason of this my terror, that I was, especially at sometimes, as if my breast-bone would split in sunder; then I thought . . . of Judas, "who by his falling headlong burst asunder, and all his bowels gushed out."[2]

These words are, admittedly, extreme; yet our religion has often augmented our instinctive fear of death. What do you suppose was the effect of singing a hymn with the following lines?

> There is a dreadful hell,
> And everlasting pains:
> There sinners must with devils dwell
> In darkness, fire, and chains.

> Can such a wretch as I
> Escape this cursed end?
> And may I hope, whene'er I die,
> I shall to heav'n ascend?

> Then will I read and pray,
> While I have life and breath;
> Lest I should be cut off to-day,
> And sent t'eternal death.

Isaac Watts penned these words. They appear, not in the current Presbyterian Hymnal, but in *Divine Songs, attempted in Easy Language, for the Use of Children*. Published in 1715, this was evidently the first hymnal written for youngsters. It's gone through hundreds of editions and been in print ever since, and I read somewhere that it was the best-selling children's book of all time until the twentieth century, when *The Cat in the Hat* or some such overtook it.

....

Of course it's untrue that nobody wants to die. Death can be a consummation devoutly to be wished, as those who've spent time in a nursing home well know. Ecclesiastes recognizes that the days of trouble come and the years draw near when we say, "I have no pleasure in them." Nevertheless, for most of us most of the time, breathing our last is an odious prospect. Plutarch wrote: "All men and all women are ready to match their teeth against the fangs of Cerberus . . . if only they may still continue to be and not be blotted out."[3]

But, one might ask, doesn't religion make a difference here? Doesn't faith help us fret less about mortality? I wonder.

When pondering death, I sometimes think about the *Testament of Abraham*, a Jewish pseudepigraphon written perhaps in the time of Jesus. It's a transparently fictional and comedic account of the final days of the great patriarch. As the book opens, Abraham is 995 years of age. That beats Methuselah, who made it only to 969. So God, deciding that Abraham's time is up, sends the archangel Michael to convey the bad news. But Abraham, although full of years, and although the paragon of obedience in the Bible, tells Michael to get lost: "I know that you are the angel of the Lord, and that you were sent to take my soul. Yet I will not follow you."

Michael accordingly ascends to heaven to inform the Lord of what has happened. God promptly composes a speech for the angel to recite to Abraham, a speech designed to make the old man see reason. Among its words are these: "Do you not know that all from Adam and Eve have died? Not even kings are immortal. Not one of the forefathers has escaped the treasury of death. All have died, all have been taken down to Hades, and all have been gathered by the sickle of death."

After Michael delivers God's eloquent oration, Abraham strikes a bargain: "Lord, hear my prayer. While I am yet in this body I wish to see all the inhabited earth and all the things made . . . and after I have seen these things, then I shall not grieve when I depart from this life." So the archangel unparks the chariot of the cherubim and takes Abraham on a sightseeing tour of everything, including the judgment of saints and sinners in the afterlife. Yet after beholding all this, after getting exactly what he's asked for, the old man reneges: "I will not follow you."

At this point, God has no choice. Having played nice with Abraham by sending to him the forbearing Michael, God now summons the savage angel of Death. That being's appearance is so hideous, and his stench so horrific, that Abraham faints when they meet. Even so, the saint somehow revives and continues struggling to push away the inevitable. Finally, Death holds out his right hand, promising the exhausted man that, if only he kiss it, cheerfulness, life, and strength will return. But it's a trick. When his lips touch Death's hand, Abraham's soul gets stuck, and Death yanks it out. The end.

The moral of the story? Even someone who lived to be a thousand wouldn't want to die; and even a saint who, like the great Abraham, otherwise obeyed God to a tee, would, if possible, disobey the order to depart. The patriarch, who obediently took a knife to kill his only son, was unwilling to lay down his own life. Long before Ernest Becker's *The Denial of Death* (1973), and long before anyone had heard of "terror management theory," the author of the *Testament of Abraham* knew that we all run away from the inevitable, and that, on this score, religion doesn't make much difference.

....

Why does the apprehension of death so trouble us, faith or no faith? The obvious answer is: genetic programming. Our recoil is a biological reflex, bestowed by an evolutionary process that instills the instinct to survive. In this we're like all the other animals. Even the spider is afraid of death, or at least is designed to flee it, as you witness when you try to squash one and miss: it vanishes in an instant.

The spider's genetically encrypted behavior, its frantic impulse to escape death, is also encoded in us. Here there are no lines between species. When an untimely end approaches, all healthy members of the animal kingdom scurry in the opposite direction.

Human beings alone, however, verbalize their fear of death; and it's intriguing that, when we do this, we don't often say, "It's my genetic programming that petrifies me." We instead come up with all sorts of other explanations for what we feel. We may say that the thought of not existing alarms us, or that the loss of our memories haunts us, or that the possibility of hell terrorizes us. Or perhaps we imagine that it's the unknown, the uncertainty of what awaits, that unsettles us. As Bacon put it, "Men fear death as children fear to go into the dark."[4] Then again, we may reason, we hate death so much because our lifelong goals are yet unrealized. What's worse than dreams forever foiled? Or, yet again, maybe we suppose that our distress derives from contemplating the physical pains that can precipitate and surround death. The great Quaker scholar J. Rendel Harris often confessed that the fear of death was strong in him, "not the fear of what lay beyond, but of the actual passing."[5] (Incidentally, this may have been Jesus' problem in Gethsemane. He'd sought to steel himself and his disciples for the inevitable—"The Son of Man must suffer many things . . . and be killed"—and yet, when the hour had come, the prospect of torture terrorized him: "Remove this cup from me." I'd guess he wasn't afraid of being dead but of dying.)

Although death is a constant, our verbal responses vary. One wonders, then, to what extent our sentences are what the neuroscientist Michael Gazzaniga dubs post-hoc rationalizations, the best guesses of conscious minds to explain to themselves why they feel a certain way.[6] We first sense an innate fear. Then our reflective selves seek to account for that fear. It's like the split-brain patient whose right hand selected a picture of a chicken when his left hemisphere was shown the image of a chicken leg, and whose left hand selected a photograph of a shovel when his right hemisphere was shown a landscape full of snow. Only his left hemisphere could verbalize, so when later asked to explain why he chose a shovel, he came up with this: "Well, you have to clean up after those chickens."[7]

Whatever one makes of my suggestion that our accounts of why we dread death can be secondary rationalizations of an evolutionary instinct, we can't doubt that our anxiety becomes, through reflection, protean; that is, it takes various and sundry forms. Those forms, moreover, differ not only from individual to individual but also, as Philippe Ariès famously urged a few decades ago, from era to era and place to place.[8] Death is like life: it's not one thing but many.

....

This makes our theologizing more difficult, because the Scriptures, which pastors recite as they stand over our graves, come to us from another time, another culture, another world. The cover of your Bible may say New Study Edition or New Revised Standard or New International Version, but it's all a lie. There's nothing up-to-date about the two Testaments. As dispiriting as this may be for consumers in love with incessant innovation, the Bible is, despite the latest covers, old and distant, and it gets older and more distant with each passing day.

What does this have to do with death? Beyond being a biological fact, death is also a cultural construct, and it would be foolish to assume that the ancients who authored our Bible felt and thought about death as do those of us who, centuries later, read what they wrote. For one thing, they lived much shorter lives, frightfully shorter by our standards. Most of us confidently stride through life presuming that we'll survive into our seventies or beyond. This is, to be sure, a myth. Cancer, strokes, and car wrecks cut lives short. Nonetheless, no one knows in advance whose ill-fated lives those will be, and the myth works for the statistical majority. Right now, the average life-span in the United States is approaching eighty.

It's hard to fathom the gulf this fixes between us and our forebears. If one goes through the published Jewish epitaphs from 300 BCE to 700 CE and averages the ages of death, the result is 28.4.[9] That pathetic number, moreover, must be higher than the historical reality. For one thing, we have more epitaphs for men than women, and then, unlike today, men tended to live longer. For another, most infants and many younger children were buried without markers, and the infant and child mortality rates were atrocious. In any case, half of all Jews didn't make it past twenty, and of those who did, perhaps half didn't make it past thirty. So the young did most of the dying, and nobody could've reasonably presumed, as a matter of course, that he or she would live until seventy. Or fifty. Or even forty. On the contrary, people must, from an early age, have recurrently observed contemporaries dropping all around them. It says much that the Greek word for "untimely," *aōros*, is all over old Jewish epitaphs. For us, death is the exception until we're decades old. For them, it was ever present. They were in the valley of the shadow of death the moment they were born.

I'm no psychologist, but surely life—and thus God—looked very different to people who could only hope to make it to thirty, as opposed to those of us who expect to see eighty. Whereas death was, for them, always near, for us it's typically remote. I remember an old girlfriend who bit off a hangnail. Two days later, a little blue streak appeared on her finger. She went to a doctor, got a shot, and that was that. Had she lived in the first century, she would have been sick unto death, a victim of blood poisoning within a week.

This stands for a thousand related facts. All manner of ailments that we now, as a matter of course, effectively treat or prevent—tetanus, TB, typhoid—once carried multitudes to the grave long before threescore and ten. The ancients must have felt very differently than do we when they heard Psalm 37:20—"like smoke they vanish away"—or 1 Chronicles 29:15—"our days on the earth are like a shadow"—or James 4:14—"you are a mist that appears for a while, after which it disappears." And when Rabbi Eliezer said, "Repent one day before your death," the impact wouldn't have been quite the same had his hearers, immunized against infectious diseases, been firmly persuaded that, with only a smidgeon of luck, they still had decades to go.

....

Pondering how differently death must have appeared to people in times gone by is an instructive exercise. Yet rather than further underline the relativity of death by contrasting the past with the present, I'd like now to pursue the same end by contrasting the present with the future.

Although we live much longer than our predecessors, we've likely witnessed only the beginning. Some experts avow that there's no reason the human life-span can't be multiplied many times over. Aubrey de Grey, co-author of *Ending Aging*[10] and editor of the scientific journal, *Rejuvenation Research*, believes that medical advances will soon allow us to become as old as the mythical characters in the early chapters of Genesis. Indeed, de Grey holds that some now alive may live to see 1,000. Most experts, to be sure, deem him unduly optimistic about how soon we'll get there as well as about whether we'll get there at all. Yet many concur that we're already glimpsing the possibility of postponing decrepitude by decades and perhaps, eventually, even centuries.

What if these latter-day Ponce de Leons are right? What if the graph of human longevity continues its rapid upward climb? (The average age of death has nearly doubled since 1900.) What if Homo sapiens can be reprogrammed to operate like *Turritopsis dohrnii*, the so-called immortal jellyfish, the small invertebrate that, after fully developing, begins to age in reverse, until it reaches its earliest developmental stage and then starts over again? What if the last enemy to be defeated is death, and the victor isn't God but modern medical researchers?

We should, of course, not get ahead of ourselves. Radical life extension is in its infancy, and biological immortality is nowhere in sight. Aging has turned out to be an exceedingly complex phenomenon, and the experts are still very far from sorting out the relevant variables. Certainly we can't postpone old age just by containing mitochondrial decay or eliminating free radical damage. Nonetheless, the assault on the citadel of death has begun. So as a thought experiment, ask yourself, What will happen to our religion when people begin to envisage for themselves multiple centuries?

The consequences will likely be far-reaching. Consider, as one illustration, Jesus' word about divorce. What might a five-hundred-year-old Christian make of it? If our future is de Grey's future, might Luke 16:18—"anyone who divorces his wife and marries another commits adultery"—come to command as little authority as Deuteronomy 23:19—"You shall not charge interest to another Israelite"? Modern capitalism obliterated the rejection of usury, and perhaps the extension of life will obliterate the rejection of divorce. How many people are going to confine themselves to one matrimonial adventure before their 500th birthday? One of the reasons the divorce rate has skyrocketed in recent times is that people have been living a little longer. What will happen when they live a lot longer? It's just statistics. The fewer years one has, the fewer occasions for divorce. The more years one has, the more occasions for divorce. How high was the divorce rate when the average age of death was less than thirty? And how high will it be when the average age of death is thirty times thirty? I recall news reports of a pair of 115-year-old giant turtles in a zoo in Klagenfurt, Austria. After living together for decades, they suddenly refused to tolerate each other. The female started biting off chunks of her partner's shell. Counseling—whatever that means for turtles—didn't work. It was time to move on. Will it be any different with long-lived humans, Christian or not?

That, however, is just the matter of divorce. What about the heart of Christian faith? Christianity is, at its birth at least, a proposition about death: "God raised Jesus from the dead." Moreover, one of the reasons the faith won antiquity is that it brought psychological liberation to many haunted by death. So what will happen when death, although not exactly defunct, becomes, on average, such a long way off that it disappears from day-to-day consciousness? What will happen when people no longer feel, as they used to say, *media vita in morte sumus*: "in the midst of life we are in death"? What good is a religion whose chief promise resolves nobody's problem? Or will our future churches be populated solely by gray-heads approaching the 900 mark, they being the only ones left to fret seriously about their mortality?

Maybe even the 900-year-olds won't show up. It's conceivable, to be sure, that the more people live, the more they will want to live, just like Abraham in the old pseudepigraphon. Yet judging from the people I've known, the lengthier the life, the easier it is to die. And isn't this precisely what we might expect from evolution? If we're designed to pass on our genes, shouldn't the craving to live diminish once we've sired children and they've reached reproductive age? Why would evolution push us to survive at all costs after we're postmenopausal and post-andropausal, after our procreative and protective roles are passé? After finishing with sex, the selfish gene no longer cares about us. There's a time to be born, a time to reproduce, and a time to die.

Beyond all that, one must wonder whether protracted life might not, after a certain point, become tedious. We're already, without radical life extension, fighting boredom. That explains why electronic screens keep proliferating at a seemingly exponential—and to me alarming—rate. But will there be enough new entertainments to fill up the centuries as opposed to the decades? Only God knows. After the years pile up, however, it could be that enough will be enough, that we'll be literally bored to death, in which case the hooded fiend with the sickle will morph into a friendly ally who spares us further ennui and a fate worse than death.

Yet whether that's so or not, it takes little imagination to see that a religion which flourished by promising resurrection to people surrounded by death on all sides might not do so well in a world in which death is only an ever-decreasing sliver of an ever-lengthening life.

....

If the diversity in perceptions of death raises questions about moving from ancient text to present experience, there's another critical problem. In order to unfold the difficulty, permit me to indulge in some autobiographical reflections.

I recall a conversation in my twenties with an MIT-educated friend. He was railing against scientists, how they waste their time investigating geological formations and spinning cosmological theories. What, he asked, is wrong with them? Why don't they, every blasted one of them, research the process of aging with the goal of reversing it? Compared to that project, everything else is trivial amusement. Once we all live forever, there'll be plenty of time to study Boolean circuits and whale migration.

I didn't argue with him. For much of my life, I shared my daughter's revulsion at the prospect of expiring. I felt just like Brigid O'Shaughnessy in *The Maltese Falcon*: "I'm not heroic. I don't think there's anything worse than death."

I also felt like the ethicist Paul Ramsey, who once wrote these words, which I wrote down because someone had finally said what I'd so often and so deeply felt: death is "an irreparable loss, an unquenchable grief, the threat of all threats, a dread that is more than all fears aggregated together, an approaching 'evil' . . . the background of every background . . . a murmuring music rising to a cacophony and then receding which . . . we hear behind all themes of life whether well or poorly sung."[11]

The vexatious cacophony became deafening one evening, when I was twenty-three, and a drunk driver sped through a red light and rammed into my car. After regaining consciousness, I asked the ambulance attendant, "Am I going to die?" His appalling response was: "Not yet."

A little later, when I was flat on a cold table in the ER, some nameless doctor told me that I might have a busted aorta, and that my odds of making it through the night were 50–50. I've no words for the utter panic, the abject horror that his estimate of my chances awoke within me. The woeful experience was as ineffable as the mystic's ecstasy, although antithetical to it in every other way. My desperation, my anxious terror couldn't have been exceeded.

I did what I later learned almost everyone in our culture does when facing premature death, which is exactly what the *Testament of Abraham* says our cowardly forefather did: I bargained with the deity. Oh Almighty God, I inwardly screamed, if you save me tonight, I will—well, I forget my side of the bargain. Whether I've kept my vow, I don't know. What I do vividly remember, however, is the unprecedented alarm and unspeakable distress. Nothing before or since has been comparable.

Now here's the problem. By the time I was twenty-three, I was a pious, well-educated Christian. I said my prayers. I went to church. I knew my Bible, and also the better-known theologians. I ruminated on the mystics and had even enjoyed mystical raptures of my own. And none of it seemed to matter when death came calling. I doubt that I could've been more terrified had I been an atheist sure of oblivion. It was as though my genetic programming trumped everything and I became a scurrying spider. My religion was just pious overlay. Faith didn't count when it really mattered.

....

I have, in the years since, much reflected on this discouraging fact. Perhaps I shouldn't be too hard on myself. After all, I was young, and death appeared in an instant. One moment I was idling at an intersection, happily singing with Deep Purple; the next moment my lungs had collapsed. There was no time to take stock.

The point here, however, has to do with the state of my religion at the time of my accident. From an early age I'd been taught that the soul at death goes to heaven and, further, that on the day of resurrection, it'll be reunited with its body for life eternal. All of which, I suppose, I trustingly accepted as a child. But when I began, a few years before my accident, to study in earnest, I quickly became confused and apprehensive.

I learned that the idea of a soul bound for heaven was in disrepute. Its few defenders seemed to be fighting a rearguard action. Democritus, Epicurus, and Lucretius—the old materialists—had finally, to all appearances, won. Reductionistic physicalism dominated the sciences, while in philosophy Gilbert Ryle had banished the ghost from the human machine. Above all, the neuroscientists hadn't found the soul. The accredited apostles of science seemed by and large to agree with Bertrand Russell "that what we regard as our mental life is bound up with brain structure and organized bodily energy. Therefore it is rational to suppose that mental life ceases when bodily life ceases."[12] Don't mind and body work and not work in tandem? Don't they develop and deteriorate together? The mind or the soul, if we should even speak of such, must be the same as the brain, or at least the product of the brain. When the lyre is broken, the music is gone. No bulb, no light. It was dreadfully disconcerting.

Some theologians were trying to save the day by disparaging immortality of the soul and trumpeting resurrection of the body. I wasn't comforted. If you take a bit of copper wire, dissolve it in silver nitrate, pour the liquid into the ground, and wait two thousand years, where is the wire? Isn't it gone for good? So too the long-since-decayed cadavers of most who've ever lived; and how can a body whose disbanded components have been scattered abroad for ages ever be numerically identical with some later body? Even if such were conceivable—I can't conceive it—even if one could solve what philosophers call the problem of gappy existence, why would the deity bother to keep track of our atoms since, according to modern physicists, every atom of every element is wholly interchangeable with every other atom of that element? Who would care whether he or she gets these fifty carbon atoms over here as opposed to those fifty over there? Furthermore, as we are ever-changing streams of molecules, which body from which instant of our lives will God raise—the approximately 10×10^{27} atoms we had at the moment of death, or some other collection when we were younger? We weren't the same yesterday as today, so how can we be the same tomorrow? Maybe we can't step into the same body twice. Moreover, if you respond to these conundrums by urging that resurrection isn't about getting back old bodies but about receiving brand new ones, then such is demonstrably not the mainstream Jewish or Christian tradition.

The Bible was of no help here. On the contrary, it was precisely the problem, because it presupposes beliefs that were no longer credible to many highly intelligent, well-informed people; and I, after being awakened from my dogmatic slumbers, had to wonder whether I could retain those beliefs. My religion had backfired. Instead of helping me with death it perplexed me. I had become Unamuno, with death my one great problem. I found myself in Psalm 88:

> Do you work wonders for the dead?
> Do the shades rise up to praise you?
> Is your steadfast love declared in the grave,
>   or your faithfulness in Abaddon?
> Are your wonders known in the darkness,
>   or your saving help in the land of forgetfulness?

To my dismay, I learned that some modern theologians had already capitulated; that is, for them the afterlife and the two traditional means of getting there—the soul and the resurrection—belonged to the past, and they were trying to refashion Christianity without them. Gordon Kaufman clearly affirmed that this life is all we have. Tillich said the same thing, albeit less clearly. And they were latecomers. As early as 1869, the Swiss pastor and theologian A. E. Biedermann had dispensed with personal immortality. I had to ask myself whether the Christian religion as I knew it was obsolete before I was catechized into it. I didn't want to slaughter my intellect on the altar of faith. I had no desire to clap my hands and try to believe in fairies.

Back then I felt on my own as I tried to make sense of modern science and modern philosophy, which seemed to be doing just fine without my religion. It was acutely unsettling. The traditional hope for a life to come, a hope that had formerly functioned for me as consolation and moral imperative, had ceased to be either. It'd instead become a complex of disturbing intellectual conundrums.

To my embarrassment, I recall being in church one Easter Sunday morning. An acquaintance approached me, elated and full of good will. He offered the traditional greeting: "Christ is risen!" Of course I responded: "He is risen indeed!" But in my gnostic self-conceit, my historical-critical arrogance, I wondered to myself, How in the heck do you know that? Have you worked your way through the dense historical evidence? Do you know the scientific issues that attend such an astounding claim? Have you read Troeltsch?

Perhaps I was so annoyed because it seemed so easy for him. It hadn't been for me. I lived in libraries, pulling from their shelves book after book on the brain-mind problem, and book after book on neuroscience and the nature of consciousness. Suffering from a quenchless thirst for assurance, I also urgently pored over dozens and dozens of tomes on the paranormal—apparitions, mediums, reincarnation, near death experiences—anything that might shed some light on the upsetting issues with which I was struggling. In my vanity, I sometimes thought I was approaching a tentative judgment on this or that issue. But it was like playing Whack-a-Mole. Every time I seemingly pounded down one problem, another instantly popped up. So everything was unsettled when death stared me down. Naturally I flinched. I'd been interrogating my religion more than benefiting from it, and fear and trembling assailed me.

....

Three-and-a-half decades later, I remain full of questions. At the same time, I've drawn a few conclusions with which I'm almost comfortable. In the end, my study has been, I'm happy to report, like that of Boethius: it's brought consolation. I like to think that, were death to return tomorrow, I'd be more composed.

Yet study hasn't been the only thing that's helped soothe the sting of death. Several years ago, in the middle of a classroom lecture, it occurred to me, for the very first time, that everyone who's ever lived has died or will die, so how hard can it be? Although I'd somehow missed it, the point is beyond obvious. If every human being has managed to do this thing, then so can I. These days, when pondering my demise, this thought always returns, and it brings solace.

Even more important is what happened when, a few years after my own accident, another drunk driver plowed into the car of one of my dearest friends. Unlike me, she didn't survive. After a few weeks in a coma, she, along with her unborn child, went away. Less than a week after the funeral, however, she came back. I was awakened in the night to behold Barbara standing at the foot of my bed. She said nothing. She just stood there— beautiful, brightly luminous, intensely real. Her transfigured, triumphant presence, which lasted only a few moments, cheered me greatly.

Then, one afternoon, several weeks after that, I was typing in my study, wholly focused on my work. Suddenly I sensed someone else in the room. The presence seemed to be located up, behind, and to my left. I understood immediately, I know not how, that it was Barbara. Unlike the first time, when I saw her and heard nothing, this time I heard her and saw nothing. She insisted that I visit her distraught husband as soon as possible. Overwhelmed by this urgent communication, I immediately picked up the phone.

Now there's a large, critical literature on ostensible post-mortem encounters, and I don't wish to argue here that my experiences with Barbara were veridical. My purpose is only to be candid and to confess that, whatever others make of such experiences, they can profoundly affect percipients. Both vision and voice were, in the moment, absolutely real and so foreign to the rest of my experience that I then took them to originate in something other than my own subjectivity. Indeed, I've difficulty thinking otherwise even now, years later. As a result, death feels less final.

Undeserved good fortune has also mitigated fears. Although life's not always been enjoyable, things have worked out pretty well of late, and as sixty comes into view, I've achieved the major goals that I long ago set for myself. I clearly recall, while mowing a lawn as a teenager, fantasizing about authoring a large commentary on Matthew, just like Theodor Zahn, and contributing to the quest of the historical Jesus, just like Joachim Jeremias. Years later, I've done those things and more, and with my chief ambitions realized, it feels that I've just about made it through life's gauntlet. I think I can see the end. And it's OK. I recall that David Hume, the great skeptic, whose serenity when dying so confounded Boswell, stated: "I have done every thing of consequence which I ever meant to do. . . . I, therefore, have all reason to die contented."[13]

I've urged that we may think and feel very differently about death than did the Bible's ancient authors, and that the distance between past and present on this matter will likely grow as time moves on. I've further observed that the Scriptures presuppose beliefs about an afterlife that many bright people, including some theologians, now find incredible, even unworthy of attention. And I've confessed that, in my own life, the life of a so-called biblical scholar, the Scriptures have instilled as much doubt as consolation; and in this I can't be alone. So where does that leave us?

We can attempt to cope with our mortality by studying philosophy, or by inquiring whether, once in a while, some mediums are in touch with more than their subconscious minds, or by exploring whether certain elements of near-death experiences might be extra-subjective, or by some other line of investigation or reflection. None of which, in my judgment, the open-minded should despise.[14] All this, however, effectively sets the Bible to one side. What then, notwithstanding all the issues introduced above, might it have to contribute?

I have some suggestions. They grow out of reflection upon the closing chapters of the Gospels and the opening chapters of Acts, and they have to do chiefly with the character of the Christian God.

The acclamation of those who initially proclaimed the resurrection of Jesus featured the third person and the past tense, not the first person and the future tense. Their touchstone wasn't "God will raise me from the dead" or "God will raise us from the dead." Rather, it was "God has raised him from the dead." Later on, to be sure, as with Paul in 1 Corinthians 15, some did, naturally enough, move from Jesus' resurrection to their own. But when Mary Magdalene and her friends returned from the tomb, their message wasn't about themselves but another. In the words of the angel, "He has been raised." Likewise, when Peter stood up at Pentecost, the topic was neither his own existential anxiety nor the persistence of his own ego in the face of death but instead what'd happened to someone else. So the initial point to contemplate is that the chief concern of Peter and Mary wasn't their inevitable death but another's triumphant life. They seemingly—in contrast to most of us most of the time—weren't looking firstly at themselves.

My next point is that the earliest Christians spoke of the post-mortem vindication of Jesus using a concept—resurrection—which, historians tell us, grew in part out of Jewish wrestling with the problem of evil. For many in the post-exilic period, it became more and more difficult to credit divine faithfulness without positing the transcendence of death. The character of the biblical God increasingly seemed to require that the righteous, especially martyrs and victims of extreme injustice, not languish interminably in Sheol but that they participate in God's ultimate victory. Resurrection would make that possible. The developing doctrine was a theological inference about the future: if God wins, death will lose.

My third point is this: With reference to both Jesus' resurrection and the general resurrection of the dead, the chief actor, and the exclusive agent, is the God of Israel, who in Jesus' proclamation is the Father who gives good gifts, including eternal life, to his children. What might we make of this particular God?

Many—including some of my close friends and lots of intellectuals I much admire—regard this miracle-working deity, who makes things right by raising the dead, as an outdated myth. On their view, we should, in the light of modern knowledge, doubt or deny that Jesus was raised, or that anyone else will ever be carried from this world to another. The well-known New Testament historian John Dominic Crossan is in this camp. He has confessed that, as a Christian, he thinks about life after death what he thinks about UFOs: he doesn't know and he doesn't care.[15] Crossan's professed passion is for justice in this present world of misery. He deems the afterlife a distraction from the one thing needful.

Although I understand, I don't agree. I don't know how to be indifferent to the possibility of a world to come. For me, Christianity without hope beyond death is of reduced relevance and of diminished interest.

I put off for later the question of whether any concept of an afterlife is credible given what our scientists now know and what many of our philosophers now teach. Here I only confess my inability to tell the hapless parents of eight-year-old Amanda, as they're checking out of the Ronald McDonald House, that their daughter is forever gone, they will never see her again, yet God is good and God is love. Perhaps I'm sentimental and weak-kneed, yet if words have meaning, these things don't cohere. Indeed, putting them together strikes me as absurd. We're left, of course, with notorious conundrums, such as why anyone should expect God to act differently in the future than heretofore. Still, it's one thing to wonder where God has been in the past or is in the present, and quite another to give up on the future. If we're without hope, aren't we without God?

It's suggestive that, in poll after poll of religious opinion, faith in God and hope for an afterlife are strongly correlated. Those who believe in the one typically believe in the other. Those who reject God but entertain the possibility of an afterlife—such as philosophers J. M. E. McTaggart and C. D. Broad—are a negligible percentage of the population. The cynical interpretation of this circumstance is that people need a supreme being to make them live again. Perhaps, however, there's more to it than this. Maybe some moderns aren't altogether bereft of theological intuition, and perhaps they sense what some Second Temple Jews increasingly felt, that eternal death and a truly good God don't go together. In the ancient world, beliefs about the afterlife developed in order to keep pace with evolving beliefs about the deity. In the modern world, it remains hard to decouple the two subjects.

....

John Donne famously wrote: "Any man's death diminishes me."[16] Speaking for myself, anyone's death diminishes God—unless, that is, there's something more than this vale of tears. If the brooding grave is everyone's finale, if existence runs out into pitiless nothing, if nihility is everyone's *telos*, then the forgotten and marginalized will remain marginalized and forgotten for all time. What good is God to them?

I at least need a God whose love and rule don't leave us alone with our greatest existential evil, a God who descends into hell to rescue the dead. I need a God who places heavenly crowns on the heads of the slaughtered infants of Bethlehem. I need the God of the old Roman catacombs, which are full of scenes representing delivery from death—Noah's ark, the sacrifice of Isaac, Ezekiel's valley of dry bones, the three youths in the furnace, the raising of Lazarus.

Maybe some, for whom life hasn't been solitary, nasty, brutish, and short but rather enjoyable, happy, wonderful, and long, don't need such a God. Maybe they've reached their goals and can rest content. But the fortunate few don't represent the less fortunate many; and that some of us, like the Sadducees of old, are happy to live and die, doesn't entail that everyone else should buck up and feel the same way. Shouldn't it distress us, if we're not self-contained, that most haven't been as lucky as Hume, while countless others haven't even had the chance to set goals, or have seemingly done little more than suffer a thousand plagues of pain, with death their only escape? Do their circumstances make any difference to God, and will God make any difference to them? Is God the everlasting bystander, so that deism is forever true? Are we all like the prophets of Baal, who called on the name of their god again and again, but there was no answer?

....

After Gollum and the great ring of power fall into the fires of Mount Doom, Frodo and Sam sit on a little ashen hill. As lava rises around them, Frodo speaks the obvious: "An end comes. We have only a little time to wait now. We're lost in ruin and downfall, and there is no escape." The two friends then slip into unconsciousness. But that's not the end. The eagles come, and the hobbits are borne away to safety. Later, when Sam awakens and sees Gandalf, he gasps: "I thought you were dead! But then I thought I was dead myself. Is everything sad going to come untrue?"[17]

There must be some analogue to this scene in the universal human story. If not, then the cosmos is finally apathetic, and death can separate us from the love of God; and if that's so, then love doesn't endure all things but finally fails. Which cannot be.

CHAPTER 2

Resurrection and Bodies

A man may fish with the worm that hath eat of a king,
and eat of the fish that hath fed of that worm.

HAMLET

Often in such cases it is possible to see that the idea which is no
longer a current belief is yet a representation (a kind of picture) of a
conviction that is still held—something we believe to be true at the
core; and we are right in pointing to that conviction as the "religious
value" of the old belief that has died out and been discarded.

J. F. BETHUNE-BAKER

The enemy here is system.

MICHAEL WYSCHOGROD

MY STUDENTS DIDN'T always fret about cannibalism. That changed a
few years ago, when I began lecturing on the resurrection of the dead.
On rare occasions, someone in the last straits of starvation will eat another human being. The repugnant fact generates a notorious and once-
famous conundrum. If the flesh of one becomes the flesh of another, and if,
on the last day, both eater and eaten arise, what will become of the particles
belonging to both? To which body will God assign them?
Although always new to my students, the puzzle of shared matter has,
in its various forms, long vexed many, beginning with the church fathers.
What if a sailor drowns at sea and is devoured by fish, and what if the fish
are in turn caught, cooked, and eaten? Or what if a tree in a cemetery sends
forth its roots and gathers nutrients from a decaying corpse, nutrients that
go into a ripening apple, which a hungry passerby plucks for a snack? Or

what if, when you die, some of the water that makes up so much of your body evaporates, becomes rain, and enters the water table, so that others drink you? Or what if a body returns to the dust and the dust becomes top soil and the top soil nurtures wheat and the wheat is turned into bread and the bread is distributed through the Eucharist?

These aren't, however, hypotheticals. They're rather facts of life on earth. We're all cannibals, feeding upon the remains of our ancestors.

Augustine solved the enigma of cannibalism by urging that consumed flesh, like many objects lost and found, will be returned to its first owners.[1] His verdict, however, hardly halted discussion. I once ran across a sermon preached before the king and queen of England in 1689, a sermon by Edward Stillingfleet, in which the Bishop contended that, when someone is eaten, only a smidgen of the devoured flesh becomes a permanent part of the diner's bulk. To this consoling fact the Reverend added that God will make up for any consumed, and so missing, pieces by collecting matter that belonged to the victim in better days, matter sloughed off long before the hapless party was digested. The same divine action will, Stillingfleet observed, take care of those who die emaciated because of consumption.[2]

This of course resolves nothing. The longer the world continues, the less likely it is that elements constituting one human being haven't belonged, at some earlier moment, to another human being. Worms and bacteria dissolve the dead, whose molecules reenter the carbon cycle, the water cycle, and the nitrogen cycle, all of which supply our food and drink. Imagine, then, what would happen if, ten seconds from now, all the dead, beginning with those most ancient, were to rise and, like magnets, draw to themselves every atom they once possessed. The world as we know it would instantly be full of holes, and some things altogether gone, including lots of saints, for when God returns all matter to its original owners, how much will be left for the late-comers? It gets even more difficult if you want God to resurrect animals, because we eat them all the time. From conception on, all of us are recycled elements.

So what other solutions are on offer? It's possible—or rather was at one time possible—to contend that human flesh can't, by its nature, be assimilated, that it always passes, unaffected, through digestive systems. A few church fathers and medieval theologians imagined this, and the opinion wasn't wholly extinguished until the early nineteenth century. A closely related view is that, although the human body could in principle be assimilated, God intervenes to make sure this never happens. The great Hugo Grotius (d. 1645) thought this a good guess. I've also run across the fantastic view, of a certain George

Hodgson, in a book published in 1853, that nothing we eat or drink—not just human flesh—joins the human body. Everything rather passes through. Food and drink are for us like gas is to the hot air balloon: the gas makes the balloon rise but is no part of it. According to Hodgson, Scripture teaches this very thing, for Jesus says in Matthew 15:17: "Do you not see that whatever goes into the mouth enters the stomach, and goes out into the sewer?"[3]

There's also the option, tentatively forwarded by Humphrey Hody (d. 1707), and to my knowledge never seconded, that maybe a cannibal doesn't die until every particle of human flesh has, via Providence, exited one way or the other.[4] This, to be sure, generates its own riddle. Might not a theologian who knows this, a theologian who loses his faith and turns evil, make human beings his only entree and so live forever?

. . . .

At this point, my students, worrying that I might be serious, become incredulous and impatient. What does all this have to do with Christian faith? None of this is in the Bible, and none of this has troubled them before. Surely, they think, my introduction of obscure and irrelevant conjectures epitomizes the sort of unedifying, egg-headed nonsense they were warned about when they decided on ministerial studies. Didn't Calvin wisely condemn the "superfluous investigation of useless matters"?[5] God, moreover, can do anything, so why think it a thing incredible, that God should raise the dead? Let's get on to something worthwhile.

I respond by asking my students what they're thinking when they utter the Apostles' Creed, which includes the line, "I believe in the resurrection of the body." To be sure, it may be that, when they're in church, they're not thinking anything. Nonetheless, shouldn't they hope that their recitation isn't empty, that their faith is more than vague and dreamy imaginings? And if so, what can their profession mean given that nature inexorably recycles everything, even corpses full of formaldehyde and sealed in bronze caskets? Or do we just throw up our hands and call it a mystery, because faith is where reason goes to die? That Jesus' tomb was empty may be good news. That so many other tombs are empty is a problem.

This settles them down for a bit, long enough for me to introduce more stuff that leaves them nonplussed. I inform them that some rabbis, recognizing that bodies inexorably disintegrate, posited that all we need for resurrection is the coccyx bone:

Hadrian—may his bones rot—asked R. Joshua b. Hananiah, "From what part in the body will the Holy One, blessed be he, make a person sprout up in the age to come?" He said to him, "He will make him sprout out of the nut of the spinal column." He said to him, "How do you know this?" He said to him, "Bring one to me, and I will explain it to you." He put it [the nut brought to him] into the fire, yet it did not burn up. He put it into water, yet it did not dissolve. He pulverized it between millstones, yet it was not crushed. He put it on a block and smashed it with a hammer. The block split, the hammer was cleft, yet it remained undamaged.[6]

Don't gardeners harvest a new plant from a twig or cutting? Didn't Eve come from one of Adam's ribs?

Christian tradition has tried out related ideas. One of the more poetically pleasing appears in a nineteenth-century book written by a Presbyterian minister, George Scudder Mott. He believed that, despite appearances, the earth never extracts all that constitutes a human body, that neither sunshine nor frost nor vegetation nor any other agency utterly undoes the human frame: some small part ever endures, and resurrection will begin with that. It's like a seed planted in the soil. The seed "sprouts, it grows, it blooms, it yields. Now where does it get material for all this? Not from the seed, for that was merely the starting point. Not alone from the soil, but also . . . from the air, the rain, and the sun. Surrounding nature furnishes the supply." And if God does this for a mere plant, surely those created in the divine image can expect no less.[7]

Not as aesthetically pleasing is the well-known proposal of the modern Christian philosopher Peter van Inwagen. Since he doesn't believe in a traditional soul and holds that human identity resides in bodies alone, his philosophy leads him, like the rabbis and Mott, to posit some solid, physical nucleus that never dissolves. He suggests that, "perhaps at the moment of each man's death, God removes his corpse and replaces it with a simulacrum which is what is burned or rots. Or perhaps God is not quite so wholesale as this: perhaps He removes for 'safekeeping' only the 'core person'—the brain and central nervous system—or even some special part of it."[8] In this scenario, God furtively snatches the body or parts thereof for storage until the last trump. This is just another way of denying that bodies in their entirety really disappear. Yet surely they do, and if Christians are compelled to deny this, if we're obliged to hope that God runs something like a cryonics lab, which keeps heads in the deep-freeze for later revival, aren't we in trouble?

. . . .

That bodies share matter and that they cease to be are just two of many puzzles occasioned by belief in resurrection. Here, however, I introduce only one more.

Natural selection has designed us for life on earth. Teeth are for chewing food, and lungs are for breathing air, and all for the purpose of keeping us alive. Christians hold, however, that, once we rise, death will be no more. The exegetical justification is 1 Corinthians 15, where Paul foresees an imperishable body, a spiritual body, a glorious body. Mortality will put on immortality, so that death will be swallowed up in victory.

Why, then, with death passé, would resurrected saints need to eat? Or why would they need to breathe? If they're invested with immortality, death won't be able to touch them, so eating or not eating and breathing or not breathing should be matters of indifference. What could be the purpose, in an immortal state, of organs that evolved in the struggle for survival, organs designed to keep us alive on earth for a few decades?

Gregory of Nyssa inferred that, when Jesus rose, he didn't take his intestines with him and that, in the world to come, we won't need ours either. As Paul wrote in 1 Corinthians 6:13: "Food is meant for the stomach and the stomach for food—and God will destroy both one and the other." Gregory, like so many after him, answered the obvious objection—Doesn't Jesus, in Luke 24, eat a bit of fish after rising from the dead?—by arguing that the act was one of condescension, for the sake of the disciples, so that they'd know he wasn't a ghost.

It takes only a little reflection to hollow out resurrected bodies entirely.[9] If, as Jesus teaches, we'll neither marry nor be given in marriage but will be like the angels in heaven, then we won't require ovaries or fallopian tubes, prostate glands or seminal vesicles. And if, as 4 Ezra avows, illness will be banished, we won't need white blood cells, antibodies, and the rest of the immune system. And if, as Revelation promises, we'll neither hunger nor thirst any longer, then we won't require kidneys to reabsorb water. Nor will we, if immortal, need blood, veins, arteries, and a pumping heart to circulate nutrients and remove waste products. One understands why Calvin proposed that plants in the world to come won't be for food but for pleasantness in sight, and why the eighteenth-century preacher, Samuel Johnson, argued that Jesus, after he lost all his blood on the cross, didn't need it back.[10] The former things will pass away.

Everything about us has been fashioned for life on earth, so that we might grow, repair, and reproduce ourselves; but if, in the future, we no longer grow, repair, or reproduce, won't stomachs, intestines, and the rest necessarily be vestigial, so that glorified bodies will be, in their entirety, akin to our irrelevant tailbone, that is, eternal relics of a one-time utility? Or should we look forward to something like what biologists call "exaptation," the process by which a trait serving one function comes to serve another function, such as bird feathers evolving from temperature regulators into instruments for flight? Maybe teeth won't be for chewing but, at least for those in hell, for gnashing.

That sounds a bit like Tertullian, who did in fact hazard that maybe old organs might take on new functions. He asked: "What will be the use of the entire body when the entire body will become useless?" He answered by observing that organs may have more than one function—the mouth, for instance, not only chews food but makes speech—and by affirming, rather cryptically, that "in the presence of God there will be no idleness."[11]

....

Despite conceding that, in the world to come, we won't need what we need now, some nonetheless have, in their eschatological imaginations, refused to part with their current organs. One early apologist observed that, as celibates prove, one can have organs one doesn't use. Others have insisted that, while our bodies may no longer serve biological purposes, they may nonetheless endure so that we're able to behold and recognize one another. Matthias Earbery (d. 1740) averred that "Seeing is one branch of Coelestial Enjoyment,"[12] for which he thought eyes necessary; yet eyes in turn require "an organical Brain to receive the Impressions from the optick Nerves."[13] At least our heads won't be empty.

There are, however, other options. You can distinguish, following the Book of Revelation, between the first and the second resurrection. In the first, at the beginning of the millennium, when Jesus comes to reign on earth, the righteous dead will arise, whereupon they will, like Adam in paradise, eat from the tree of life. To do so, they will need teeth, intestines, and so on. But then, after the millennium, there will be a second resurrection, when the rest of the dead will arise. Some will be thrown into the lake of fire. Others will become like angels and enter into the new heaven and the new earth. At that point people may finally abandon their corporal appliances with their animal functions. Maimonides, on the Jewish side, taught something like this.

The idea of a first resurrection to earthly life in the millennium neatly skirts all the indelicate questions about resurrected organs. It doesn't, however, let anyone off the hook. We still have to wonder about the transition from the millennium to the eternal state. What will happen to human bodies once the first earth passes away and the sea is no more? The solution of two resurrections just punts the problem down the road.

There's another difficulty, although we've learned of it only lately. The average human body harbors, according to recent estimates, at least ten thousand species of parasitic microbes. There are about 46,000 of these tiny organisms under each fingernail. The total number of individual microbes in a human body is around one hundred trillion (which bests by a factor of ten the total number of cells we have). Many microbes, such as digestive flora, are required for healthy functioning. So if we'll indeed need functioning intestines in the millennium, won't our microbial ecosystems have to be resurrected, too? Without the bugs we host, the intestines won't work.

....

Enough of that. It would be tedious to continue piling up the obtuse questions that people have worried about and the apologetical tales they've spun when pondering resurrection. After a while I sympathize with my students, who hope that deliberations about intestines can't really have much to do with faith. So let's ask a different question. How is belief in the resurrection of the dead now faring?

Many years ago I asked my father, a sometime Presbyterian, to read Wolfhart Pannenberg's *What Is Man?*[14] This book argues that modern science has shattered the old metaphysics and slain the soul. Pannenberg thought this not bad news but good, for he took the Bible to teach resurrection, not immortality. My father was of another mind. After a few weeks, he returned the book, saying that he preferred New Age guru Shirley MacLaine and reincarnation to theologian Wolfhart Pannenberg and resurrection.

My father represents many. Recent surveys show little belief in bodily resurrection among Protestants and Catholics in Western Europe and the United States, even among those who recite the old creeds. Indeed, in some polls of North Americans, Western Europeans, and Australians, belief in resurrection is less popular than belief in immortality of the soul, belief in reincarnation, and belief in extinction.

This shouldn't be news. Here are three sentences from three nineteenth-century writers:

From 1864: the resurrection of the dead "lingers in the minds of most people only as a dead letter."[15]

From 1867: "The Resurrection of the Dead is a doctrine which has ... fallen out of notice."[16]

From 1872: the resurrection of the body "is very generally rejected by the most intelligent, thinking, and inquiring minds of the age, both in the Church and out of it."[17]

One suspects that the undeniable decline in belief is reflected on our grave markers. For although my personal sampling has necessarily been circumscribed, I've seen enough to surmise that, were one to gather statistics regarding the sentiments carved on tombstones in Europe and North America over the last four hundred years, one would discover that resurrection is mentioned less and less as the centuries move forward.

The waning of literal resurrection belief is likewise reflected in the general public's growing acceptance, over the course of the last two centuries, of the dissection of the human body for anatomical instruction. (In nineteenth-century Britain the question wasn't whether dissection should be legal but whether the knife should carve executed murderers or the unmourned and "friendless poor."[18]) Also telling is the phenomenon, which has increased dramatically since World War II, of people bequeathing their bodies to "science." As our commodified corpses have become objects of physical study and items of medical utility, their traditional eschatological meaning has ebbed.

As illustration of the current moment, which includes unbelief even in conservative circles, consider the Roman Catholic theologian, John Michael Perry. Although at ease with the supernatural, he rejects resurrection. He believes that Jesus' soul triumphed over death and communicated with the disciples. And yet, according to Perry, Jesus' body, being unnecessary for life in the world to come, rotted in the tomb. In Jesus' time and place, however, most people mistakenly believed that survival required a body. Thus for the disciples to embrace the truth of Jesus' victory over death, God had to arrange things so that the tomb would be void. The deity worked this trick by hurrying up the natural processes of decay. The body remained where Joseph of Arimathea laid it, but its disintegration was so rapid that, when the tomb was entered shortly after Jesus' interment, it appeared that its occupant had vanished.[19] Now I think it would've been easier for God just to have told the angel who rolled away the stone to hide Jesus' lifeless body behind the bushes. The point, however, is that while Perry is comfortable with miracles and life after death, resurrection is out.

These days, even many professing belief in resurrection don't really believe. I've spoken with several pastors who hope that God will fashion for them new, heavenly bodies. They anticipate not repair but replacement. They may preach resurrection, but they don't envisage bones being knit together in the graveyard.

....

This isn't the dominant Christian tradition. Jerome was convinced that "it is this very flesh in which we live that rises again, without the loss of a single member."[20] According to Augustine, God will revive and restore "bodies that have been consumed by wild beasts, or by fire, or those parts that have been disintegrated into dust and ashes, or those parts that have dissolved into moisture, or have evaporated into the air."[21] Canon 1 of the Fourth Lateran Council declared that all "will rise with their own bodies which they now bear about here." Sir Thomas Browne wrote: "Our estranged and divided ashes shall unite again . . . our separated dust, after so many pilgrimages and transformations into the parts of minerals, plants, animals, elements, shall at the voice of God return into their primitive shapes and join again to make up their primary and predestinate forms."[22]

Until recent times, most theologians and preachers taught this. The idea is reflected in our religious art, where bodies sometimes climb out from the ground, or in the old church cemeteries, where the feet of the dead are laid toward the rising sun, so that, when Christ returns, like lightning from the east, everyone will stand up facing the right direction.

Why did people believe such things? Why did some even wonder what happens to clipped hair and cut nails when the dead rise on the last day?[23] Part of the answer is the Bible. Jesus' tomb, the Gospels report, was empty. They also tell us that he displayed his scars to his disciples, presumably for the purpose of proving that the body which was buried was the same body which arose. John 5 says that "the hour is coming when all who are in the tombs will hear his voice and come forth, those who have done good, to the resurrection of life, and those who have done evil, to the resurrection of judgment." This is a prophecy about burial places. Matthew 27 purports that, when Jesus died, "the earth shook, and the rocks were split; the tombs also were opened, and many bodies of the saints who had fallen asleep were raised, and coming out of the tombs after his resurrection they went into the holy city and appeared to many." Second Maccabees 14 tells of a certain Razis, an elder of Jerusalem, who died like this: "with his blood . . . completely drained from him, he tore out his entrails, took them in both hands and hurled them at the crowd, calling upon the Lord of life and spirit to give them back to him again." Such texts inevitably move minds in a certain direction. In short, the Bible itself occasioned the now unfashionable debates about entrails and cannibalism.

. . . .

When did the traditional doctrine begin to lose favor? Surely there was always some popular incredulity, maybe a lot of popular incredulity;[24] but if we're considering major theologians, the first large blips of doubt show up, as far as I've been able to learn, in the seventeenth century. John Locke, picking up on the work of Thomas Hobbes, stressed that personal identity lies in continuity of consciousness, not in physical stability. He may have been the first to speak of "resurrection of the person." He in any case preferred that expression over "resurrection of the body." Locke found support in Paul, who on his reading taught the reception of new heavenly bodies, not the gathering of dispersed particles.[25]

In the century after Locke, literalism, although still loudly defended, was being revised. David Hartley (d. 1757), obviously influenced by the biological preformationism of his day, inferred that there may be "an elementary infinitesimal body in the embryo," a body invulnerable to death, and just as it directs development in the womb, it will later be the "vegetating" power or organizing center of the resurrection body.[26] Charles Bonnet (d. 1793) forwarded a related idea: within the visible brain is an invisible, indestructible brain, a "little ethereal machine" that will be the nucleus of glorified bodies.[27] Variants of this notion—always supported by appeal to Paul's remark that a sown body is like a bare seed—are all over the eighteenth-century literature.

It's telling that, around this time, few any longer worry whether every human being who has ever lived could be raised and, in accord with Joel 3, squeezed together for judgment in the Valley of Jehoshaphat (identified with the Kidron Valley). The problem, once discussed by such luminaries as Aquinas and even, incredibly, Leibniz, just goes away.[28]

By the middle of the nineteenth century, books on resurrection with "same body" in their titles ceased to appear. Edward Hitchcock could then write: "If only a millionth part, or a ten thousand millionth part, of the matter deposited in the grave, shall be raised from thence, it justifies the representations of scripture, that there will be a resurrection of the dead."[29] A bit later, the influential Charles Gore insisted that belief in resurrection "does not mean that the particles of our former bodies, which were laid in the grave and which have decayed and passed into all sorts and forms of natural life, will be collected together again."[30] That was "the old view," not "the new view."[31]

In 1911, William John Sparrow Simpson documented how theologians had, in the previous hundred years, steadily moved away from the literalism of Tertullian and Augustine toward the more ethereal understanding of Origen.[32] The latter disbelieved in a millennium, stressed the radical otherness of transformed, eschatological bodies, and posited within us a life principle from which, as from a seed, future lives will sprout.

A decade after Sparrow Simpson, the Anglican H. D. A. Major, founder of *The Modern Churchman,* promoted personal survival unfettered by an earthly body. "I do not hold," he wrote, "in the mode of the resurrection of the dead which has been held by the Catholic Church for eighteen centuries."[33] Although charges of heresy were brought against Major, the Bishop of Oxford exonerated him: "I am satisfied that Mr. Major's teaching does not conflict with what Holy Scripture reveals to us of the Resurrection of the Body."[34] Soon enough the Archbishop of Canterbury's commission on doctrine declared that "we ought to reject quite frankly the literalistic belief in a future resuscitation of the actual physical frame which is laid in the tomb."[35] Emil Brunner, not long thereafter, showed himself to be of the same mind: "The flesh will not rise again. . . . The resurrection has nothing to do with that drama of the graveyard pictured by medieval fantasy."[36] The same opinion has been held by those Christian thinkers, such as B. H. Streeter, Ladislaus Boros, and Gerhard Lohfink, who've argued that resurrection takes place at the moment of death, when the body is still in plain sight.[37]

....

The move away from literalism hasn't been reversed. I remember a dinner with N. T. Wright. Given that he has been so insistent that Jesus' tomb was empty and that God will raise the dead for life on a refurbished earth, I asked him what he makes of all the old riddles, such as the puzzle of shared matter. Unruffled, he opined that Origen long ago had solved most of the issues. So the great modern apologist for resurrection turned out to be less than a full literalist. His view wasn't that of Jerome. He was rather closer to a church father who minimized material continuity and thereby secured for himself widespread condemnation.

Wright's judgment stands for a dramatic change in Western Christianity. Locke has won, which means Origen has won. Even those who still defend resurrection no longer fret about diffused particles. There is, for example, the theory which posits that, at death, the so-called "simples" that make us up will fission into two spatially segregated sets of "simples" with different causal paths. One will be a corpse. The other will be a body in heaven.[38] This is akin to splitting the planarian flatworm: if the worm is cut in two, the head half grows a tail and the tail half grows a head. In the resurrection, however, one half never makes it.

Then there's the idea—sponsored recently by John Polkinghorne and, a century before him, John Harvey Kellogg, the inventor of breakfast cereal[39]—that the soul should be conceptualized as an information-bearing pattern. Someday God will remember you and will upload your pattern into a new environment. That'll be your resurrection. This way of understanding resurrection is unsurprising in a world of computers, where information is conceived of as separate from the physical states that carry it.

I don't like either of these theories, although they're philosophically entertaining. I'm especially unconsoled by the idea of God implanting my memory pattern into some future frame. That won't be me but a duplicate, so what do I care? God could've done the same thing five minutes ago, and I wouldn't take the other guy to be me. Moreover, it's not clear that it takes omnipotence to work this trick. Some modern transhumanists, such as Ray Kurzweil, already dream about future technology making us immortal by uploading cellular brain maps into supercomputers.[40] The only point here, however, is that all such proposals leave our bodies in the ground, which is indeed and emphatically a "new view."

....

What then happened? Doctrinal revolutions, like all other revolutions, have manifold causes. In the nineteenth century, some Jewish prayer books substituted language about immortality for language about resurrection; and in 1869 and 1885, in Philadelphia and in Pittsburgh respectively, liberal Jewish authorities issued statements that dismissed, as antiquated, belief in bodily resurrection. These developments had something to do with the desire to sunder religion from politics. Historically, resurrection was a collective event for the Jewish people. It was indeed to take place in the Land of Israel and to inaugurate the Messiah's reign from Jerusalem. Many modern Jews, wanting to be good citizens in America and Europe, didn't like the nationalistic associations. Immortality, by contrast, wasn't sectarian. It was cosmopolitan.

As is obvious by now, however, unbelief in old-fashioned resurrection wasn't confined to Judaism. Further, politics wasn't everything. Of direct relevance for Christianity as well as Judaism was the rationalism of the Enlightenment, which generated in educated quarters so much suspicion about miracles. To hope for resurrection is to hope for a miracle—indeed, a miracle beyond all others. This didn't, as the old debates over the resurrection of Jesus show, suit a deistically inclined age. The skeptics, such as Thomas Woolston (d. 1733), protested that bodies are law-governed, and that reanimation would break all the laws. Impossible.

While the deists gave up resurrection, which belonged exclusively to revealed religion—as Robert Boyle wrote: "If God had not in the scripture positively revealed his purpose of raising the dead, I confess I should not have thought of such a thing"[41]—many of them retained immortality, which required neither the Bible nor divine intervention. Hadn't Pythagoras and Plato, as well as Hindus, believed, without benefit of Scripture, in a self inherently immune to death? In addition, some thinkers, such as Moses Mendelssohn (d. 1786), thought immortality to be, unlike resurrection, the conclusion of a sound argument. Kant, eschewing all natural theology, disagreed, yet he nonetheless posited immortality on the basis of practical reason. He didn't posit resurrection.

Deistic predilections worked their way into much of nineteenth-century German theology, so much so that major figures such as Ritschl, Harnack, and Bousset didn't entertain resurrection for a second. Immortality, by contrast, was still on the table.

In addition to qualms about miracles, disbelief in the historicity of Genesis—a disbelief fostered in part by geological discoveries—had its effect. The end has always been correlated with the beginning, so when scholars began to question the literal sense of the Bible's early chapters, second thoughts about the literal sense of its final chapters followed. If the opening is theological projection, maybe the conclusion is no different.

We should remember in this connection that comparative religion was arising when deism was thriving, and comparison of what the Bible teaches about the end with what other religious texts have to say raised tough questions. Charles Daubuz (d. 1717) found Egyptian and Chaldean materials in Revelation, and when the Zend Avesta—a collection of old Zoroastrian texts featuring a lot of eschatology—was translated into German in the eighteenth century, the parallels with the Bible were obvious. The eventual upshot of such discoveries was the conviction that resurrection stemmed not so much from the Old Testament as from later Judaism, and that Judaism in turn derived its hope from other cultures. In short, resurrection turned out to be like other ideas, that is, it had a human history. It wasn't a doctrine invented by God and spoken from heaven.

More recently, cremation and organ donation have played their roles in distancing us from old-fashioned resurrection. Of course, the causation is bidirectional. On the one hand, the decline of the old doctrine emboldened some rationalists in the eighteenth century, some Protestants in the nineteenth century, and some Roman Catholics in the twentieth century to tolerate or even promote cremation. On the other hand, the growing acceptance of cremation—the British Cremation Society was founded in 1874; Parliament officially allowed crematoria in 1902; the influential Charles Gore gave his blessing in 1924; and the Archbishop of Canterbury, William Temple, was cremated in 1944[42]—must in turn have made the resurrection of the flesh seem less instinctively plausible to many. How important can our remains be if we scruple not to reduce them to ashes? The British sociologist Tony Walter has written that the crematorium may be a setting "in which the materialist belief that death is the end makes sense and in which reunion of the immortal souls of lovers makes sense, but any recognizably Christian belief in resurrection does not."[43] The psychology of organ donation must be similar: leaving our organs to others is proof that we won't need them back.

I've wondered about another possible factor. It has to do with modern mobility. There was a time when most people died and were buried near their place of birth, so they lived out their lives not far from the graves of their beloved. In such a setting, attachment to physical remains was possible. One could, and people often did, reminisce and weep above bones. What's happened, however, as more and more of us have failed to stay put for long? Today we often bury our dead, move away, then mourn and remember them from afar. In such a context, continuing ties must be unrelated to burial plots and tombstones. If we recall the dead, it's because we carry them around in our hearts and minds, not because we visit their remains. Graves and bones are irrelevant.[44] Might this not be another circumstance that has nudged us away from finding religious meaning in corpses?

....

To this point, I've discussed resurrection faith as though it were an isolated belief. It's not. It's rather part of a traditional complex, part of the web of Christian eschatological expectations. It's only one event in a sequence of end-time events: Jesus returns, then the dead are raised, then they are judged, then they enter heaven or depart to hell. Now this entire scenario has, in the last two to three centuries, fared poorly—above all, perhaps, because the old-style hell has become, for reasons to be reviewed in a later chapter, about as unfashionable as any belief could be. One guesses, then, that insofar as resurrection has been associated with that beleaguered, widely despised doctrine, to that extent its credibility has suffered. In other words, as hell has sunk, it's dragged allied expectations, including resurrection, down with it.

....

Notwithstanding everything said so far, resurrection hasn't been banished; it isn't universally held in low repute. It retains stout defenders, even if they don't champion the old literalism. In the middle of the twentieth century, Oscar Cullmann famously urged that the Bible teaches not immortality of the soul, a Greek idea, but resurrection of the dead, a Jewish idea.[45] More recently, philosopher Nancey Murphy and biblical scholar Joel Green, among others, have similarly advocated resurrection and depreciated immortality, or at least the traditional conception of an immortal soul.[46]

This camp repeatedly makes two points. First, the Bible doesn't sponsor a dualistic anthropology but is rather holistic. Second, modern science makes talk of immaterial souls obsolete.

At the risk of being both unbiblical and unscientific, I'm not on board.

In several important respects, to be sure, we should be sympathetic, or rather more than sympathetic. It'd be beyond inane to close our eyes to the irrefragable results of modern science, and it'd be thoughtless to sponsor an easygoing immortality that makes light of death, of the fear and pain that can attend the dying, and of the grief and loneliness that can afflict survivors. Furthermore, it'd be intolerable to say anything that denigrates material bodies or the physical world—although we should admit, when we take our perfunctory swipes at Platonism, that modern medicine makes it much easier to celebrate bodies. Our progenitors didn't have Novocain, C-sections, or sodium pentothal. The burden of the flesh was much heavier upon them.

Still, I'm not on board.

One problem is the Bible, or at least the New Testament. Although a few have taken it to teach soul sleep, and although William Tyndale (d. 1536), long before Cullmann, held the biblical idea of resurrection and the Hellenistic idea of immortality to be mutually exclusive, the New Testament doesn't anticipate modern physicalism. Matthew, Mark, the author of Luke-Acts, John, and Paul as well as the authors of Hebrews, James, 1 Peter, 2 Peter, and Revelation all believed that the self or some part of it could leave the body and even survive without it.

When Jesus, in Matthew and Mark, walks on the water, his disciples fear that he may be a *phantasma*, a ghost; and when, risen from the dead, he appears to his own in Luke, he denies that he is a *pneuma*, a spirit. The concept of a disembodied spirit wasn't foreign to first-century Jews.

In accord with this, Matthew's Jesus exhorts his followers not to "fear those who kill the body but cannot kill the soul [*tēn psychēn*]; rather fear him who can destroy both soul and body in Gehenna." Implicit is the notion that body and soul are separated at death and joined later for the Last Judgment. Similarly, Luke's Jesus promises the so-called good thief, "Truly, I say to you, today you will be with me in Paradise." Wherever this paradise is, it's not on Golgotha, and they're not going to get there on foot. (Incidentally, the old comeback, sponsored by, among others, Milton, that we should move the comma—"Truly, I say to you today, you will be with me in Paradise"—so that the reunion might be put off until the end of time, is far-fetched. It's true that a few Byzantine manuscripts place the comma after "today," but the tendentious punctuation was designed to obviate the puzzle of how Jesus could be in heaven when he was supposed to be harrowing Hades.)

Paul's letters hold more of the same. Despite his hope to see the second coming and his insistence on resurrection, his true home is in heaven (Phil. 3:20), and he desires to depart and be with Christ, for that is far better than remaining in the flesh (Phil. 1:23–24). The apostle also relates that he was once caught up to the third heaven, to paradise, and that he may not have been in his body at the time (2 Cor. 12:2–3). Paul even, at one point, sounds a bit Platonic: "we look not at what can be seen but at what cannot be seen; for what can be seen is temporary, but what cannot be seen is eternal" (2 Cor. 4:18).

....

In more than one place, then, the New Testament takes for granted that the inner person or sprit is potentially independent of the body and isn't inert after death. This shouldn't surprise. By the first century, all of Judaism was Hellenized, and Greek ideas about immortal souls had been assimilated. This explains why some old Jewish texts plainly speak of souls being separated from bodies at death while others teach that, when the righteous die, they return to God and adore the divine glory. There are even books in which souls exist before taking bodies. In accord with all this, one pseudepigraphon—the so-called Apocryphon of Ezekiel—features a story in which, at the great judgment, the soul excuses itself by blaming the body while the body excuses itself by blaming the soul. Although this book is all about resurrection, it's thoroughly dualistic.

The old Jewish cemetery at Bet She'arim contains some inscriptions that speak of immortality, others that refer to resurrection. They're all from the same community, and some of both kinds of inscriptions are from the same hand. It's also telling that, unlike many moderns, the church fathers, with very few exceptions, didn't take immortality of the soul to be pagan. Nor, with a few exceptions, such as Aphrahat, an early fourth-century Syrian, did they countenance soul sleep.

....

Calvin wrote a short treatise entitled *Psychopannychia*, which is Greek for "falling asleep all night." The splendid subtitle is *A Refutation of the Error Entertained by Some Unskillful Persons, who Ignorantly Imagine that in the*

Interval between Death and the Judgment the Soul Sleeps, together With an Explanation of the Condition and Life of the Soul after this Present Life. In my judgment, Calvin—who reviews the same texts I've cited and more—got it right. The New Testament teaches neither the sleep of the soul (psychopannychism) nor the death of the soul (thnetopsychism), and it doesn't hope only for resurrection. New Testament anthropology remains, in certain respects, dualistic.

For Calvin, this settled what we should think. I'm not like-minded. For me, things are more complicated. I doubt that the New Testament instructs us about brains and minds. Its dualism is naive and unreflective, not dogmatic. To think otherwise, to attempt to distill from the New Testament a metaphysical scheme that directly addresses the ongoing scientific and philosophical debates regarding human nature, human brains, and human consciousness, is like hunting for science in Genesis. We don't do that anymore. Whether we should be monists or dualists or pluralists or idealists or whatever can't be resolved by appeal to chapter and verse.

....

So how do we make a decision? Here's where the Christian materialists are confident. Modern science, they believe, has established that human beings are physical objects. Neurobiology, for instance, demonstrates that everything once attributed to a soul is instead the product of complex brain organization. So the traditional soul is superfluous, a myth, and if Christians are to hold any credible hope for an afterlife, physical resurrection is the only option. To contend otherwise is to kick against the scientific goads.

The opinion is startling. Materialism was defended by ancient skeptics such as Democritus and Lucretius, and by modern rationalists such as Diderot and Feuerbach. The reduction of human beings to a contingent collection of atoms has typically been coupled with the view that our universe is a meaningless, mechanistic, apathetic drama, and that death is oblivion. In Wisdom 2:2, it's the skeptics who proclaim that "reason is a spark kindled by the beating of our hearts." Their modern counterparts are Owen Flanagan and Stephen Hawking. The former weds materialism to naturalism and deems belief in "non-natural things," including souls and God, to "stand in the way of understanding our natures truthfully and locating what makes life meaningful in a nonillusory way."[47] For the latter, the brain is "a computer which will stop working when its components fail. There is no heaven or afterlife for broken down computers; that is a fairy story for people afraid of the dark."[48] It's no wonder that Pope John Paul II declared materialism to be, for Catholic theology, out of bounds.

Observation about the company one keeps isn't, however, an argument. Neither is my suspicion that the new Christian physicalism is a way of making the best of a bad situation, a rationalization to reduce cognitive dissonance, a strategy which enables "climbing on the bandwagon of modern progress."[49]

....

Yet what if one has reasons for being ill-at-ease with the totalizing claims of scientific materialism, whether reductive or nonreductive? My personal library contains books with these titles: *After Physicalism*, *Objections to Physicalism*, *The Waning of Materialism*, and *Irreducible Mind*.[50] Each is a volume of collected essays whose contributors—philosophers, neuroscientists, psychologists—contend that physics-based materialism is a simplification that doesn't cover all the evidence. I also own books with less aggressive titles that nonetheless come to related conclusions. Some of their authors qualify as highly informed critics—Wilder Penfield, the neurosurgeon who first mapped the sensory and motor cortices; Sir Karl Popper, the great philosopher of science; Sir John Eccles, the Nobel Prize–winning brain scientist; Thomas Nagel, one of America's most famous living philosophers; Alvin Plantinga, the eminent analytical philosopher; and Raymond Tallis, the distinguished polymath and Emeritus Professor of Geriatric Medicine at Manchester.[51] In the cases of Popper, Nagel, and Tallis, one can't attribute their views to religious sentiment. Popper was an agnostic. Nagel and Tallis are atheists.

One might respond that I've been reading the wrong books, and that equally prominent authorities, in far greater number, affirm that varied configurations of matter explain everything. But I have read what I have read. Some arguments, moreover, stay with me. This, of course, isn't the place to introduce them. All I can do is insist upon this: not being a materialist doesn't entail being philosophically or scientifically illiterate. It's not like being a young-earth creationist. There's a large literature on materialism, and not all of the erudite contributors come down on the same side.

Scientific materialism may be an extraordinarily productive working hypothesis, as far as it goes in the lab. That's not far enough, however, to make it a metaphysical principle that decisively settles the truth about everything, including human nature. A scientific program—Newtonian mechanics, for instance—can reveal much without revealing everything.

....

But to deny isn't to affirm, and although I'm dubious about materialism, I've nothing to offer in its place. Maybe there's truth to the hypothesis of

William James and neuroscientist Mario Beauregard, that flesh-and-blood brains don't manufacture consciousness but rather regulate, limit, and restrain it—sort of like a TV deciphering electromagnetic waves.[52] Or maybe some part of the self exists in a higher dimensional space, so that our world is like E. A. Abbott's *Flatland*, and we're four- or five-dimensional beings living in a three- or four-dimensional world.[53] The neurobiologist John Smythies has defended an experimentally grounded version of this thesis, arguing that phenomenal space is ontologically distinct from physical space, and that conscious perception exists in a parallel slice of our multidimensional hyperspace.[54]

But then maybe some part of the mind is, following physicist Henry Margenau, a nonmaterial field, analogous to a quantum probability field.[55] Or maybe there's something to the theory of Sir Roger Penrose and Stuart Hameroff, that consciousness is a quantum phenomenon, and that it could, theoretically, exist independently of its current biological home, as a collection of "entangled fluctuations" in quantum space-time geometry. Hameroff has even speculated about a "quantum soul."[56] Or maybe, as the late philosopher C. J. Ducasse insisted, some part of us is indeed an extraordinarily subtle, supersensible substance, more elusive than neutrinos, and we each "carry a future Ghost within" (Thomas Carlyle).[57] One recalls that Hilary of Poitiers and other church fathers, like traditional Hindu metaphysicians, took the soul to be like an exceedingly very thin or diaphanous substance.

I neither believe nor disbelieve any of these hypotheses. I'm neither a dualist nor a pluralist nor a dual-aspect monist but rather, on this subject, an agnostic, intrigued by various possibilities, committed to none. For all I know, matter is congealed spirit. My only conviction is this: despite all our scientific progress, matter remains a profound mystery, consciousness remains a profound mystery, and the self remains a profound mystery, so their relationship remains a profound mystery. One sympathizes with Colin McGinn who, although a naturalist, has argued that consciousness lies forever beyond human understanding.[58] Whether or not he's too pessimistic, I haven't a clue. In the meantime, however, I don't feel compelled to cast my lot with the materialists.

....

This conclusion, I confess, comes as a relief, for if I were obliged to infer that my self is essentially what I've eaten—I'm a pure biological byproduct—I'm not sure what I'd do. The problem is this: If the strict materialists are right, I don't see how, once dead, we can ever live again.

If you leave home and later return, those who welcome you back unthinkingly presume that you continued to exist during your absence. If instead they learn that, after you left, you ceased to be, then they'd regard the thing at the door as an imposter. The return of what doesn't exist makes no sense.

This matters because resurrection is our return, the continuation of our lives. So must there not be continuing selves of some sort between death and resurrection? And if that's so, don't we have to be something more than what the undertaker handles? If you're instead your body and only your body, and if that body disintegrates, aren't you gone for good?

You might respond by waving the magic wand of divine Omnipotence: God can do what we can't imagine. Yet who believes that God can do absolutely anything? Can God make 2 + 2 = 5, or give Lee the victory at Gettysburg after the fact? Even if you hold that the deity can do such things, because with God all things are possible, should you be sanguine about contradictions between your faith and what you otherwise deem credible? If there are mysteries, there are also absurdities. Maybe believing that we're nothing but matter and that we'll nonetheless live despite death is simply nonsense. What if I were to observe that, according to scientists, the world is about 4.5 billion years old, but that its age in Scripture is about 6,000 years, after which I urged assent to both estimates, because we have here a great mystery, beyond understanding—like Jesus being divine and human at the same time? You'd decline to go along. In like fashion, I decline to go along with the notion that, without a soul or some functional equivalent, eternal life is nonetheless possible. Some things just can't be.[59]

....

I've another reason for hoping that materialism isn't compulsory. This one's not philosophical but pastoral.

A Presbyterian minister once shared with me that, when he attended seminary in the 1950s, he was taught that immortality is unbiblical and bad, resurrection scriptural and good. Trusting his teachers, he took their claim to heart. So when, after getting his first church, a grieving widow asked him where her husband had gone, he told her: your beloved is in the ground, dead to himself and the world, awaiting resurrection. Other mourning parishioners received the same news. In each case, the pastor perceived, they took no comfort. On the contrary, their anguish was augmented. His people wanted to hear that their loved ones were in heaven, or with Jesus, or in a better place. Imagining them cold in the dirt didn't console.

This occasioned much reflection on the pastor's part. He eventually decided that, if the gospel is good news, and if his doctrine was bad news, something was amiss. Souls, heaven, and immortality returned to his ministerial vocabulary.

I'm with the pastor on this one. Shouldn't we comfort those who mourn? Shouldn't we tell the grieving that nothing can separate them or those they cherish from the love of God? Yet how does such encouragement comport with teaching that we all rot in the ground for ages untold?

There's also a psychological issue. A recent experiment showed that, when you ask people whether they believe in an afterlife, there's a bit of a falloff if the question comes with a foot massage.[60] Now this seems silly to me, and I wonder how the researchers won funding. But they did, and when their work was finished, they inferred that, the more people are reminded of their embodiment, the harder it is for them to imagine a life beyond this one. If they're right, won't preaching materialism make it harder for pew-sitters to hope for more? Maybe we have here a recipe for the further decline of the mainline churches.

. . . .

Even if one agrees with me that Christian materialism is unnecessary and unattractive, our creeds speak of resurrection, so the question of meaning remains. What then, finally, given all that we know, might we think?

Interpretation is potentially unbounded. One can, for instance, turn resurrection into a political metaphor, as in Ezekiel 37. Or one can make it an effective symbol of personal, existential renewal, as in so many Easter sermons. It'd also make sense for a Christian who believes that God has given us only this life to construe resurrection as a symbol of the circumstance that our molecules will, after we're gone, pass into the ecosystem and be resurrected as vital parts of other living things. What, however, might we make of resurrection if we hope that death isn't extinction?

Surely part of the answer is that the old literalism must be scrapped. As the convoluted debates attest, there's no adequate solution to the problem of shared matter; and it's mighty hard to fathom that bodies designed for earthly life are, with only modest revision, equally designed for life eternal. The discontinuity between now and then must be extreme.

The New Testament isn't all against us here. Jesus, in Matthew, Mark, and Luke, gets after the Sadducees for their slavishly literal and unimaginative critique of resurrection; and Paul, when defending resurrection in 1 Corinthians, doesn't write about bones in the ground. He rather draws an analogy involving seeds and plants, after which he calls the whole thing a mystery. The Bible itself isn't consistently literalistic here.

One can of course retort that Jesus' tomb was empty, and that if our fate is akin to his, then our flesh must also be taken up. Since the body of Jesus that rose was the same that was spat upon and crucified, won't we too rise in the same body in which we suffered and died?

The argument isn't hollow. Nonetheless, substantial discontinuities between his resurrection and whatever awaits us are undeniable. His body, as Acts 2:31 puts it, saw no corruption. Our bodies will decay. He rose on the third day. We'll be in the ground longer than that. And so it goes. Christ's victory over death can't be the blueprint for our victory. First John says that we'll be like him, but that's the end, the goal, and maybe there's more than one means of getting there. As Aquinas put it, "Christ's resurrection is the exemplar of ours as to the term 'whereto' but not as to the term 'wherefrom.'"[61]

. . . .

If we cast aside literalism, resurrection language must be a way of suggesting an eschatological future that transcends prosaic description, a future that can only be intimated through sacred metaphor and sanctified imagination. In other words, resurrection, like the parables of Jesus, characterizes God's future for us via an analogy, in recognition of the fact that we can't do any better. We see dimly.

But what might resurrection, understood as picture language, help us to fathom?

The beginning of an answer comes from considering the historical context in which Jews first embraced the doctrine. For them, resurrection wasn't the antithesis of nonexistence, as it might be for a modern materialist. It was rather the antithesis of being in Sheol, the Bible's name for the land of the dead. This realm was thought of as wholly undesirable. Its wraith-like inhabitants were enfeebled shades, pale phantoms of their former selves, without hope of egress. Pathetically weak, they couldn't even praise God. The miserable place was the Hebrew's counterpart to the Greek Hades, which in Homer houses the "mindless" dead, who are nothing but images of mortals who've come undone. For the old Israelites, death meant Sheol, and Sheol meant existence without life.

One guesses that ideas about Sheol grew out of human experience. Apparitions of the dead are a cross-cultural reality.[62] Indeed, and however one explains the fact, people frequently see the departed. Moreover, while many apparitions are lifelike and comforting, others are transparent, mechanical, and inexpressive. Presumably it was this latter type that informed Jewish ideas about Sheol. To be in the Pit was to be like the stereotypical ghost—an insubstantial vestige, desolate and lost.

Resurrection, when it finally entered Jewish theology, was the negation of all this. It was the belief that God won't permit Israel to pine away in hopeless misery. It was the faith that the bars of Sheol won't ultimately prevail: the prisoners will be set free. It was the conviction that God isn't the God of the dead—that is, of ghosts—but of the living, so what awaits the saints can be hoped for instead of dreaded.

We may, if we choose, share this conviction, even while jettisoning the old literalism. Of course, how such a future might come to pass, or what it might mean concretely, who knows? One could fantasize, on the basis of the stories where the risen Jesus appears and disappears and seems to be material and not material, that resurrected life will mean the ability to participate fully in whatever worlds or dimensions we find ourselves. What counts most, however, is the hope that what lies ahead is not less but more.

....

If resurrection effectually communicates the hope that life in the world to come is full rather than attenuated, it also effectually conveys that the fate of the one is bound up with the fate of the many. Bodily resurrection isn't about the lone individual. It's rather a public and communal event at one point in time. In Matthew 25, all the nations are gathered before the Son of Man, and in Revelation 20, all the dead stand together before the great white throne. Here Christian art follows the Bible and gets it right. Scenes of the resurrection typically depict large crowds. Even Jesus, in the old icons of his resurrection, isn't alone. As he departs from Hades and rises from the dead, he hauls others up with him, including Adam and Eve, representatives of fallen and redeemed humanity. His defeat of death is their defeat of death. His victory is their victory. So resurrection is about the human collectivity. It puts everyone in the same story by giving us all the same ending. In this resurrection differs from and is superior to that other chief symbol of the afterlife, immortality. Resurrection isn't about you or about me but about us, and about a kingdom. When, in the Revelation of John, the saints rise from the dead, they enter the New Jerusalem, with its twelve open gates. That means they enter a city, which by definition shelters a large collection of people.

That we will, if we continue to exist, be our true selves only in community is a sensible projection from life as we now know it, and it's a projection encouraged by the image of bodily resurrection. For bodies are more than biological machines. They're also the vehicles by which we establish and maintain social relationships. Bodies make it possible for us to know others and for others to know us. So profession of the resurrection is a way of saying that the world to come will be, like this one, communal. Here I recall some words of A. E. Taylor: "to be in Heaven, as Christianity conceives of it, is to be a member of a society of persons who see God, themselves, and each other as all truly are, without confusion or illusion, and who love God, themselves and each other with the love of this true insight; what is more than this is imaginative mythology."[63] Origen has a beautiful passage in which he ponders why Jesus took a vow not to drink again of the fruit of the vine until the coming of the kingdom. He proposes that, as long as others suffer or sin, the risen Jesus, even though he's in heaven, can't but grieve. So too, according to Origen, is it with the apostles: they can't know perfect joy as long as earth's miserable affairs continue as ever. They are like the saints of olden times: "Abraham is still waiting to obtain the perfect things. Isaac waits, and Jacob and all the prophets wait for us, that they may lay hold of the perfect blessedness with us."[64] Even after death we are members of one another.

....

However helpful resurrection may be as a symbol of life in its fullness and of a shared future, its chief service may lie elsewhere. For if one thing seems assured, it's that we have no power in the face of death. We may, with diet and exercise or whatnot, fend off the sickle for a bit, but the hour comes when none of us will work; and if we aren't to be vanquished utterly, it won't be because we've got something up our sleeve.

Some modern theologians underline the point by insisting that to be dead means not to exist. God, they say, brings life out of things that are not. They're like Milton and Thomas Hobbes, who thought that the death of the soul followed by resurrection would be the best way to preserve God's grace and omnipotence.

I think of things a bit differently. It's true that God is the subject of our sentences with "will raise" or "will resurrect" in them. Yet neither the New Testament nor the dominant Christian tradition teaches that to die is to cease to be. Resurrection isn't the gift of existence as such but the end of being ghosts. It's like Christ harrowing Hades. The dead who rise with the savior are already there when he shows up. They're waiting, hoping to exchange the desolation of the underworld for the joys of heaven.

Nonetheless, death would indeed seem to be the utter end of all human effort, of any illusion that we're masters of our fate. You can't resolve either to be extinguished or to live on after brain death. And if you do somehow live on, you can't choose which part of you does so, or where it goes, or how it gets there. If there's an agent in death, it can only be God. We're reduced to hope. Our incapacity makes us like Jesus on the cross. All he could do was close his eyes and commit his spirit to Another.

Maybe, once we become acclimatized to whatever ultimately awaits us, there'll be a place for our decisions and our efforts. But at the moment when we pass from here to there, it'll be like our first coming into this world. When born, we were ignorant and passive, and we couldn't provide for ourselves. All we could do was instinctively cry out for nourishment and comfort. And as it was in our beginning, so will it be at our end.

....

Some people feel that they've been thrown into this world. Although I don't dispute their experience, mine is different. I feel that I was gently laid down here. Maybe that's why so much of life has seemed to be a gift, including my body, which I didn't design or build. As soon as I became aware, it was just there, going about its manifold business.

Furthermore, I don't really understand much about it. I don't know how to break down food or how to distribute nutrients. I don't know how to heal cuts or how to battle infections. I don't know how to manufacture saliva or how to contract muscles. All these things, and a million more of which I'm the beneficiary, just happen. I do none of them. Science, to be sure, helps me to understand some of what goes on, but it was all going on long before my teachers and my books taught me anything.

We're all immersed in a great Wisdom that we didn't invent and don't control, a great Wisdom that's been with us since birth. Hope in resurrection is the conviction that this Wisdom won't abandon us as death approaches but will accompany us to whatever awaits us.

CHAPTER 3

Judgment and Partiality

....

> Just as bread is the most necessary of all foods, so the
> thought of death is the most essential of all works.
>
> JOHN CLIMACUS

> We are called upon to trust, not Jesus' knowledge
> of the future, but his imagination.
>
> GARRETT GREEN

> I am like a man on a sea voyage nearing his destination. When I embarked I
> worried about having a cabin with a porthole, whether I should be asked to sit
> at the captain's table, who were the more attractive and important passengers.
> All such considerations become pointless when I shall soon be disembarking.
>
> MALCOLM MUGGERIDGE

....

ALTHOUGH ICONS FILL my study, only one sits on my desk, staring me in the face. It's not Isaac of Nineveh, who makes me feel that all shall be well. Nor is it one of my non-canonical icons of Origen, who should have been sainted rather than anathematized. It's rather Sisoës the Great, an Egyptian anchorite of the fifth century, about whom we know little.

His icon, which appears first in the fifteenth century and presumably depicts an imaginary event, has the aged saint standing behind a casket. His bearded face stares through the glass cover, at the skeleton inside. Lying haphazardly on the ground, in front of the coffin, are a shield, a scepter, a sword, and a crown. The inscription reads: "Sisoës, the great among ascetics, stood before the tomb of Alexander, emperor of the Greeks, who at one time had shone with glory; and, horrified by the inexorable passing of time and the vanity of this transient world, he cried aloud: 'Lo! Beholding thee, o grave, I fear the judgment of God and I weep, for the common destiny of all humanity comes to mind! Oh death, who can escape thee?'"

This icon is my *memento mori*, my daily reminder that night comes, when I shall no longer work. For me, its image and inscription evoke Shelley's famous "Ozymandias," which tells of the wrecked statue of a defunct king of kings, a colossal memorial that lies in ruin, half-sunk beneath the desert sands. The poem, like the icon, forcefully communicates that all human achievement, however grand, must fade, and that, from this point of view, all is vanity.

The saint, however, says something that Shelley doesn't. Sisoës confesses: "I fear the judgment of God." For the horrified monk, death doesn't just lay waste to all that we do. It's also the portal to judgment, when even saints must give an account to God.

This is a pretty old-fashioned idea. Not that the judgment has disappeared utterly. Its prominence in the Bible and the creeds requires that at least theologians and biblical scholars pay it some heed. But books and articles written by the professionals needn't tell us much about the amateurs, which means almost everybody.

From the approximately 2,000 Sunday mornings I've gone to church, I recall no mainline Protestant pastor exhorting me to fear the judgment of God. Divine judgment also hasn't been a hot topic in the e-mails I receive. "Dear Professor Allison: Have you changed your mind about the resurrection?" "Dear Professor Allison: Is it possible that Jesus never existed?" "Dear Professor Allison: What do you think of Bart Ehrman's latest book?" These are the sorts of questions that typically show up in my Microsoft Outlook inbox. No one ever solicits my views about the Last Judgment. There's the occasional query about hell, but that's almost always about who's in and who's out.

A seeming lack of concern with judgment is also evidenced in our Protestant liturgies. Maybe the Eastern Orthodox still regularly pray "that we may have a good response at the fearful judgment seat of Christ," but their petition has no weekly equivalent in the Protestant services known to me. The closest we get is when we recite the Apostles' Creed: "He shall come to judge the living and the dead." But one theologian has dubbed this the "least-loved statement of the Creed,"[1] and the words rarely if ever resonate with anything else in the rest of the service. I'd bet that, for most, the line is largely or wholly empty.

Representative of the modern outlook is a revision made to the Book of

Common Prayer. The 1928 edition, in its wedding service, had these words: "I require and charge you both, as ye will answer in the Dreadful day of Judgment, when the secrets of all hearts shall be disclosed, that if either of you knows any impediment why ye may not be lawfully joined together in Matrimony, ye do now confess it." In the 1979 Episcopalian version, this eschatologically braced imperative becomes: "I require and charge you both, here in the presence of God, that if either of you know any reason why you may not be united in marriage lawfully, and in accordance with God's Word, you do now confess it." The dreadful day of judgment, when the secrets of all hearts shall be disclosed, has been scratched.

The deletion typifies our age. Heaven and hell, it's true, still make it now and then to the covers of popular magazines. When, however, was the last time the newsstands featured an article on the great assize? In like manner, although polls of religious opinion regularly take the pulse of belief in the afterlife, what pollster has measured sentiment about the Last Judgment?

The pollsters haven't been reading the Bible, where heaven and hell are subsets of the much larger theme of judgment. The Scriptures say very little about hell or about heaven as usually understood. Judgment, by contrast, is everywhere. "If you are angry with a brother or sister, you will be liable to judgment" (Matt. 5:22). "The people of Nineveh will rise up at the judgment with this generation and condemn it" (Matt. 12:41). "We will all stand before the judgment seat of God" (2 Cor. 5:10). "The time has come for judgment to begin with the household of God" (1 Pet. 4:17).

. . . .

Why, despite the numerous biblical texts, are most mainstream pulpits mum about eschatological judgment? Part of the explanation must lie in the demise of hell. As attested by numerous old paintings, in which the fiery pit is at the bottom of portrayals of the returning Christ, hell was historically imagined to be the immediate upshot of judgment. We might, then, expect the cultural fate of the one eschatological conviction to correlate with the cultural fate of the other. And so it is. Hell is at the periphery of modern culture and modern theology, and judgment is likewise at the periphery. Hell, however, is the chief topic of another chapter, so what else might one observe regarding modern apathy regarding judgment?[2]

Maybe it's relevant that, in our everyday conversations, the verb "judge" and the noun "judgment" typically carry negative connotations. "Who are you to judge?" is a refrain in our collective conversations. It's a sign of our easy relativism that the biblical words perhaps most often heard in our culture come from Jesus' rebuke of the crowd in John 8: "Let whoever among you is without sin cast the first stone." Biblical literacy may be low, but everyone's heard these words. Another imperative known to all appears in Matthew and Luke: "Judge not." Tellingly, the command is, most often, unaccompanied by its conclusion, "so that you may not be judged."

It's instructive to contrast, over against the generally pejorative connotations of "judge" and "judgment," the typically positive connotations of the closely related word, "justice." "Justice for all" emphatically concludes our Pledge of Allegiance, and the phrase is the motto for the Campaign for Human Rights in the Philippines. The old Superman was introduced, on both radio and TV, with the assertion that the superhero fights a never-ending battle for, among other things, justice; and the Justice League of America is full of likeminded others—Batman, Wonder Woman, Flash—for whom we all cheer. Martin Luther King Jr.'s "I Have a Dream" speech pleads for "racial justice," augurs "the security of justice," and anticipates "the bright day of justice." A "just war" is, we are taught, a good war, and bad people, we hope, get their "just deserts." The reason we fret when justice and love seem to travel divergent paths is that we value the one almost as much as the other. People of different political persuasions may debate issues surrounding "social justice," "economic justice," and "restorative justice," but no one goes to bat for "injustice." One guesses that theologians wanting to say something about the final judgment might gain more attention if they spoke and wrote about "the ultimate justice."

....

However that may be, we're not coherent when we applaud justice and jeer judgment. In a fallen world, it's often impossible to have one without the other. Justice at Nuremberg only followed judgment at Nuremberg. And on a personal level, we all expect the courts to take our side and uphold justice when we've been wronged, which requires that a judge or jury pass judgment. Nevertheless, "judge not" is a rhetorical staple.

What's the upshot? If, as a rule, we don't want others judging us, perhaps this affects, on some level, our feelings about God. If everyone else should reserve judgment, why should the deity be so very different? Who appointed God judge, jury, and executioner?

Our modern relativism might also move us to wonder by what criteria a final judgment, a separation of the tares from the wheat, could be conducted. Doesn't a universal judgment imply a universal standard? If, however, as we commonly suppose, there's no one-size-fits-all religion or one-size-fits-all morality, how could there be a one-size-fits-all doomsday?

One may protest, of course, that the Supreme Being should be up to the task, and further that the current culture shouldn't set the agenda for the churches. Yet it won't do much good. If, as John A. T. Robinson remarked over fifty years ago, "judgment is an embarrassing theme,"[3] many pastors will preach, or rather not preach, accordingly.

If they're Presbyterians, the hymnal will help. The current PCUSA hymnal has a topical index at the end. "Justice" has nine entries. "Judgment" isn't there. (The ratio in my 1845 edition of the complete hymns of Isaac Watts is, by contrast, almost exactly the other way around: eight for judgment, one for justice.)

....

If there's a cultural problem with the concept of judgment, there's also a theological problem. It has to do with justification by faith. The New Testament teaches that grace, not works, is the source of eschatological salvation, and that believers have already passed from death to life. Yet the New Testament likewise insists that one is justified by works, which will be reviewed at the Last Judgment. We have here a well-known puzzle.

The difficulty arises not only because Paul's letters seem to be at odds with the Epistle of James and the Gospel of Matthew. The problem is also internal to the Pauline corpus, which champions justification by faith yet also teaches that all must appear before the judgment seat of Christ, in order to receive good or evil, according to what they have done in the body (2 Cor. 5:10). If the faithful have already been acquitted and saved, if the verdict's already in on the basis of faith, how can there be a coming judgment according to works? There seems to be, in Paul, a formal contradiction between judgment by works and justification by faith.

Historically, however, Christians have been loath to espy such conflict within the canon. They've accordingly offered various rationalizations, whether their topic has been Paul against Paul or Paul against others. It's been common, for example, to opine that the denial of justification by works refers to deeds antecedent to faith and baptism whereas the affirmation of justification by works refers to post-baptismal behavior, to deeds that follow faith. Some with this view hold that, for Christians, the judgment won't determine their salvation but rather establish their reward, their rank in heaven's hierarchy. As John Gill put it: "this judgment will not be of their persons, on which their final state depends; but of their works; and that it might appear, that the distribution of favours to them, in this kingdom-state, is just and equitable."[4]

Others have collared the problem by appealing to divergent historical contexts: dissimilar sentiments were appropriate for different congregations or different states of mind. Maybe, for instance, as Bede argued, the author of the Epistle of James perceived that his audience needed to hear more about works whereas Paul, for the most part, thought his readers needed to hear more about faith.[5] Or maybe, as some modern commentators have urged, with reference to the tension internal to Paul, the message of justification was directed to scrupulous legalists whereas warnings of judgment were for those who thought they could live as they pleased.

There's no need to catalog further opinion. The sole point here is that, rightly or wrongly, many have sensed that justification by faith and judgment by works are antagonists. The consequence is this: The more one stresses justification by faith, the more one tends to neglect, consciously or unconsciously, judgment by works. This explains why many of my born and bred Protestant students, when asked to contemplate certain New Testament texts, become unsettled. Persuaded that justification by faith is everything, they find Luke 12:41–48, where one servant gets a severe beating while one gets a light beating, perplexing. They're also usually nonplussed by 1 Corinthians 3:10–15, where Paul teaches that those who've built on the right foundation will receive a reward whereas those who haven't done so well will see their work "burned up" and "will suffer loss," being saved "only as through fire." Reading the Bible with the assumption that works count nothing for salvation, many are uneasy with eschatological promotion and demotion on the basis of works. They fend off cognitive dissonance by disregarding the doctrine of judgment.

Some theologians have made related moves. William Ames, the early Calvinist, spoke for many when he asserted that "the sins of the faithful will not come into judgment. In this life they are covered and taken away by the sentence of justification; the Last Judgment will be a confirmation and manifestation of that sentence. It would not be right that they should again be brought to light."[6] Two centuries later, the German theologian Heinrich Heppe wrote to like effect: "the godly will not really be judged, but Christ will separate them from the others, that they may be witnesses of his real judgments, by which he turns over . . . men from their own works to their godlessness and worthy condemnation."[7] The same idea appears already in Luther, who boldly insisted that "the judgment is abolished; it concerns the believers as little as it does the angels. . . . We who believe shall not be judged. . . . All believers pass from this life into heaven without any judgment."[8]

Incidentally, art history reflects the impact of Luther and like-minded others. Before the Reformation, the psychostasis, or weighing of a soul in the pans of judgment, was a prominent element in depictions of the grand assize. After the Reformation, the scales began to move from the center of paintings to the periphery, and they got smaller and smaller. The Reformers' stress on faith and justification over against works marginalized the pans.

Rendering the Last Judgment anticlimactic wasn't, however, without some pre-Protestant precedent. In the fourth century, Jerome, influenced by John 5:24 ("anyone who hears my word and believes him who sent me has eternal life, and does not come under judgment, but has passed from death to life"), insisted that faithful Christians will not be judged, that only the wayward need much worry.[9] Zeno, bishop of Verona, had similar thoughts,[10] as did, later on, Gregory the Great, Maximus the Confessor, Julian of Toledo, and Peter Lombard.[11]

....

So far I've suggested that the Last Judgment is peripheral for many, partly because relativism is our prevailing ideology, and partly because belief in justification by faith has inhibited some from envisaging eschatological judgment for themselves. There's something equally obvious and important to consider, however. The Last Judgment presupposes that we're accountable for our actions. So what happens when new knowledge assails traditional notions of personal responsibility?

My public education, from grade school on, impressed upon me that genes and environment determine who we are. As to whether nature or nurture is more significant, whether it's toilet training and parental discipline or DNA and the extra Y chromosome that make all the difference, my teachers disagreed. But whichever side of the debate they championed, none ever spoke of a third factor. So when I added up the percentage of influence assigned to genes and the percentage of influence assigned to environment, the total was always one hundred. The implication was patent. Factors beyond our choosing steer our destinies.

Since leaving college, I've run across countless claims that reinforce my old school lesson, claims such as these:

The religious opinions of identical twins separated at birth are closer than the religious views of non-identical twins separated at birth.

Brain scans reveal that the prefrontal cortices of imprisoned murderers are likely to be less developed than those of other citizens, and further that the smaller a convict's amygdala, the more likely that individual will, upon release, return to jail.

If you were abused as a child, and if you carry the monoamine oxidase A gene, the odds that you will abuse others are greater than if you were abused as a child and don't have that particular gene.

When patients with Parkinson's take a drug called Pramipexole, some of them with no prior history of gambling turn into passionate gamesters.

Certain defects involving the hippocampus and the corpus callosum seem to play a role in psychopathology, because they correlate with excessive aggression, reduced empathy, and diminished conscience.

Now if these are indeed facts, and if the stack of such facts continues to grow—as the new discipline of neurocriminology assumes it will—it's obvious that our behavior can't be understood apart from our biology. Indeed, maybe in certain important respects biology is destiny. How responsible can we be if biomarkers are statistically significant predictors of our behavior?

....

It gets worse. The neuroscientists who peer into our skulls see no breaks in the chemical and electrical chains of causation, so some of them, such as Paul and Patricia Churchland, regard free will, which they can't locate, as an illusion, or even insist that our thoughts and feelings are epiphenomena, by-products of complex neural activities.[12] To them we're effectively meat puppets. Those in this camp always refer to the experiments of Benjamin Libet, who famously showed that, milliseconds before we consciously will an action, the brain displays a so-called readiness potential.[13] In other words, before we decide to do something, the cascade that will lead to our action has already commenced. So maybe the so-called hard determinists are right. Maybe we don't consciously decide what to do. We just go along with what some unconscious process has already decided. Our decisions are downstream from the main events; they're figments, rationalizations *ex eventu.*

More recently, in 2013, experiments established that, when people are asked to decide between adding or subtracting numbers, their likely decision can be, more often than not, decoded from neural activity three to four seconds before they report themselves coming to a decision.[14]

Even without such experiments, introspection reveals that our conscious minds do less than we typically imagine. I've often awakened in the morning, thought about getting out of bed, and then gotten up before deciding to do so. My conscious assent didn't lead. It followed. It's the same sometimes when I'm lying on my back, trying to psyche myself up for the next series of bench presses. I frequently start before I resolve to begin. How often, I've got to wonder, am I my own by-stander, a self-deluded Johnny-come-lately?

Even though I don't worship at the shrine of free will, I'd like to think, despite much expert opinion to the contrary, that I'm an actor in my life's drama, not an onlooker. I want my thoughts to disrupt the world's chain of causes and effects. Thus I'm tempted to muster here some reasons for hoping that they do so. It would, however, take us too far afield to introduce the criticisms of Libet, or to explore why brain plasticity may suggest a place for the conscious will, or to ponder experiments which show that we cheat less when told that we have free will and cheat more when told we're determined.[15] All that would, moreover, be beside the main point, which is that much modern knowledge conspires to make us second guess our sense of responsibility.

....

We're left with two questions. The first is sociological. In a world where we think of ourselves as products of genes and environment, in a world where the idea of personal responsibility has been dismissed as folk psychology and dubbed a "cultural construct," a fiction that's convenient for some, inconvenient for others, won't the doctrine of the Last Judgment become less and less plausible for more and more people? The second question is theological. How can God hold us accountable for what we've said and done when we're not wholly accountable for what we've said and done?

One might launch a response to these queries by observing that our tradition hasn't been naively overconfident regarding human freedom. Language about sin has often been coupled with language about slavery, and talk about salvation has often been joined to talk about election. That we're not wholly in charge has always been evident to honest reflection. Saints know what it's like to do the very things they hate. They likewise testify to having been rescued and led by a Reality beyond themselves.

Our subjection to outside forces and our restricted autonomy aren't, however, the topics I shall pursue in the rest of this chapter. I wish rather to suggest that, whatever we make of the complex, ongoing philosophical and scientific debates regarding human accountability, the biblical idea of eschatological judgment may be profitably related to a little-studied but fascinating human experience.

....

The account of the vision of the Last Judgment in Daniel 7 includes this sentence: "The court sat in judgment, and the books were opened" (7:10). Revelation elaborates: "And I saw the dead, great and small, standing before the throne, and books were opened. Also another book was opened, the book of life. And the dead were judged according to their works, as recorded in the books" (20:12). Because omniscience doesn't need written records to jog the memory, we shouldn't take the language of Daniel and Revelation literally. The biblical scenes must be figurative ways of saying that, in the end, the whole truth without disguise will come to light.

Some of the church fathers agreed. They developed the idea of judgment by borrowing from Romans 2:14-16: "When Gentiles . . . do instinctively what the law requires . . . they show that what the law requires is written on their hearts, to which their own conscience also bears witness; and their conflicting thoughts will accuse or perhaps excuse them on the day when . . . God, through Jesus Christ, will judge the secret thoughts of all." Cyril of Jerusalem taught that we will, on the last day, be judged in the light of our own conscience; and according to Basil the Great, God will illumine our hearts so that our memories will pass before us and our own sins will testify against us.[16] Dorotheos of Gaza identified the accuser of Luke 12:58—"when you go with your accuser before a magistrate, on the way make an effort to settle the case, or you may be dragged before the judge"—with the conscience, which will reproach us when we come under judgment.[17]

Augustine also adopted this idea. With reference to the books in Revelation 20, he wrote: "we must understand this to mean a kind of divine power which will ensure that all the actions, good and bad, of every individual will be recalled to mind and presented to the mind's view with miraculous speed, so that each person's knowledge will accuse or excuse his conscience, and thus each and all will be judged simultaneously. This divine power is no doubt called a 'book' because it ensures the recollection of the facts, and those facts are, as we may say, 'read' in this process."[18]

These words, which Aquinas and other theologians later endorsed, and which have a striking parallel in Dorotheos of Gaza,[19] much intrigue me. The reason is that they are astonishingly close to what we often find in modern accounts of so-called near-death experiences (NDEs). People who've been to the brink of death and returned to tell about it commonly report that their lives were reviewed along the lines Augustine indicated. Here are four accounts:

1) All of my life up till the present seemed to be placed before me in a kind of panoramic, three-dimensional review, and each event seemed to be accompanied by a consciousness of good or evil or with an insight into cause or effect. Not only did I perceive everything from my own viewpoint, but I also knew the thoughts of everyone involved in the event, as if I had their thoughts within me. This meant that I perceived not only what I had done or thought, but even in what way it had influenced others, as if I saw things with all-seeing eyes. . . . And all the time during the review the importance of love was emphasised. Looking back, I cannot say how long this life review and life insight lasted . . . but at the same time it seemed just a fraction of a second, because I perceived it all at the same moment.[20]

2) I saw everything happen from birth till then in fast motion. Also, while this was happening I could feel the feelings of these events. I could also feel any pain I gave out to others. I also felt the goodness I'd given out.[21]

3) It's like climbing right inside a movie of your life. Every moment from every year of your life is played back in complete sensory detail. Total, total recall. And it all happens in an instant.[22]

4) Everything seemed to be at one moment, even when "events" seemed to occur in a sequence. . . . It *was* a re-experiencing of my life, but from three different perspectives simultaneously. One perspective was my version of my life as I might have recounted it. . . . However I was also experiencing my life from the perspective of those with whom I was involved. I felt what they felt, I lived their emotions as they acted with and reacted to me. This was *their* version of my life. . . . I felt the pain and frustration my actions caused *them*. It was an absolutely different view of my life and it was not a pretty one. . . . At exactly the same time I experienced a *third* view of my life. . . . It was an unbiased view, free of the subjective and self-serving rationalizations that the others and I had used to support the countless acts of selfishness and lack of true love in our lives. To me it can only be described as God's view of my life. It was what had *really* happened, the real motivations, the truth. . . . All of

this—the three-way re-experiencing of my life and self-judgment—was simultaneous and yet separate and distinct.[23]

There's a reason we've all heard the phrase "My whole life flashed before my eyes." We've heard it because it happens.

Now perhaps you're allergic to NDEs because, unlike me, you're queasy about paying much attention to anything outside the scientific mainstream. But for our immediate purposes it's moot whether NDEs are wholly endogenous or incorporate authentically transcendent elements. What counts is only that the experience, whatever the explanation, is subjectively real and common: the great cloud of witnesses bars all doubt. Their testimony, moreover, is cross-cultural and cross-temporal. Accounts of life-reviews—which sometimes move from the present to the past, other times from the past to the present—come not just from the Americas and Europe but from Saudi Arabia, China, India, Thailand, Sri Lanka, Tibet, and Melanesia;[24] and if you know where to look, you can find them sprinkled throughout history. Of course, like every other human experience, it's remembered, interpreted, and written up differently in different times and places. In India, for example, the myth is that, when you die, the god Chitragupta consults the Akashic record that's he kept, over the course of your lifetime, of all you've done. But that people in multiple cultures and for centuries have had the same basic experience is patent.

....

In 1892, the Zürich geology professor Albert Heim published an article entitled "Notes on Death through Falling."[25] He interviewed climbers who had fallen off mountains and yet survived. They often reported to him that they had, while falling, experienced a review of their entire lives. This matched Heim's own experience, because he too had once fallen and seen his whole life pass before him. Heim's goal in writing was to console the families of individuals who had died in the mountains. On the basis of his interviews, he felt confident assuring them that, in their loved ones' final moments, they had "reviewed their individual pasts in states of transfiguration."

Decades before Heim wrote, Rear-Admiral Sir Francis Beaufort (1774–1857) came close to drowning at sea. After his last gasp of breath, his body went limp, but internally

thought rose above thought with a rapidity of succession that is not only indescribable, but probably inconceivable by anyone who has not himself been in a similar situation. . . . Travelling backwards, every past incident of my life seemed to glance across my recollection in retrograde succession; not, however, in mere outline . . . but the picture filled up with every minute and collateral feature. In short, the whole period of my existence seemed to be placed before me in a kind of panoramic review, and each act of it seemed to be accompanied by a consciousness of right or wrong, or by some reflection on its cause or its consequences.[26]

Evidence for the life review goes back millennia. Pythagoras purportedly taught that, when death approaches, the soul sees its earthly existence in abridged scenes rapidly succeeding one another, with startling clearness.[27] Then there's *The Teaching for King Merikare*, which comes from the First Intermediate Period in Egyptian history, which means it comes from before 2055 BCE. The text teaches that, at death, the deceased's deeds are "set before him as a sum," and that the judges "view a lifetime as but an hour." Jan Assmann interprets the text this way: the deceased is accountable for a lifetime that's replayed "in a single hour, as though it were a biographical film. . . . Here we already see the Judgment of the Dead in its classic form: as a scene in which the deceased is confronted no longer by his enemy but by his own life, his own guilt, and by his judge."[28]

. . . .

Why does Augustine's idea of the Last Judgment line up with a well-attested human experience? It's a good guess that he or his tradition merged the biblical idea of a last judgment with the testimonies of people who, near death, had viewed, in a moment, the gallery of their personal memories.

What I postulate for Augustine is clear in a passage written by the nineteenth-century Bishop of Dublin, Richard Whately. In his treatise on the last things, Whately wrote this: "There are some persons to whom it occasionally happens, that at some particular moments, the events of many past years flash across the mind . . . very distinctly, in a very short time; though it would take many hours to record them in words."[29] The Bishop then went on: "It is neither impossible, nor even improbable, that in another life, a single moment may set before us a vivid, complete, distinct recollection of all that has passed in this [life]; and that each may thus have as sudden, as clear, and as complete a view of his own character, as he has of his person when a glass is placed before him."[30] Whately consciously projected the life-review known from human testimony onto the biblical prospect of the judgment of the dead. On his view, the conscience of each individual, vivified, impartial, and informed by an accurate life review, will, at death, pass sentence on that individual's life.

Whately was followed by the Scottish theologian Alexander Macleod,[31] who drew attention to Coleridge's idea that a quickened, comprehensive memory could be "the dread book of judgment, in whose mysterious hieroglyphs every idle world is recorded."[32] The same notion appealed to Thomas de Quincey:

> I was once told by a near relative of mine, that having in her childhood fallen into a river, and being on the very verge of death but for the critical assistance which reached her, she saw in a moment her whole life, in its minutest incidents, arrayed before her simultaneously as in a mirror; and she had a faculty developed as suddenly for comprehending the whole and every part. . . . I have . . . seen the same thing asserted twice in modern books, and accompanied by a remark which I am convinced is true, namely, that the dread book of account, which the Scriptures speak of, is, in fact, the mind itself of each individual.[33]

Jewish tradition attests to the same merger, for it too knows the idea that death leads to a comprehensive viewing of one's life, interpreted as the judgment of God. The Hasidic Rabbi, Yitzhak Meir of Ger, taught that "what man fears is the moment [at death when] he will survey from the other world everything he has experienced on this earth."[34] Centuries before Rabbi Yitzhak, the Talmud attributed to "the Rabbis" the view that, at the hour "when a man departs to his eternal home, all his deeds are enumerated before him and he is told, Such and such a thing have you done, in such and such a place on that particular day."[35]

....

The life review raises challenging questions. What accounts for this thing, which is so often profoundly meaningful? How can hitting the wall of death sometimes cause a lifetime of memories to replay themselves coherently? Why, if it's a defense mechanism, as a few have urged, are some NDErs so enthralled that they subsequently long for death more than life? Maybe someday the scientists will find the chemical or electrical trigger, but that still won't explain why evolution selected for this startling talent. What is its survival value or biological benefit?

One likewise wonders how so much can be perceived in an instant. The cognitive scientists have established that time can be experienced at different rates, but the instantaneous presentation of a whole life pushes credulity. How can it happen? And what does it say about the relativity of time and the nature of consciousness? Beyond that, doesn't full recollection imply the controversial thesis that we never really forget anything? Here are two testimonies:

"It was amazing how my life was shown with events I had completely forgotten about and others that were so insignificant that it felt like I was seeing each frame of the personal movie of my life on earth."[36]

"Many trifling events which had been long forgotten then crowded into my imagination, and with the character of recent familiarity."[37]

What is going on here? Wilder Penfield, the famous neurosurgeon, was able to summon disremembered facts by electrically stimulating the temporal lobes of his epileptic patients,[38] and we all know what it's like to be struck, out of the blue, by something we haven't thought of for decades. Most of us also have had the experience of waking up, not remembering any dreams, and then, later on in the day, in response to some random prompt, recalling one of them. Somewhere inside was a dormant memory. Maybe, then, there are a million more of them in each of us. Maybe our past isn't dead but sleeping. Maybe there's a video recorder in our heads that never shuts off. Scientists have now found four people who appear to have near perfect, plenary recall over most of their lives. My hunch is that they're different not because their memory vaults are larger but because, for reasons unknown, they have unrestricted access.

Another question. How reliable is the outpouring of memories near death, and is the answer the same for everybody? Recent studies have abundantly documented the rampant sins of ordinary memory. We're constantly revising, abbreviating, and contaminating recall. Is the life review similarly infected by such distortions, or does it hold up better? I've no idea—although it's intriguing that one reviewer of hundreds of NDEs claimed to have come across nothing "unrealistic."[39] Unlike dreams, life reviews, it appears, aren't phantasmagoric or bizarre. I can also add, for what it may or may not be worth, that one NDEr reported that he was able to recall an incident of which he had no previous conscious knowledge,[40] and further that we have a story from the nineteenth century in which somebody claimed to have recovered a lost contract after nearly drowning and seeing, in his life review, where he'd hidden it.[41]

One last puzzle. According to many, the life review brought home to them the supremacy of love and/or knowledge, or helped them to understand the consequences of their actions, as in this account: "Everything I ever thought, did, said, [everyone I] hated, helped, did not help, should have helped was shown in front of me . . . like a movie. How mean I'd been to people. . . . I saw how my acting, or not acting, rippled in effect towards other people and their lives."[42] Yet we also have an occasional report such as this one: "There flashed . . . a perfect picture of my past life in every detail. . . . Conscience appeared to play no part in the matter."[43] What are we to make of this? Memories, it seems, can come to life while one's conscience remains inert. Viewing one's past doesn't always stir regret or inspire repentance.

. . . .

However one sorts through the issues that I've just introduced, it appears to me that historians of doctrine shouldn't ignore the life review.

Christians have commonly believed that we're all judged at death. As Hebrews says: "It is appointed for mortals to die once, and after that the judgement" (9:27). But we're also taught that all will stand before God's throne when history comes to its climax. As Revelation prophesies: "And the sea gave up the dead that were in it, Death and Hades gave up the dead that were in them, and all were judged according to what they had done" (20:13).

Putting these two things together has always been a problem. As one old theologian put it: "If the soules of the Elect goe presently after their death to heaven, and the soules of the Reprobate to hell, what neede a general Judgment?"[44] According to Gregory the Great, Aquinas, and the dominant Catholic tradition, the particular judgment is for the soul, the general and public judgment—which will be able to take into account the long-term effects of one's deeds—for soul and body. But according to Lactantius and Cyril of Alexandria, the exegetical basis for a preliminary judgment is dubious. There's only one judgment, the final judgment. William Newton Clarke and John Mackintosh and purportedly the Cathars long before them held the opposite view: judgment takes place at death. Then there are those, such as T. F. Torrance, who imagine (appealing to Einstein) that both prospects amount to the same thing because our time is relative over against God's eternity.[45]

Christianity, one should keep in mind, isn't the only religion with apparent redundancy. The same inconcinnity appears in Zoroastrian and in some Jewish and Islamic texts, for while these religious traditions envisage a universal, end-time judgment, they also often teach that human beings are judged upon death.[46]

What accounts for the phenomenon of two judgments, one of them seemingly otiose, in more than one tradition? Maybe the life review is part of the answer. Zoroastrianism, Judaism, and Christianity dogmatically affirmed judgment at the end of history. Human experience, however, was equally clear: Some people near death felt judged when they saw their lives pass before their eyes. Such testimony, I suggest, wasn't ignored. It affected religious traditions, so that the one judgment became two.

Perhaps something analogous occurred in Chinese Buddhism, for it presents a similar oddity. In some texts the soul is judged at death, but then a second judgment occurs forty-nine days later.[47] Maybe, once more, the duplication owes something to the life review. Perhaps the forty-nine-day idea was the dogma that came first, after which it was supplemented by knowledge of what happens to some who come close to death but don't pass over.

....

I wish to be clear: I'm neither insisting that the life review is there because God put it there nor confidently equating the experience with divine judgment. My discussion is rather a way of fumbling toward some constructive analogy or useful parable. My goal is to find a helpful myth as opposed to an unhelpful myth. Michelangelo's *Last Judgment* in the Sistine Chapel is, for me, just art. It's aesthetically profound, and its nudity, the absence of all earthly covering, is highly appropriate; but its frightening serpents and contorted faces are, for me at least, too fantastic and too foreign to nurture my theological imagination.

By contrast, the idea that we'll be compelled to understand our lives in their entirety, the bad along with the good, and enabled to grasp the consequences of all that we've done makes good sense, so imagining divine judgment as including a life review of some sort likewise makes sense. Furthermore, the life review is, for now at least, a mystery, so it fittingly stands for another mystery. To be sure, the life review is likely to be at best only another imperfect image of some aspect of whatever awaits us. Still, some images are better than others, and this one is imaginatively attractive. It also has the benefit of being congruent with one possible rendering of 2 Corinthians 5:10: "before the tribunal of Christ we must all be seen to be as what we are."

Thinking along the lines of a life review is further compatible, I submit, with portions of the canonical gospels. Luke 8:17 proclaims that "nothing is hidden that will not be disclosed, nor is anything secret that will not become known and come to light." Something like this happens in life reviews, when the forgotten past becomes remembered, and when people see things they'd have preferred not to recall. Then there's the fable of the Rich Man and Lazarus, where Abraham enjoins the dead Dives, "Remember that during your lifetime you received your good things, and Lazarus in like manner evil things" (Luke 16:25). Here memory is the rich man's introduction to his post-mortem fate. There's likewise Matthew 12:36, which warns that "on the day of judgment you will have to give an account for every careless word you utter." This correlates with those life reviews which purport to encompass absolutely everything one has said and done. Finally, the dramatic depiction of the Last Judgment in Matthew 25, where the Son of Man separates the sheep from the goats, is, like the life review, all about revelation: in the end, the true meaning of what we've done and haven't done will be made plain.

·················

The life review is the inverse of amnesia. Amnesiacs, bereft of memory, suffer the loss of identity. Observers of a life review, by contrast, gain self-understanding.

Most of us are more like amnesiacs than those who've benefitted from a life review. We may look at ourselves in the mirror, but we never see who or what is there. We perceive rather the temporary social constructions of our earth-bound egos. We behold the illusions we project. Wittingly and unwittingly, we fabricate identities. We selectively forget and remember, distorting and concealing ourselves from everyone, including ourselves. If, then, the truth about us is ever to come to light, if our self-idealizations and self-centered conceits are ever to be canceled, if we're ever to distinguish the authentic from the inauthentic and the eternal from the temporal, our memories and consciences will need to be enlivened, so that we can perceive and evaluate ourselves as we are, not as we vainly imagine ourselves to be. Indeed, the *visio dei*, the vision of God, must be subjective as well as objective: our hope is not only to see God but also to see ourselves as God sees us, to know ourselves even as we are known.

Kierkegaard wrote in his journal: "It is quite true, what philosophy says, that life must be understood backward. But then one forgets the other principle, that it must be lived forward. Which principle, the more one thinks it through, ends exactly with temporal life never being able to be properly understood, precisely because I can at no instant find complete rest and adopt the position: backward."[48] Maybe that resting place, which we can't find in this life, is the judgment, when lame self-justification will halt, when we'll be enabled to surmount *maya* and perceive the folly of our vain pursuits, when we'll experience ourselves in the third person, from a perspective that transcends and shatters our absurdly partisan self-perception.

....

To this point I have, despite quoting Scripture and church theologians, offered little that's distinctively Christian. I've been able to do this because multiple faiths have versions of post-mortem and/or end-time judgment. It's common religious property, not something unique to the Bible and biblically-inspired faiths. Moreover, NDEs with life reviews come from all sorts of people, including agnostics and atheists, so the phenomenon, like discussion of it, doesn't belong to Christians alone.

There are ways, however, in which Christian theology distinguishes itself in the matter of eschatological judgment, and I'd like, in winding down, to contemplate two of them. The first is the identification of the judge of the last day. According to the New Testament, Jesus Christ will return as the Son of Man to sit on the throne of his glory. All the nations will then be gathered before him, and he will separate them as a shepherd separates the sheep from the goats, for God the Father has given him authority to execute judgment.

Equally distinctive is the idea, associated especially with the Fourth Gospel, that the eschatological judgment isn't confined to the future. Somehow, it's already taken place in Jesus' passion. John's Jesus declares, as he nears the cross: "Now is the judgment of this world; now the ruler of this world will be driven out" (John 12:31); and again, with an emphatic perfect tense: "the ruler of this world has been condemned" (16:7–11). Furthermore, those who hear Jesus' words and believe the One who sent him have eternal life even now; they don't come under judgment but have already passed from death to life (5:24).

I'd like to put together these two ideas—Jesus as judge and judgment as past—in order to suggest a Christological approach to the Last Judgment.

The interpretation of Jesus' crucifixion as the eschatological turning point isn't unique to the Fourth Evangelist. It's rather part and parcel of an early Christian habit of associating the passion and resurrection of Jesus with properly eschatological motifs.

In Mark, for example, the passion narrative in chapters 14–16 exhibits a series of striking parallels with chapter 13, the eschatological discourse that immediately precedes it. Jesus prophesies that, in the latter days, the temple will be destroyed (13:2), and when he is on the cross, the veil of the temple is rent, symbolizing that the building and what it stands for have just become passé (15:38). He prophesies that the saints will be "delivered up" (13:9, 11), which is exactly what happens to him (14:10, 21, 41). He prophesies that, as part of the eschatological tribulation, his followers will appear before Jewish councils (13:9), and he is soon enough arraigned before a Jewish council (14:53–15:1). He prophesies that the saints will be beaten (13:9), and he himself is beaten (14:65). He prophesies that the disciples will, in the end, stand before governors (13:9), and he appears before the governor Pilate (15:1–15). He prophesies that the disciples will be "led away" (13:11), and a bit later he is "led away" (14:44, 53; 15:16). He prophesies that, before the Son of Man comes, brother will hand over brother to death (13:12–13), and he is betrayed by one of the twelve, a member of his surrogate, inner family (14:10, 20, 43). He prophesies that people will flee (13:14–16), and his disciples, when he is arrested, flee (14:40–52). He prophesies that, when the old age convulses and nears its end, the sun will go dark (13:24), and when he is crucified, darkness falls upon the earth (15:33). Finally, Jesus admonishes his disciples to watch for the day of the Son of Man, lest the master come and find them sleeping (13:35–36); and in Gethsemane, after Jesus exhorts James, Peter, and John to watch, they fail to do so, whereupon the master comes and finds them sleeping (14:32–42). It's clear, then, that the end of Jesus foreshadows or inaugurates or belongs to the end-times.

It's the same in the First Gospel. Not only does Matthew reproduce the correlations in Mark, but he adds an earthquake at the cross (27:51) and another at the tomb (28:2), which forges yet another link with the eschatological discourse, where Jesus avows, "there will be . . . earthquakes in various places" (24:7). Matthew also contributes the astonishing tale in which Jesus' death occasions the opening of tombs and the resurrection of saints (27:51–53). Once more, then, Jesus' end is the beginning of the end, or the end of the world in miniature, or the proleptic realization of the last times.

In this particular, Paul falls in line with the Gospels. For the apostle, the crucifixion is the rift between the old evil age, over which principalities and powers rule, and the new creation, over which Jesus the messianic Lord reigns (1 Cor. 15:25–27). Through Jesus' death, the saints have been "set free from the present evil age" (Gal. 1:4). Because the Messiah has died and risen from the dead, "the end of the ages has come" (1 Cor. 10:11), "everything old has passed away" (2 Cor. 5:17), and there is a "new creation" (2 Cor. 5:17; Gal. 6:15). Paul can, moreover, characterize Jesus as "the first fruits of those who have died" (1 Cor. 15:20), an expression which assumes that the eschatological harvest is underway, that the resurrection of Jesus has inaugurated the general resurrection of the dead.

The tradition, astonishing to my mind, of construing the end of Jesus as though it were the eschatological turning point, must, given its appearance in Paul, the Synoptics, and John, go back to very early times. Explaining its origin is a fascinating historical exercise.[49] Here, however, I wish rather to offer a theological interpretation.

....

What does Jesus, the judge of the last day according to the New Testament, do as he faces the apocalypse of his passion and resurrection?

When one of his disciples draws a sword, to defend him in the garden, he rebukes him: "Put your sword back into its place; for all who take the sword will perish by the sword" (Matt. 26:52). Although Jesus could call an army of angels to wreak vengeance on his enemies (Matt. 26:53-54), he refuses. In like manner, when he appears before the High Priest or Herod or Pilate, he says next to nothing in his defense; and when he is struck, slapped, and spit upon, he turns the other cheek. Above all, as he dies on the cross, Jesus prays: "Father, forgive them; for they do not know what they are doing" (Luke 23:34).

A pattern runs throughout the passion narratives. It's summed up in 1 Peter 2:23: "When he was abused, he did not return abuse; when he suffered, he did not threaten; but he entrusted himself to the one who judges justly." In the Synoptics and John, Jesus refuses to answer violence with violence. He instead responds with forbearance and forgiveness. Beyond that, nothing in the passion narratives hints that while he's helpless now, he'll wreak vengeance later, when the tables are turned. When he promises the repentant thief that he will soon enter paradise, he doesn't rebuke the unrepentant thief and condemn him to Gehenna. Nor does Jesus revile or pronounce judgment upon the High Priest or Pilate. On the contrary, the man of sorrows forgives all those who've conspired to brutalize and slay him.

The resurrection narratives reveal the same longsuffering character. For Jesus forgives those who forsook him, who left him alone in his hour of despair. This includes Peter, who adamantly denied him not once but three times. Upon rising from the dead, we might expect Jesus to return to Galilee and to begin afresh by looking for a more promising bunch of disciples. He instead finds Peter and his companions and commissions them for service. This entails that he has forgiven them. Further, although the fact is often missed, in order to do this, he has to negate his own somber warning: "Whoever denies me before others, I also will deny before my Father in heaven" (Matt. 10:33). Peter denies Jesus. Jesus doesn't deny Peter. He rather says to him and his miserable fellows, "Peace be with you" (John 20:19). In the resurrection appearances, the unqualified admonition about denial is set aside, and mercy triumphs over judgment. Threats, it appears, aren't binding.

What follows? If the Gospels identify Jesus with the judge of the last day, and if they construe his passion and resurrection as a mini-apocalypse, then Christian readers might well ask, Haven't we seen how the judge once acted when the end came, and why shouldn't we expect more of the same in the future? If Jesus has rehearsed the end, don't his followers have some idea of what's coming? Will the one who repudiated violence and vengeance think better of it down the road and adopt a different policy? Will the one who forgave his enemies once refuse to do so again? Will he finally call a halt to forgiving seventy times seven?

Large parts of the Christian tradition, including a few paragraphs in the New Testament, have imagined that things will indeed be different next time. When the judge appears, forgiving enemies will belong to the past. He will have had enough of the Sermon on the Mount and of turning the other cheek. It'll be time to revert to an eye for an eye and a tooth for a tooth. The sun will no longer shine on the just and unjust, but only on the just. Evil will be requited with evil.

All this, however, requires that Jesus' behavior in the passion narrative is a temporary strategy as opposed to a demonstration of God's deepest character. On this view, how Jesus behaved on one occasion says little or nothing about how he will behave on another, or is even altogether misleading. Yet how then will a Christian plausibly insist that the cross discloses the divine identity, or that God is the same yesterday, today, and forever? Is it credible that the figure in the passion narratives is a passing anomaly, that Jesus acted the part of a lamb led to slaughter only as some sort of provisional strategy which will, in the end, be abandoned for some radically different tactic? Does the risen Christ bear his scars as justification for revenge or as a sign of his everlasting character?

....

I don't wish to be misunderstood here. I'm not optimistically forecasting, on the basis of the New Testament, the happy upshot of God's evaluation of our completed lives. To forgive people is one thing. To fix them is another. And we all need fixing, which will surely entail forfeiture and the pain of remorse all around. As Paul says, when our work becomes visible, it will be revealed with a fire that will test what sort of work each has done; and some will suffer loss (1 Cor. 3:12-15).

Nonetheless, the passion narratives do more than suggest the judge's goodwill. Here, it seems to me, Calvin catches part of their spirit:

> How could a most merciful prince destroy his own people? how could the head disperse its own members? how could the advocate condemn his clients?.... It certainly gives no small security, that we shall be arraigned at no other tribunal than that of our Redeemer, from whom salvation is to be expected; and that he who in the Gospel now promises eternal blessedness, will then as judge ratify his promise. The end for which the Father has honored the Son by committing all judgment to him, was to pacify the consciences of his people when alarmed at the thought of judgment.[50]

Contrast Calvin's encouraging words with the following, from a late-nineteenth-century theologian:

> If it is so hateful to a criminal to be brought before an earthly magistrate, well may the poor soul quake with fear when she is introduced into the presence of God, the strict and omniscient Judge, and required to give the most accurate account of all the thoughts, words, deeds, and omissions of her past life.... The most powerful reason of all why the soul fears to appear before the judgment seat is because she knows not what the sentence of the Judge will be. She has far more cause to fear than to hope.[51]

Our Western theological tradition, with its love of jurisprudence, has gone astray when it's extended the courtroom metaphor too far and turned divine judgment into a legal and impersonal affair, as though God were as blind and impartial as Lady Justice with her scales.

. . . .

I was once called to jury duty. When I walked into the courtroom and saw the defense attorney, I smiled and waved. He waved and smiled back. He was a friend, and my family's lawyer. The judge quickly sent me home. There was to be no favoritism in his courtroom.

The divine court, on a Christian view, must be radically different. For the judge isn't the detached enforcer of some inflexible law. The judge is rather the author of the parable of the Prodigal Son; and as shepherd and savior, as advocate and physician, he's wildly biased in favor of all the defendants. There's something theologically right about the old paintings of the Last Judgment in which Michael the archangel furtively pressures the scales of justice, in order to obtain a favorable outcome.

The New Testament isn't Kafka's *The Trial*, where an unknown, mysterious court is conducting business while anxious people are kept in the dark. Rather, light has shone in the darkness, and for the express purpose not of condemning the world but of saving it. The mercy of its long-suffering judge, who makes no pretense to neutrality but has an overriding personal interest in a favorable outcome, is not strained. So even if lives must be reviewed and egos reconstructed, even if the crooked must be made straight and works tested by fire, the court is rigged. Judgment, like death, has lost its sting.

....

John Pearson, the seventeenth-century Bishop of Chester, isn't really a name with which to conjure. He doesn't even make my list of the top one hundred greatest theologians. He didn't, however, go infallibly wrong, which means on occasion he got something right. That's true of the following words, with which I should like to end this chapter:

> we shall receive our sentence not according to the rigour of the law, but [according to] the mildness and mercies of the gospel . . . [so] whatsover sentences in the sacred Scripture speaketh any thing of hope, whatsoever text administereth any comfort, whatsoever argument drawn from thence can breed in us any assurance, we may confidently make use of them all in reference to the judgment to come.[52]

CHAPTER 4

Ignorance and Imagination

···

I believe that it would be worth trying to learn something about the world
even if in trying to do so we should merely learn that we do not know much.
This state of learned ignorance might be a help in many of our troubles. It
might be well for all of us to remember that, while differing widely in the
various little bits we know, in our infinite ignorance we are all equal.

KARL POPPER

No theories about the future of the Kingdom of God are likely to be
valuable or true which paralyze or postpone redemptive action on
our part. To those who postpone, it is a theory and not a reality.

WALTER RAUSCHENBUSCH

Is it not the role of religion, as well as art, to speak in excess, to
break the bondage of everyday caution, to be hyperbolic? . . .
Can we today learn again to imagine more than we know?

STEPHEN H. WEBB

···

PERHAPS I SHOULD be embarrassed for publicly pondering the world to
come. Haven't scientists demonstrated that we're essentially physical
beings, so that the end of our earthly existence must be the end of us? Don't
we also know that death isn't, whatever Paul wrote, a post-Edenic curse but
evolution's friend? Natural selection wouldn't work without it.

Beyond that, doesn't contemplating an otherworldly future disincline
us from attending to the urgent problems of an anguished present? History
supplies unedifying examples of eschatology acting as an anodyne when
resistance was the one thing needful.

Isn't it further evident that the idea of life after death is a self-serving projection, a prolongation of infantile desire? Isn't its chief purpose to console fearful egos unwilling to face their own demise? Because we shun the thought of death, we compensate by fantasizing about a pleasant alternative. Aren't we like the raven Moses in Orwell's *Animal Farm*? The bird "claimed to know of the existence of a mysterious country called Sugarcandy Mountain, to which all animals went when they died. It was situated somewhere up in the sky, a little distance beyond the clouds. . . . In Sugarcandy Mountain it was Sunday seven days a week, clover was in season all the year round, and lump sugar and linseed cake grew on the hedges."[1]

Finally, how can one doubt that claims about a future life, even if there is one, are merely shadows cast by anxious imaginations upon the walls of our ignorance? Debates about heaven, hell, purgatory, resurrection, the millennium, and the like are inevitably interminable and contribute nothing to knowledge, for no one can talk intelligently about an unknown country. That the afterlife in the world's religions is an overgrown labyrinth of contradictory conjectures is no mystery. Their competing testimonies establish their ignorance. Certainly there's no way to confirm or refute their propositions. The closest we ever get is when messianic prophets or Bible pundits of a certain stripe predict the date of the end. That history meanders on, discrediting them by taking no notice, is fodder for cynicism—and all the more if one concedes that the New Testament itself sponsors a near expectation that was disappointed. If that sad fact doesn't dishearten you, what will?

The problems with a future life, whether set in heaven or on a new earth, are such that, for many of our contemporaries, it's an antiquated folk belief, an illusion without a future. How can anyone intellectually up to speed take the thing seriously? Bertrand Russell was dismissive: "emotions . . . cause belief in a future life."[2] Princeton philosopher Mark Johnston is equally condescending: "You either rehearse a scientifically established materialism about life and death, or you preach."[3]

....

Some church-goers concur with the naysayers. Years ago, after I'd finished a Sunday school class on the last things, an elderly woman raised her hand. Having patiently listened to me for an hour, she confidently voiced what was to her self-evident: "Of course, young man, it'd be lovely to believe some of the things you've shared with us. I'm afraid, however, that death is the end." Conversations with others during coffee hours over the years have revealed that she's scarcely alone in her unbelief, a fact opinion polls confirm. More than a few Christians expect nothing beyond this world.

How should I, who am of another mind, respond to them, to those who reject or are on principle suspicious of the topics with which this book concerns itself from beginning to end? I've never quarreled with such folk. I've rather listened to what they've had to say and tried to understand it, after which, if there's been time, I've respectfully shared why I'm not death-tolerant, and why I want and expect more than a coffin.

To some extent this is what the following pages attempt to do. Leaving scientific and philosophical issues for another chapter,[4] I'd like to address three complaints commonly lodged against hope for something other than oblivion. The first is the moral problem, that such hope, far from being a quaint, pleasant dream not much affecting daily lives, is actually injurious, for it relaxes the tug of conscience, lessens outrage, and diminishes efforts to repair a broken world. The second complaint is psychological, that such belief is defensive, a cowardly, self-centered refusal to concede the inevitable. The third is the epistemological problem, that such belief, because it presumes to know the unknowable, must be a mirage.

....

First, then, the moral issue.

Francis Newman, the younger and lesser-known brother of Cardinal Newman, when looking back on his religious pilgrimage, which included time among the eschatologically oriented followers of John N. Darby, wrote this:

> Those who stick closest to the Scripture do not shrink from saying, that "it is not worth while trying to mend the world," and stigmatize as "political and worldly" such as pursue an opposite course. Undoubtedly, if we are to expect our Master at cockcrowing, we shall not study the permanent improvement of this transitory scene. To teach the certain speedy destruction of earthly things, as the New Testament does, is to cut the sinews of all earthly progress; to declare war against Intellect and Imagination, [and] against . . . Social advancement.[5]

Newman's testimony has support from my own experience. During the early 1970s, I spent a year among middle-class evangelicals of the dispensationalist variety. They ardently discussed Hal Lindsey's *The Late Great Planet Earth*, and they expected to be raptured to heaven in short order. Now most of them were, if I may generalize, decent and sincere. They did their best to live according to the light they'd received. Their eschatology—their fatalistic, pessimistic eschatology—didn't, however, make them better citizens. Their rapture culture deterred them from wonder-ing about, or at least publicly addressing, long-term solutions to concrete social problems. They didn't need to change anything because God was about to change everything.

I recall being dismayed by what they often made of baneful news, such as military conflicts or earthquakes. These weren't troubles to be ame-liorated but tidings of great joy, tokens that the end was near. We never prayed for peace in the Middle East. We implicitly rooted for things to get worse. Cataclysm was a rousing prospect. It was also, in Salem Kirban's fifth-rate novel *666* and other precursors of the *Left Behind* series, morbid entertainment.

I get it, then, when people declaim that the more we worry about escha-tology, the less we'll worry about our earthly responsibilities. Fixing your eye on heaven or expecting God to wrap things up shortly isn't obvious incentive for conserving wilderness. In the words of Nicholas Lash, if only we could quit construing the present as "the antechamber of the eternal," we'd be better able to take more "seriously the responsibilities of our his-torical existence."[6]

Nonetheless, Lash's claim, if intended to be a generalization covering all times and places, is dubious. Similar beliefs—or, in this case, a similar un-belief—need not instill similar practices. One must assume much to imag-ine that simply subtracting hope for a life to come will foster righteousness. Lash's logic seems to be this: if we deem ourselves to have only this world, then we'll take better care of it.

One is reminded of Heidegger's avowal, that "once one has grasped the finitude of one's existence, it snatches one back from the multiplicity of possibilities which offer themselves as closest to one—those of comfort-ableness, shirking, and taking things lightly."[7] Someone could, however, counter: if this world is all we have, then let us eat and drink, for tomorrow we die. Philip José Farmer was of the opinion that "without a belief in eter-nal life for us . . . terrestrial existence is something to be gotten through with as little pain and as much pleasure as possible."[8] Why should expect-ing oblivion keep us from being, if we want, narcissistic coveters of enter-tainment? Why should it, all by itself, dissuade us from passing our time watching YouTube, or from abandoning ourselves to inert melancholy?

John Lennon, in his musically beautiful but lyrically vapid "Imagine," invited us to disbelieve heaven and hell, so that we might live for today. Yet doesn't everything depend upon who's doing the imagining?

A friend once confided to me that, since he doesn't believe in an afterlife, he'd commit certain criminal acts were he really persuaded that he had little time left, for then he wouldn't have to suffer the consequences. He was serious, and there's nothing wrong with his reasoning. This man just doesn't live in Lash's moral universe. That the two share a common disbelief in a world to come doesn't lead to their sharing a common ethic. Not all consciences are on the same wavelength.

....

Lash's argument, at least in the bald form he presents it, isn't logically sound. There must be a missing premise. Perhaps, however, the argument is empirically plausible; that is, maybe, as a matter of the historical record, when good people buy into an afterlife or await an imminent end, they tend to help their neighbors less than they otherwise would. If, perhaps, the early Christians had paid as much attention to the sanitization of Tarsus as to the second coming of Christ, they'd have better served their fellow citizens.

Yet how could one ever prove that eschatology is everywhere and always a sedative? If one can cite, as anecdotal support, case histories of groups that were preoccupied with the end and so unoccupied with the present, it's just as easy to name individuals who've managed to care about this world and the world to come at the same time, or who've testified that eschatological beliefs reduced their vice and fostered their virtue.

Josephus, the old Jewish historian, thought it self-evident that "the good are made better in their lifetime by the hope of a reward after death, and the passions of the wicked are restrained by the fear that, even though they escape detection while alive, they will undergo never-ending punishment after their decease."[9] Pious individuals from many times and various places have expressed like sentiments. The Lutheran theologian Johann Gerhard (1582–1637) affirmed that "consideration of the last judgment keeps our lives straight and corrects our habits, for it calls us away from impiety and carelessness. For it is inevitable that we are driven to God by fear and kept from sin if the thought of that judgment comes strongly into our mind."[10]

When I run across sentences such as those of Josephus and Gerhard, I think two things. First, I wish it were otherwise. I'd prefer to imagine that human beings can be good without anticipating personal reward or punishment. I like the medieval tale of the woman—in some versions she is Hypatia, the Neo-platonic philosopher—who carried around a torch and a pitcher of water, using the torch to burn the pleasures of heaven and using the pitcher to drown the fires of hell, so that people would love God for

God's own sake. And I understand Einstein's remark that a person "would indeed be in a poor way if he had to be restrained by fear of punishment and hope of reward after death."[11] Wasn't Gregory of Nazianzus right to affirm that, for virtue to be virtue, it must be "without reward"?[12]

But, second, I see no reason to assert that Josephus and Gerhard were deceived. Surely in some cases, maybe in many cases, people have assessed themselves rightly when claiming that they've behaved better because of their eschatological hopes and fears. Was Max Weber wholly wrong to urge that anxiety over whether one belonged to the elect and so was bound for heaven motivated our Protestant ancestors to work hard and stay on the straight and narrow? Was it all for naught that old European town halls sometimes featured depictions of the grand assize, depictions intended to warn the participants in a trial that they would, on the last day, be accountable to the all-knowing judge on high? I'd bet that, on occasion, some wavering individuals made up their minds to do the right thing after staring at the wall.

Two psychologists, on the basis of their experiments, recently concluded that "fear of supernatural punishment may serve as a deterrent to counter-normative behavior, even in anonymous situations free from human social monitoring." They indeed discovered that "viewing God as a more punishing, less loving figure was reliably associated with lower levels of cheating. This relationship remained after controlling for relevant personality dimensions, ethnicity, religious affiliation, and gender."[13]

I'm not cheering this result. I'd prefer to believe that human beings can do better than this. Solomon Stoddard's 1713 sermon *The Efficacy of the fear of Hell, to restrain Men from Sin*, whose title describes the entirety of its contents, makes me cringe. My sole point here, however, is this: one can't, as a generalization about the human race, claim that eschatology makes lousy citizens.

If it were otherwise, what would we make of William Booth, the founder of the Salvation Army? He was a Finneyesque evangelist tormented by the prospect of unsaved multitudes flailing in literal hell-fire. At the same time, this soul-saver preached a Jesus who delivers in the here-and-now as truly as in the future, a Jesus who's anxious to deliver from temporal misery as well as from eternal misery, a Jesus who wants to eliminate poverty and turn east end London into the New Jerusalem. Booth wrote:

> I saw poor women and children compelled to live in hovels of the most wretched squalor and filth, from which light and air were all but excluded.

I saw the people dying prematurely of disease from the want of food and attention. I knew that thousands of young women were being sacrificed to the gratification of the lusts of men who bought and sold them, body and soul, for the most paltry prices; and, worst of all—most agonizing of all—I saw the indifference of those who had the means to help, or I heard those whose place it was to deliver them say that there was no remedy, or, at least, no remedy on any scale at all adequate to the length and breadth and depth and height of these horrible evils.

Booth professed the discovery of "two gospels of deliverance . . . one for each world . . . . I saw that when the Bible said, 'He that believeth shall be saved,' it meant not only saved from the miseries of the future world, but from the miseries of this also. That it came with the promise of salvation here and now" and of deliverance "from poverty and disease, and the majority of kindred woes."[14]

There's much in Booth's theology and in his strategies for social ministry with which to take issue. Nevertheless, it remains clear that, according to his own testimony, end-time beliefs didn't push him away from the world but toward it. As this is likewise true of others, it's a mistake to insist that eschatology, in and of itself, leaves us in the privacy of our own religious minds, indifferent to the misfortunes of others, unmotivated to confront the evils that pervade our world.

Although the fact may surprise, the "Rapture Index," a Web site that purports to be "the prophetic speedometer of end-time activity," has a link labeled "What should Christians be doing?" If you click and read through the entries, you find discussion of community service, prison ministry, and soup kitchens, as well as encouragement to fund homeless shelters, volunteer in hospitals, and support Habitat for Humanity.

. . . .

The facts, insofar as we can measure them, don't support the allegation that eschatology necessarily reduces good deeds whereas incredulity must multiply them. Indeed, the sociologists inform us that, at least in North America, the most religious, who statistically have a higher faith in an afterlife than others, are the most charitable: they give more time and more money to both religious and secular causes. The explanation of this circumstance is unclear. It may have little to do with doctrine, much less anything to do with eschatological doctrine. Perhaps, as David Campbell and Robert Putnam have argued, the key is social networks: the greater the number of good friends you have in a close-knit subgroup, the greater your commitment to charitable causes.[15] But however one tackles that issue, empirical study doesn't establish that institutions which inspire eschatological convictions thereby impede altruism.

A similar result follows from study of so-called near death experiences (NDEs) and their effects. Whatever you make of such experiences— whether you think them wholly endogenous or authentic glimpses of the beyond or something in between—one thing is clear: the vast majority of NDErs return not only with enhanced belief in an afterlife but also with increased determination to serve others. This isn't an artifact of their having almost died. NDErs, as opposed to individuals who've suffered cardiac arrest without an NDE, are more committed to faith in an afterlife and also score higher on questionnaires designed to gauge love and compassion for others.[16]

....

Historically, eschatological doctrine has mediated moral instruction. The *Apocalypse of Zephaniah*, a Greek text of Jewish provenance likely composed around the turn of the era, offers illustration. In this, the seer has a vision of a scroll on which all of his sins are written. He observes: "If I did not go to visit a sick man or widow, I found it written down as a shortcoming on my manuscript. If I did not visit an orphan, it was found written down as a shortcoming on my manuscript. A day on which I did not fast (or) pray in the time of prayer I found written down as a failing upon my manuscript" (7:1-6).

Using the Last Judgment to inculcate social teaching is conventional in ancient literature. The instance best known to Christians is the picture of the Last Judgment in Matthew 25, where the sheep and goats appear before the enthroned Son of Man and his angels. Those who enter the kingdom of heaven are those who've fed the hungry, given drink to the thirsty, welcomed strangers, clothed the naked, cared for the sick, and visited prisoners. Those who depart into "the eternal fire prepared for the devil and his angels" are those who've failed to undertake such tasks. Here a vision of the end-time judgment outlines a social program and eschatology is ethics. The passage, moreover, hasn't just been read: it's been lived. It motivated Mother Teresa of Calcutta. It inspired the founding of medieval hospitals. And it's undergirded the hospitality of Benedictine monasteries. As the *Rule* says: "Let all guests who arrive be received like Christ, for He is going to say, 'I was a stranger and you welcomed me.'"

Christianity and Judaism are scarcely the only faiths that have attempted to instill ethics via eschatology. The Egyptian *Book of the Dead*, in its famous 125th chapter, contains this string of negative confessions, to be recited in self-defense when one is judged on the other side:

> I have not mistreated cattle.
> I have not done violence to a poor man.
> I have not defamed a slave to his superior.
> I have given no order to a killer.
> I have not caused anyone suffering.
> I have not added to the weight of the balance.
> I have not taken milk from the mouths of children.

Returning to Lash: the problem isn't eschatology in general, nor is it this or that particular expectation, not even misplaced faith in a near end. Eschatological doctrines are malleable. They don't dictate their application or determine how believers behave. Institutional contexts and numerous other variables prompt people to put their eschatology to good use or to bad use or to no use.

In this, eschatological expectations are like so much else under the sun. They become what you do with them. The apocalyptic visions of Daniel have inspired both militant messianists and pacifistic messianists; and hell, which has led some to despair, has led others to the mission field. Blanket statements about the behavioral consequences of eschatological belief are akin to sweeping simplifications about the behavioral consequences of belief in God: they're not very helpful.

....

Despite the length of the foregoing rebuttal, more remains to be said on the subject of eschatology and ethics, and I shall return to it below. For the moment, however, all that matters is this: otherworldly concern isn't incommensurate with this-worldly involvement.

What, then, of the second common objection to taking eschatology seriously, the objection that heaven, hell, and the rest are self-serving projections, wistful illusions that disavow the reality of death? Aren't they the proof that we're excessively preoccupied with our own piddling significance? Isn't ego maintenance the inspiration for otherworldly paradises?

It'd be folly to set oneself wholly against this objection. Heaven often functions to reassure us that what we value above all—our individual selves—will endure and indeed prosper, just as hell often serves to reassure us that what we despise above all—our enemies—will fitly suffer. The afterlife is a genie that grants our wishes.

This isn't the end of the matter, however. The objection from desire, if analyzed as an argument, is an *ad hominem* fallacy. That I desire dinner doesn't establish that I'll never eat it, and that some of us want to live forever doesn't prove that we won't. We can crave things that exist as well as things that don't exist.

In addition, it's easy to invert the psychology. Maybe some who are so strongly set against a life to come are victims of what the psychoanalysts term reaction formation. This involves exchanging a rejected impulse for its opposite. Repudiating an afterlife can be sour grapes, an act of repression, a means of coping with your own death-related anxiety. It can be a way of stoically proving to yourself that you don't need the crutch others require, that you're more rational and less sentimental than the weaklings who believe.

....

Whatever one makes of that suggestion, there are Christian versions of the objection that an afterlife is egoistic indulgence. I first learned this when I read, as a college student, Krister Stendahl's 1972 Nobel Conference Lecture, "Immortality Is Too Much and Too Little." Stendahl, a New Testament scholar who became the Lutheran Bishop of Stockholm, advised that the traditional belief in immortality is theologically suspect because it's self-centered: it privileges the individual over wider concerns. Why should we augment our importance by hoping for more than God has given us?[17] Shouldn't we instead renounce ourselves? What counts is the victory of God's kingdom, not our perpetual existence.

The argument intrigues me. It sets one part of our tradition—hope for eternal life—over against another part—the call to lose our lives unselfishly in service of the kingdom—and argues that we must choose between them.

I didn't know what to make of Stendahl's argument when I first ran across it decades ago, and I've returned to it and wrestled with it off and on over the years, especially when I've encountered similar claims in the writings of Feuerbach and Tolstoy, Simone Weil and Don Cupitt. I've remained uneasy, because while I haven't wanted to jettison an afterlife, I also haven't wanted to endorse a sub-Christian egocentrism. I'm unhappy with the thought that my faith is third-rate because it doesn't see death as the end, that it's less noble than the faith of those—Camus, for instance—who've sponsored self-sacrificial philanthropy while conceding victory to the grave.

....

What I've tentatively decided is that we need to distinguish between being selves and being selfish. When a tree sends out roots to draw water and nutrients to its trunk, it's being self-centered, yet it isn't sinning. Neither do human beings err ethically when they eat and drink to stay alive. Such acts, although self-seeking, aren't selfish in the disagreeable, ignoble sense.

Hope for a life beyond needn't, I suggest, be different. If it's not wrong to hope that my neighbors and I will wake up tomorrow morning, how can it be wrong to hope that we'll all wake up forever?

To be sure, it's easy enough for such hope to mutate into a fantasy wherein our self-seeking desires are gratified, in which we don't lose our flawed personalities but keep our familiar, mundane selves and their longings. Yet our present life is in this regard no better, for it offers a like temptation: The earthly futures we fancy for ourselves regularly indulge our mercenary aspirations.

The problem isn't hope. Nor is it visualizing the future. We all hope and plan, whether our imaginings stop at death or not. The problem is that we view things from a predominantly self-interested point of view. Yet just as we can work to put away childish things and strive for more in the here and now, so can we aspire for more when pondering the hereafter. Indeed, we should conceive of the afterlife not as self-fulfillment or self-expansion but as self-emptying and self-abnegation, as a state or process that effects, among other things, the fulfillment of Jesus' injunction that we truly lose our marred selves.

....

How might this work? How might we lose our lives without losing everything that we are or without ceasing to be self-referentially aware? Consider the opening lines of the Westminster Larger Catechism:

Question: What is the chief and highest end of man?

Answer: Man's chief and highest end is to glorify God, and fully to enjoy him forever.

We enjoy things in two very different ways. When, for instance, we look at a large pile of money, we almost inevitably fancy what we might do with it. We enjoy not the money but its potential utility, enjoy imagining what it, under our control, could do for us. When, by contrast, we contemplate a stunning sunset, we have no such fantasy. This is because we can't own or manage the beauty of a waning sun. It transcends personal possession and utility. It has no price because it can't be bought. So we appreciate it as it is.

These two ways of seeing represent, I suggest, a fundamental difference between this world and what we may hope for in the world to come. The psychology of looking at money stands for our habitual orientation in this life, our constant self-absorption, our allegiance to the law of self. By contrast, the way we admire a sunset foreshadows our reconstruction and reorientation in a better world, in which we shall, as egos without egoism, enjoy others and God for their own sakes, unconditionally. This second sort of seeing anticipates the beatific vision.

....

It's precisely the promise of more than death that raises the possibility of unraveling our currently constructed egos, of crucifying our self-centered perceptions, of repositioning our displaced centers. Whatever else heaven may be, surely it must be the transition from vain self-importance to disinterested love, the end of the ever-grasping self, the obliteration of I Me Mine. So although the hope for a life beyond is often an extension of self-love, an escapist indulgence, a Goldilocks tale where everything is "just right," Christians can and should imagine it to be something else. It should be the prospect, perhaps quite painful, of dismantling our egos as we have known them, for the sake of something unimaginably larger and more profound than our current individual selves. Won't the new creation require that its citizens be re-created, and that the first-person singular no longer be capitalized?

The afterlife may be a screen upon which we project our wishes, but it's also a screen in another sense—a sieve that won't allow everything through. I take the old image of the Grim Reaper holding a sickle to be a personal reminder that large parts of me, maybe most of me, will have to be cut away.

....

I come now to a third common complaint regarding the afterlife, namely, that it's all fantasy. Hell's no more real than a Stephen King novel, and heaven's no less fiction than the land of Cockaigne, the peasant fantasy of the Middle Ages in which work was forbidden, rivers flowed with wine, and roasted pigs walked around with knives in their backs.[18] The empty blackness of death, like the empty blackness of the sensory deprivation chamber, has been the opportunity for humans to hallucinate. So can't we safely ignore all the flights of fancy, all the indeterminate ramblings about what lies beyond the gates of death?

I have another opinion. Even were one to concede, as I don't, that all accounts of the world to come are deceptive fiction, that wouldn't justify indifference. To suppose otherwise would be to insist that, if there's no literal truth there, there's no truth at all. But whatever may or may not lie ahead, people's hopes and fears about the future are main ingredients for cultural and religious history. Histories of hell, even if they don't tell us about hell, tell us much about those who've believed in hell; and histories of heaven, even if they don't tell us about heaven, tell us much about those who've believed in the place. Influential stories and symbols and their interpretations always repay study, so on this account alone eschatology shouldn't be swept into the dustbin of forgotten notions.

But that's to speak as a historian, and there's more to life than history.

....

We all use our imaginations to foresee the future, whether we're planning the rest of the day or the rest of our lives; and despite our best efforts, nothing guarantees that what we imagine will come to pass. Indeed, rarely does the future heed our plans. Each morning I plot the coming hours, and seldom do my designs unfold without a hitch. On most days, unforeseen circumstances interrupt, and I end up improvising, deferring activities, changing course. The same is even more true of my long-term planning: the further into the future my imagination has projected itself, the less prescient it's been. Indeed, only rarely have I seen the far future approximately as it's come to pass. My life illustrates chaos theory: I can't predict or control things because there are always too many variables. The result is that most of my personal goals have turned out to be useful fictions. They've given me something to shoot for, but they've rarely been realized, at least in the forms I'd first imagined them.

The world to come can't be much different. Here I agree with the skeptics: I doubt that we can divine much about it. We may cherish some hopes and dreams, but the odds that they'll prosaically line up with the future are negligible. Against the cynics, however, this doesn't mean that eschatology is pointless, that we have nothing save ill-informed guesses about things of which we can form no real conception. If some fictions are useless, others are useful.

Feuerbach, in his critique of Christianity, wrote: "Faith in the future life is nothing else than faith in the truth of the imagination."[19] The issue isn't whether this is correct—in large measure it is—but whether the imagination can hold truth, whether (to borrow from Plato) there are "likely myths," myths that convey appropriate theological value and meaning.

....

I need to pause here, before going further, because some might be uneasy with the notion that eschatology is, from one point of view, fiction. But this is old news. When Jesus proclaimed the future kingdom of God, he uttered parables and drew analogies. His preferred strategy was to say: It's sort of like this, and it's sort of like that. He talked about sheep and goats, weeds and wheat, debts and debtors. He spoke of grooms and bridesmaids, servants and masters, leaven and treasure. Over and over again he introduced his eschatological speech with "The kingdom of God is like. . . ." His preferred rhetoric makes him a bit like Plato, who wrote that "a person of sense will not insist that these things are exactly as I have described them. But I think that he will believe that something of the kind is true . . . and that it is worth his while to stake everything on this belief."[20]

Paul was no different. He confessed that "eye has not seen nor ear heard, what God has laid up for those who love God" (1 Cor. 2:9). The old theologians followed suit. William Whitaker wrote: "Although we generally know that the saints in heaven are blessed, yet we know not their particular state, their actions, the manner and degree of their happiness. . . . Christ revealed to the saints on earth, heavenly things, but not what was done in heaven."[21] Francis Turretin wrote that "whatever symbols are used, drawn from earthly things to adumbrate" the happiness of heaven, "it must always be recollected that they are employed allegorically and ought to be understood mystically."[22] John Rogers wrote that heaven is "transcendent, infinite, ineffable, incomprehensible, and remote from our weak senses."[23]

The future is never clear, not even in prophecy (which is one reason the Old Testament didn't enable anyone to see the New Testament ahead of time). We don't just hope for what we don't see but for what we can't see. So the world's religions and their holy books—the Bible included—are inevitably full of differing expectations and diverse scenarios about the things to come. What else could we expect from imagination, even inspired imagination? If God being all in all is our future, and if God can't be comprehended, then our future can't be comprehended.

. . . .

The end is like the beginning. We no longer find cosmological or chronological facts in Genesis. That book is a source for theology, not for science or history. Rightly interpreted, Genesis teaches us not when God created the world but that God created the world. From it we learn not that a talking snake once tricked a man and a woman into doing something stupid but that irrational human beings who don't know their place bring misery upon themselves and their world. We're accustomed now to reading Genesis as theology without reading it as history.

It should be the same with eschatology: the relevant biblical texts aren't history written ahead of time. They're rather artistic portrayals of what lies beyond the realm of our immediate, ordinary experience. Like icons or expressionist paintings, they aim not at picture-perfect representations but seek to convey meaning.

Heaven and hell are myths, or if you don't like that word, symbols of what we hope and fear lies ahead. They're more poetry than prose. They're a bit like the planetary model of the atom, or the representation of space-time as a deformed rubber sheet. They don't depict but evoke. They don't describe but suggest.

The accuracy of any description diminishes in inverse ratio to its object's distance, and as the last things aren't to hand, we—whose minds evolved in order to interact with the world of the five senses—can't depict them. We're compelled, then, either to keep quiet or to imagine; and we do the latter when we believe that the future is too important to ignore, that too much hinges upon it. To be sure, if we're being picky, good eschatology, like good theology, must be largely apophatic: our discontinuous future, the best of all possible worlds, won't really be this, and it won't literally be that. For practical purposes, however, eschatological minimalism isn't enough. Imagination abhors an aniconistic vacuum, and the theological imagination can't but draw upon its convictions about and experience of God—what, for instance, it believes about divine love and justice—or upon its ideas about human beings—what it thinks about the existence or non-existence of a soul, for example—to anticipate, however inadequately, what might lie ahead.

....

To be a useful fiction, an eschatological fiction needs to be at least two things. First, it needs to engage us where we are. I happen to hate big cities, so the last thing I want in the afterlife is another one. This means that the New Jerusalem doesn't work for me, and I'll never publish an article on Revelation 21. I prefer to look forward to the new Maine coming down out of heaven from God. Now of course I don't take my expectation literally, yet I nonetheless find it meaningful because, recalling Plato, I think: surely something of the kind must be true. Those, however, who love life in the big city may find inspiration in Revelation 21, or in Peter Berger's stunning essay on why New York City foreshadows the kingdom of God.[24] They too can say to themselves: surely something of the kind must be true.

The second thing required for useful eschatological fictions is that they be theologically sound. This means they must derive from and promote foundational convictions about God. In everyday life, we never imagine from scratch: we can only invent with the materials already to hand. It's the same with eschatology. We extend into the future what we believe about God in the past and the present. More precisely, we project our convictions about God's goodness, truth, and beauty onto the unknown. When we do this, we aren't guilty of untrammeled speculation, and our metaphors aren't mere metaphors. They're rather imaginative attempts by finite creatures to stammer about an ineffable God and an indistinct future, or rather about both at the same time, since the human *telos* is God.

So to return to the skeptics: yes, from one point of view, we don't know what we're talking about. Eschatology is sketchy fiction, not miraculous foreknowledge. Nonetheless, not all myths are equal, and eschatology needn't be fiction in the way that the Dispensationalists' bogus rapture is fiction. It can instead be fiction on the side of religious truth, as is the allegory of the sower. Mark 4 doesn't preserve the historical account of a Galilean farmer who went out to sow. That chapter instead enshrines a parable, a lie not intended to deceive, a story that's historically empty yet theologically helpful. Constructive eschatology belongs to the same genre.

I'm willing to concede that, just as we don't really know what to pray for, beyond "Thy will be done," so we don't really know what to hope for, beyond "Thy will be done." Nevertheless, just as I continue to say my prayers and to ask for this and that, so too do I continue to ponder what might lie beyond and to hope for this or that.

....

Up to this point, I've sought to address some common complaints. I'd now like to turn things around and offer a couple of reasons why, instead of discounting eschatology, some of us should consider addressing the subject more than has been our custom.

....

I understand why some preachers and teachers say as little as possible about eschatological subjects. For one thing, some believe that the scientific and philosophical objections to traditional beliefs can't be overcome, so they feel obliged to move on. For another, there's history's embarrassing mountain of eschatological nonsense, which includes not just all the banal heavens and inhuman hells but also the false messiahs and sign-board prophets, cargo cults and erroneous forecasts. Who wants to be associated with all that? It's prudent to keep a safe distance from those who don't know the history of eschatological folly and so keep repeating it.

Nonetheless, the reserve of so many mainline and liberal Protestant ministers doesn't serve us well. Despite secularization and the spread of skepticism, surveys reveal that large numbers still ponder what might lie beyond. Two out of three North Americans profess belief in heaven, and most of them claim to have thought a lot about it.[25] Why should pastors and theologians hold back on a religious topic so many seemingly care about so deeply? There's likely something to John Cobb's remark that "our sophisticated equivocations" on eschatology "have contributed to our general irrelevance to the religious interests of our contemporaries."[26]

....

Soon after it appeared, I read Dan Brown's *The Da Vinci Code*. I found it to be an entertaining potboiler, which I supposed would make a good movie, which it didn't. I thought no more about it until, a couple of months later, I learned of people in my church who'd read it and been shaken by it. They wanted to know from their pastor whether Jesus might've been married, and whether the church had covered up other shocking secrets. Their ignorance was dumbfounding. Nonetheless, they were reading, thinking, and trying to understand.

It's similar with eschatology. The subject escaped from the pulpit and control of official religious authorities long ago, and many now adopt eschatological ideas from multiple sources. Websites recount dramatic near-death experiences. Television shows feature mediums who purport to communicate with departed spirits. Movies are full of apocalyptic and post-apocalyptic themes. Books promote reincarnation and animal immortality. Graphic novels narrate visits to heavenly kingdoms and hellish realms. And dispensationalism flourishes on the radio and between book covers.

In my experience, all this goes on with insufficient commentary from those in mainline pulpits and seminaries. But shouldn't we be eager to share some prudent observations about the latest eschatological excitement, and shouldn't we be able to discuss, say, the evolution of hell and the origins of dispensationalism? Shouldn't we have the resources to explore sympathetically modern skepticism and its grounds as well as the ability to say something informed about near-death experiences? Shouldn't we want to offer criticism of sentimental, self-centered expectations, and shouldn't we aspire to share ideas that might better convey the *mysterium tremendum*?

Of course there's no reversing the long historical process that's seen secular institutions appropriate most of the responsibilities for the dying and the dead. At present, doctors and nurses surround deathbeds; and if you want a priest, pastor, or rabbi by your side—they're of course optional—he or she will come and go only as the medical authorities allow. Further, once our loved ones depart, we entrust their remains to coroners, morticians, funeral directors, and cemetery owners, who conduct their business under the laws of the secular state. There's not much left for us religious folks to do. Yet we can still converse about death and the hereafter, and some people may still want to hear what we have to say. Why disappoint them? Why be eschatologically bashful? Why not strive to offer some input about and beyond the popular culture? Why not contribute to people's stores of ideas as they go about blending their inevitably eclectic mix of eschatological hopes? If we abdicate this task, we run the risk, when it comes to death, of reducing ourselves to psycho-therapeutic bereavement counselors who have little distinctive to offer.

·················

It's possible I've overreached here. Maybe my generalizations about what pastors and teachers should expect of themselves are too much. After all, there's a variety of gifts and a variety of interests. Tempers and talents differ. Some educators and pastors, it's evident, just aren't much interested in the last things. Their minds are elsewhere, on a present that hands them enough trials and tribulations with which to cope. Why take thought for the morrow when today's troubles are sufficient for the day?

Fine. Not all are prophets, and not all care about prophecy. This circumstance, however, is all the more reason for those of us who do care to share what we know and think.

·················

I've a second reason, this one more personal, for attending to eschatology.

Lamentably, we often fail to appreciate people until they're gone, which means we take them for granted when they're around. Some say this is because we never truly and firmly grasp that people, like time, are fleeting; and doesn't eschatology get in the way here? If there's always another tomorrow, or rather eternity, what's the rush of anything? Immortality is a type of inflation, and inflation always devalues, which is why you can have too much of a good thing. To bestow indefinite life spans upon people is to cheapen them and to diminish today. It's better to live as though we have only now: *carpe diem*. As Grace Jantzen has put it: "If immortality is denied, and if moral growth is valued, there is an urgency to moral improvement, both for oneself and for others, which might easily be ignored if it were thought that there was endless time available."[27]

There's a fallacy here. It's the end of current circumstances that makes the difference, not the end of all circumstances whatsoever. That's why eschatology itself can inculcate a sense of ethical urgency, as when imminent expectation disturbs religious slumber. In Romans, salvation being nearer now than when one first believed should move one to live honorably, soberly, and without jealousy (13:11–14). And in 1 Peter, the claim that "the end of all things is near" introduces these obligations: "Maintain constant love for one another. . . . Be hospitable to one another without complaining. Like good stewards of the manifold grace of God, serve one another with whatever gift each of you has received" (4:7–10). So while, in the minds of some, the prospect of extinction heightens attention and compels us to act now, belief in the last things can achieve precisely the same result. Indeed, the purported upshot of personal extinction is also the admonitory lesson of eschatology: keep awake. Night comes, when no one can work.

. . . .

Maybe inflation isn't a problem for immortality. Some things count for more because they endure, just as some things count for less because they don't endure. Paper plates destined for the trash have little value. The old family china, passed down from generation to generation, is worth much. Indeed, as often as not, we pay less heed to things that quickly come and go and more heed to things that last.

Isn't it the same with people? As a general rule, the more time I've spent with a friend or family member, the more profound and meaningful the relationship has become. Time has always augmented the value and significance of friendship. Indeed, it's partially the long time involved that explains why my most treasured friendship goes back over half a century, all the way back to nursery school. Given this, isn't it altogether natural for me to want that relationship to extend into the indefinite future? And wouldn't it be truly peculiar if instead, in deference to the supposed principle that we prize things more when they're impermanent, I didn't lament the eventual termination of my lifelong friendship?

. . . .

It's worth candidly asking what happens to us when our loved ones leave. We mourn them for a while, and then we get on with our business. Memories fade and emotions recover. The ripples of their influence dissipate. As our companions are buried, they sink not just below the sod but also below our daily awareness. We visit their graves less often. When the phone rings, our minds cease to hope, as they once did, if only for an instant, that Mom or Dad is calling. Year after year, thoughts turn to our departed loved ones with reduced frequency. Absence makes the heart grow harder.

This much unsettles me. I'm distressed that I now go days without thinking of my late parents or weeks without thinking of my departed friends. They're receding into the past and disappearing from the present. The common wisdom may be that we need to let go; yet it seems wrong that these people are becoming less real, less distinct, and that they matter less and less to all of us who once knew them. Soon they will be altogether forgotten.

In the face of such deterioration, I'm not comforted by the proposition that finitude begets value. My experience is that, when it comes to people, finitude drains value. My only solace is that things aren't as they seem to be, that our loved ones aren't machines with built-in obsolescence.

If death is the end, then we're all snow: we arrive, we melt, we are no more. Eschatology is a way of saying that we're more. It's a way of resisting the diminishing value of the dead. It's a way of making all of our stories longer-lasting and so more meaningful. It's the claim that human beings matter greatly because they matter persistently. That claim, even if one doubts it, shouldn't be dismissed as a recipe for escapism, moral complacency, or some other social sin. Chesterton was right: "It is absurd indeed that Christians should be called the enemies of life because they wish life to last forever."[28]

....

In closing this chapter, I want to return to the relationship between eschatological convictions and historical responsibility. On this topic we can, I'd like to suggest, learn something from the modern discussion of the historical Jesus and his expectations.

Johannes Weiss and Albert Schweitzer, over a hundred years ago, famously argued that the kingdom of God was, for Jesus, eschatological in the strict sense of the word. It was, that is, inescapably bound up with the final things, with the resurrection of the dead, the Last Judgment, and the world to come.[29]

They were correct. They may have gotten many details wrong, but they got the big picture right. Jesus was an eschatological prophet with a messianic self-conception, and he hoped in a God who would radically alter just about everything.[30] When Jesus solemnly declared that the first will be last, the last first, he wasn't naively oblivious of the cruel fact that, all too often, the rich get richer, the poor poorer. He was instead prophesying, as the future tense indicates: God will, at the judgment, turn the world upside down. He was likewise prophesying when he blessed the hungry and those who mourn, avowing that they will be filled and comforted: that's eschatology, not a realistic estimate of probabilities.

What does all this have to do with ethics? Schweitzer urged—notoriously—that Jesus had an "interim ethic," that his moral teaching was inextricably united with his belief in a near end. This explains, according to Schweitzer, why Jesus didn't care much for money, why he called people away from their families and jobs, and why he said so little about the Roman occupation. If the present form of this world is passing away, you needn't bother much with the present form of this world.

Schweitzer wasn't, in this particular, spot on. While a near expectation presumably motivated some of Jesus' curious demands, and while his eschatology added urgency to all his imperatives, he drew most of his moral teaching from the Jewish Bible and attendant traditions. Although he proclaimed the near advent of God's kingdom, he reportedly summed up his moral demands by quoting two celebrated imperatives from the Torah—love God and love neighbor. Those imperatives originated apart from eschatology, and their force is independent of eschatology, and the same is true of most of his moral teaching.

It's not, however, Schweitzer's imperfect idea of an interim ethic upon which I want to reflect. It's rather these words, which appeared in the first edition of his *Quest of the Historical Jesus*:

> In reality that which is eternal in the words of Jesus is due to the very fact that they are based on an eschatological worldview, and contain the expression of a mind for which the contemporary world with its historical and social circumstances no longer had any existence. They are appropriate, therefore, to any world, for in every world they raise the man who dares to meet their challenge, and does not turn and twist them into meaninglessness, above his world and his time, making him inwardly free, so that he is fitted to be, in his own world and in his own time, a simple channel of the power of Jesus.[31]

This interpretation much intrigues me. Schweitzer is saying that Jesus, in his imagination, didn't just look forward, from the present to the consummation, but rather projected himself into the future and from there looked back, from the consummation to the present. He appraised what he saw around him over against what he saw coming. He assessed this world over against the world to come.

On this view, meditating upon the eschatological kingdom, when Torah will be done on earth as in heaven, was Jesus' way of perceiving the unadulterated will of God; and being infatuated with the possibilities of paradise regained—"from the beginning it was not so"—he tended to neglect the conventional gamut of cultural and political possibilities. He rather asked for more—far more—because, mindful of the prophecies, he saw far more coming. In this way, eschatology entered the present as a mandate.

Jesus may have hoped for a kingdom that only God could bring, but that didn't occasion passivity or flight from a world askew. As a Jew committed to the *imitatio dei*—"Be merciful, just as your Father is merciful" (Luke 6:36)—it was impossible for him to dream of the divine restoration, with its radically new social, political, and economic order, and to remain indifferent to the current order. To long for justice in the eschaton without sponsoring justice now would have made no sense to him. Rather, to imagine God's radically different future entailed intolerance of the same old same old.

Because Jesus expected toll collectors and sinners to enter the kingdom, he welcomed them today; and because he believed that the poor will inherit the earth, he embraced them now.

Jesus envisaged, in the words of Gustavo Gutiérrez, "the utopia that sets history in motion."[32] This is why Jesus was so often heedless of earthly contingencies, why he was so often radical and subversive, and why he again and again blasted complacency. He lived against injustice because he dreamed of its opposite. He disputed what is because he longed for what is not. The kingdom wasn't for him a vision opposed to praxis but a vision that commanded praxis.

Of course, such an idealistic way of looking at things has its limitations. It's not good for everything, which is why the history of Christian ethics is the history of qualifying Jesus. At the same time, an eschatological worldview that judges the transient in terms of the transcendent has the great virtue of distancing one from the present, of creating a critical perspective on, and a holy dissatisfaction with, all the contingencies that masquerade as necessities. In the words of Johann Baptist Metz, Jesus' eschatological God is not an opiate but the "guarantee of the immutable standard in the unremitting struggle for the dignity of all human beings" and "universal liberation."[33]

....

There's an analogy here with the old Christian anchorites. Despite their attempts to seek God in private, they often ended up living very public lives as rural patrons and religious oracles. After they crossed the boundaries of ordinary society by cutting familial, economic, and political ties, people came to perceive them as impartial judges. They accordingly became social legislators and personal courts of law. Simeon Stylites, as a recent commentator has put it, ran an extensive social service network from atop his pillar.[34] Simeon became a well of wisdom and a fount of fair judgments because he had severed his ties to the world and stepped away to behold it from afar.

Jesus did something analogous. His eschatological imagination loosened his personal and social ties and so helped him to live outside of what people took for granted. God's kingdom erased the finality of his historical and cultural context and so enabled him to perceive something other than the current state of affairs.

....

How might we appropriate Jesus' ethical eschatology? I briefly offer, as a conclusion, three suggestions. The first is this: we need Jesus' idealistic orientation. If our world is fallen, we should find a way, as he did, of rising above it. And the way to do that, or at least one way to begin to do that, is through prophecy, which is the gift by which we see beyond the present, beyond its lack of imagination, beyond its ruling powers and taken-for-granted interests.

Contemporary circumstances always carry inertia, their own potent momentum, which makes changing course, whether for the one or the many, no easy task. So we require a compelling vision that surpasses and so relativizes the contemporary moment, a vision that breaks our cultural hypnosis and moves us to hope for more than what we see, a vision that breeds impatience and keeps us ill-adjusted to so-called reality. We need the idealistic faith to move the mountains before us: commodity fetishism, oppressive governments, corrupting entertainment, narcissistic indifference.

For all this, utopia serves us better than Christian realism. Utopia may be nowhere, and it may be as likely as the meek inheriting the earth, but we can't give it up. To settle instead for the realistically obtainable, to be pragmatic, would be to exchange the "ought" of the city of God for the "is" of the city of man. The status quo isn't our friend, and we shouldn't acknowledge its authority. Instead of being content to make a virtue of necessity, we need to dismantle necessity. The one thing needful, as Martin Luther King Jr. understood, is to dream of what hasn't happened.

Second, if Jesus' eschatological vision tacitly pushed people to temper their own economic and familial self-interests in view of the kingdom to come, we—or rather those of us not on the lower rungs of the socioeconomic ladder—need a similar critical distancing. Modern ethical theorists have, in their own way, recognized this. Proponents of Ideal Observer Theory, such as Roderick Firth, have insisted that an act is ethically sound if an impartial, omnipercipient viewer, that is, someone without prejudice or self-interest and with a God's-eye view, would approve;[35] and John Rawls famously sought to elucidate the notion of justice by crafting his "veil of ignorance" scenario, a thought experiment in which rational agents can agree on broad moral principles when they're unaware of their own economic class, social status, political position, and other contingencies.[36]

Whatever else we make of these proposals, they rightly recognize that, in certain respects, we need to get beyond ourselves. We need to strive for something akin to objectivity, to inspect ourselves and our slice of the world from a distance, to relativize our customary point of view by seeking a much larger point of view. To do this requires prophetic imagination— and seeing with more than our own eyes: we need the eyes and dreams of others, especially the eyes and dreams of the oppressed and less fortunate. There can be no privatization of hope.

Third and finally, our idealism, like that of Jesus, should be theocentric and so grounded in the conviction that, ultimately, all will be well. There are, of course, other ways to justify one's commitment. Marxism, for instance, has its dialectical materialism, its faith in an evolutionary advance. But those of us still inspired by the biblical prophets may be sustained by hope in the ultimate, transcendent triumph of God. We aren't Sisyphus, who was condemned to futility. The object of our hope is the ground of our hope, so somewhere, somehow, the hungry will be filled, and those who weep will laugh. The eschatological kingdom isn't the unreal but the not-yet real. Someday "Thy kingdom come, Thy will be done" will no longer be our prayer but our history.

CHAPTER 5

Hell and Sympathy

....

The mysteries of God's love cannot be measured by the penal code.

SERGIUS BULGAKOV

Death, misery, and hell have an end because grace is eternal.

JÜRGEN MOLTMANN

Hell, where is thy victory?

THE APOSTLE PAUL

....

I'M A LOUSY evangelist. This became painfully obvious the first time someone tried to make me one. It was 1972, and I was attending a youth rally in Dallas, Texas. One afternoon, my group leader instructed me to ring the doorbell of every house on a particular block. When someone came to the door, I was to share the good news, pray for God's blessing, then check off the address on my clipboard. Being a severe introvert, I was mortified. Knowing the task to be impossible, and persuaded that lying is wrong, I sneaked up to the first door, rang the bell, then ran and hid in the bushes. After a woman answered the door, stared in confusion, then turned back inside, I moved on to the next house to repeat the procedure. I returned the clipboard, a check mark in front of each address.

Timidity eliminated one vocation. It wasn't, however, the only difficulty. There was also a theological problem. Even back then, I couldn't believe that those who answered the door were, unless they'd invited Jesus into their hearts, fated for hell.

I remember reading, not long after returning home from Dallas, a pamphlet on Christianity and other religions. It plainly taught that all Jews, Muslims, and Hindus will burn in fire for ever and ever. As proof, the author cited biblical texts. I recoiled. I can in fact recall standing up and anxiously pacing the room. The notion of post-mortem torture for all unlike me was, long before I encountered liberal theology, repellent. For one thing, my image of God wasn't that of a merciless tormentor. For another, hell seemed unjust. I knew that most Buddhists are Buddhists because their parents were Buddhists, and how could the circumstances of one's birth be a reliable statistical predictor of one's eternal destiny?

My youthful antipathy toward the conventional hell with its belly full of non-Christians was so profound that, had I regarded the teaching of the pamphlet as essential Christian doctrine, I'd have abandoned my religion. One can't believe what one can't believe.

In retrospect, the interesting question is why, forty years ago, a Kansas teenager was so appalled by a doctrine that others have championed, especially as my response can't be deemed idiosyncratic. There have always been Christians anxious to ameliorate hell. Their number, moreover, has burgeoned in recent times. So the autobiographical question is a larger historical question. Why now do vast numbers routinely find the old doctrine not creditable?

....

Before addressing that question, it will be useful to keep before us what many Christians have believed about hell. For this purpose, I select several troubling quotations. The first is from Jeremias Drexel, the seventeenth-century devotional writer who won an audience among both Catholics and Protestants:

> If all the most severe most barbarous tortures which were ever invented by the tyrants of the earth, who, by anxious thoughts and hellish contrivances, have improved and refined the art of cruelty, and brought it to perfection; if these, I say, were to be heaped upon the head of one man, and he were to endure them for a hundred years, yet they would not come near the pains of the damned for one day![1]

In other words, Mengele was an amateur. His unspeakably fiendish deeds pale beside what God has cooked up for sinners in hell.

My second quotation comes from Robert Bolton, an Anglican preacher whose book on the last things was published in 1633:

> I have somewhere read of the horrid execution of a Traitor in this manner: being naked, he was chained fast to a chaire of brasse or some other such

metall, that would burne most furiously, being fil'd with fiery heat; about which was made a mighty fire, that by little and little caused the chair to be red and raging hot, so that the miserable man roared hideously many houres for extremest anguish, and so expired. But what an horrible thing had it bin to have lien in that dreadful torment eternally: and yet all this is nothing. For, if the black fire of hell be truly corporall . . . it is such (say they) that as far passeth our ordinary hottest fire, as ours exceeds the fire upon the wall.[2]

In Bolton's theology, the unimaginable agony of being roasted alive is as nothing—nothing!—compared with the excruciating, mindboggling horrors awaiting the damned.

My third selection appears in an infamous pamphlet printed in the middle of the nineteenth century. It unfolds the meaning of Psalm 21:9—"You shall make them as a fiery oven in the time of your anger"—with these words:

See! it is a pitiful sight. The little child is in this red-hot oven. Hear how it screams to come out. See how it turns and twists itself about in the fire. It beats its head against the roof of the oven. It stamps its little feet on the floor of the oven. You can see on the face of this little child what you see on the faces of all in Hell—despair, desperate and horrible! . . . This child committed very bad mortal sins, knowing well the harm of what it was doing, and knowing that Hell would be the punishment. God was very good to this child. Very likely God saw that this child would get worse and worse, and would never repent, and so it would have to be punished much more in Hell. So God in his mercy called it out of the world in its early childhood.[3]

It would be less disturbing were these words authored by a devotee of the god Moloch. They instead come from the Reverend J. Furniss, a Roman Catholic priest of Ireland. They appear, moreover, in a booklet entitled *The Sight of Hell*, which was number ten in the series "Books for Children and Young Persons." The goal, then, was to petrify little ones.

The Sight of Hell is now available in a PDF file on the Internet, so anyone can peruse it.[4] My guess is that the few who've done so are like me, that is, they're historians doing research. I'd wager that nobody has downloaded the thing in order to read it to children. Today, even apologists for hell can't stomach Furniss. I recall William Lane Craig, the evangelical philosopher, once defending hell, yet dismissing Father Furniss as "ridiculous." His rationale was that the biblical language about future punishment must be metaphorical.

I'll spare you further odious imaginings, although not for a lack of material: I could go on and on. Christians of all kinds—Catholic, Orthodox, Protestant—have enthusiastically detailed the gruesome and terrifying future that God allegedly has devised for the unredeemed.

....

My next quotation is of a different sort. It doesn't warn sinners about hell but records how the doctrine profoundly disturbed some fifteenth-century Japanese converts. Here's Francis Xavier, the Jesuit missionary to Asia:

> One of the things that most pains and torments these Japanese is, that we teach them that the prison of hell is irrevocably shut, so that there is no egress therefrom. For they grieve over the fate of their departed children, of their parents and relatives, and they often show their grief by their tears. So they ask us if there is any hope, any way to free them by prayer from that eternal misery, and I am obliged to answer that there is absolutely none. Their grief at this affects and torments them wonderfully; they almost pine away with sorrow. But there is this good thing about their trouble—it makes one hope that they will all be the more laborious for their own salvation, lest they, like their forefathers, should be condemned to everlasting punishment. They often ask if God cannot take their fathers out of hell, and why their punishment must never have an end. We gave them a satisfactory answer, but they did not cease to grieve over the misfortune of their relatives; and I can hardly restrain my tears sometimes at seeing men so dear to my heart suffer such intense pain about a thing which is already done with and can never be undone.[5]

The good news Francis proclaimed was mixed with some awfully bad news. If the default setting for human beings is damnation, and if confessing Jesus is the sole escape, then all who died before the missionaries appeared are doomed. Accepting Christ, on this version of Christianity, meant not only losing forever one's dead family members and dead friends, but losing them to interminable affliction. Everybody involved, including Francis, was understandably reduced to tears. Also understandably, some Japanese thought that their native religion had more "clemency and mercy" than did the missionary's religion.[6] (Ironically, it was the other way around for many early Protestants, who worried that their deceased Catholic parents and grandparents might be in hell.[7])

My last quotation comes from Albert Barnes, the nineteenth-century Presbyterian pastor and expositor. I stumbled across it years ago and took note because I found his candor so exceptional, his confusion so moving:

> That any should suffer forever—lingering on in hopeless despair, and rolling amidst infinite torments without the possibility of alleviation, and without end. That since God can save men, and will save a part, he has not proposed to save all. . . . These are real, not imaginary difficulties. . . . They are probably felt by every mind that ever reflected on the subject—and they are unexplained, unmitigated, unremoved. . . . My whole soul pants for light and relief on these questions. But I get neither; and in the distress and anguish of my own spirit, I confess that I see no light whatever. I see not one ray to disclose to me why sin came into the world; why the earth is strewn with the dying and the dead, and why man must suffer to all eternity. I have never seen a particle of light thrown on these subjects that has given a moment's ease to my tortured mind. . . . I confess, when I look on a world of sinners and sufferers; upon death-beds and grave yards; upon the world of woe filled with hosts to suffer forever;—when I see my friends, my parents, my family, my people, my fellow citizens—when I look upon a whole race, all involved in this sin and danger, and when I see the great mass of them wholly unconcerned, and when I feel that God only can save them and yet that he does not do it, I am struck dumb. It is all dark, dark, dark to my soul, and I cannot disguise it.[8]

Barnes's theology required him to believe in eternal torment for sinners. At the same time, his theology taught him that God loves everybody, and further that Albert Barnes should love everybody. One understands why he was so distraught. If, as Charles Hodge observed, the "natural heart revolts from and struggles against" hell,[9] how much more the Christian heart, which professes that God is love?

. . . .

Hell has, from the beginning, unsettled some Christians. This is because, as Augustine conceded long ago, "eternal punishment appears harsh and unjust."[10] One understands why, in the *Vision of Paul* (from the fourth century), the damned aren't tormented on Sunday or on the great feast days of the church; and why, in the *Greek Apocalypse of the Virgin* (of uncertain date), they are released altogether from torment for the fifty days from

Easter to Pentecost; and why, according to Oecumenius, the torments of hell will be less severe after a period of time;[11] and why, according to John Henry Newman, the lost need not always be conscious of their past punishment or future suffering;[12] and why, at the Vespers of Kneeling on Pentecost Sunday, the Orthodox pray these words: "on this final and saving festival, thou art pleased to accept intercessory propitiation on behalf of those held fast in hell, and thou dost grant to us great hopes that thou wilt send down on them relaxation of their torments and consolation."[13] Doctrine hasn't always extinguished sympathy.

Not until relatively recent times, however, did hell begin to encounter far-flung, reflexive incredulity. The number of doubters swelled in the seventeenth and eighteenth centuries, when some decided that the Greek word, *aiōnios*, means not "eternal" but rather "age-long," so that hell has an expiration date. Others, such as Isaac Newton and John Locke, opted for conditional immortality, the view that the wicked will be annihilated. The 1600s and 1700s also seemingly witnessed the birth of the exegetical proposal—I haven't yet been able to ascertain its originator—that, in the New Testament, "Gehenna" signifies always and only the valley outside Jerusalem, nothing more.[14]

The shifting sentiments are discernible in a 1690 sermon by John Tillotson, who became Archbishop of Canterbury. Tillotson, who was preaching before Queen Mary II, distinguished between threat and promise, claiming that while one is bound to keep a promise, it's not morally wrong to issue a threat one doesn't execute. This raised the possibility—although Tillotson was exceedingly cautious here—that the biblical threats about hell, whose function is to alter behavior, need not precisely predict the fate of the wicked.[15]

You might protest that the fires of hell couldn't have been cooling already in the seventeenth or eighteenth century, because Jonathan Edwards (d. 1758) was around then, and he penned that staple of high-school English anthologies, "Sinners in the Hands of an Angry God." Yet hell—which Edwards, as a youngster, deemed to be "a horrible doctrine"[16]—wasn't the central theme of his theology or his preaching. Moreover, the extent to which we should regard his sermon as representative of his time and place is unclear. No one was conducting public opinion polls back then. It's suggestive that, in another sermon, "The Eternity of Hell Torments," Edwards defends hell against detractors. When he argues at length that hell is absolutely without end, that it will involve sensible misery, and that perpetual punishment will achieve various goods, he's playing the apologist. He knows Christians who disagree.

How could he not know? Forty-five years before Edwards was born, a certain Samuel Richardson authored *A Discourse of the Torments of Hell: The Foundation and Pillars thereof Discovered, Searched, Shaken and Removed. With Many Infallible Proofs, that there is Not to be a Punishment after this Life for Any to Endure that Shall Never End* (1658). This book, which is mostly scriptural exposition, was felt sufficiently noteworthy that three English divines wrote works attacking it. A few years later, *A Letter of Resolution concerning Origen and the Chief of his Opinions*—probably authored by Bishop George Rust, the Cambridge Platonist—defended the church father and his universalism. And ten years before Richardson, Gerrard Winstanley, founder of the Diggers, affirmed that "in the end every man shall be saved. . . . What is called the day of judgment is not a day but a long period. Only the Serpent remains at the end in eternal punishment."[17]

Later, during Edwards' lifetime, Jacob Ilive published a pamphlet titled *The Oration spoke at Joyners Hall in Thamesstreet on Monday, Sept. 24, 1733*, which lampoons literal hell fire as the invention of self-serving clergy. It was then too that the renowned William Law (d. 1761), author of *A Serious Call to a Holy and Devout Life*, adopted Origen's understanding of hell as mental, purgatorial, and temporal. The eighteenth century was also home to Thomas Newton (d. 1782), the Anglican Bishop of Bristol, who, although scarcely a radical, dissented from the idea that hell would have no end: "Imagin [sic] it you may, but you can never seriously believe it, nor reconcile it to God or goodness. The thought is shocking even to human nature, and how much more abhorrent then must it be for the divine perfections! God must have made all his creatures finally to be happy; he could never make any, whose end he foreknew would be misery everlasting."[18]

The tipping point came finally in the nineteenth century. Even if Charles Spurgeon was still insisting that no one fears a metaphorical fire, his era, the historians tell us, was when hell, at least in European Protestantism, quietly slunk away for good. Unless you wanted an effective metaphor or a good reason to reject Christianity, you ignored it.

Charles Darwin, who originally studied for the ministry and knew some theology, wrote this in his *Autobiography*: "I can indeed hardly see how anyone ought to wish Christianity to be true; for if so the plain language of the text seems to show that the men who do not believe, and this would include my Father, Brother, and almost all of my friends, will be everlastingly punished. And this is a damnable doctrine."[19] Before this sentence was posthumously published, Darwin's Anglican wife wrote in the margin of the manuscript: "I should dislike the passage . . . to be published. . . .

Nothing can be said too severe upon the doctrine of everlasting punishment for disbelief—but very few now wd. call that 'Christianity.'"[20] This estimate of hell's deteriorating condition is confirmed by a remark of Gladstone not long thereafter: Hell has been relegated "to the far-off corners of the Christian mind . . . there to sleep in deep shadow, as a thing needless in our enlightened and progressive age. . . . We are in danger even of losing this subject out of sight and out of mind."[21]

By 1891, Thomas Sawyer could publish *Endless Punishment*, a polemic against hell which carried the subtitle *In the Very Words of Its Advocates*. His presupposition was that "there are some opinions . . . whose honest statement is their best refutation."[22]

....

Recent decades haven't brought revival. I've been in church most Sunday mornings for almost sixty years now, and I recall only two sermons on hell. One was in a Congregational church, and the pastor's main point was that there is no hell. The other sermon was in a PCUSA church, not so long ago. The pastor did strive to take hell seriously. Yet compared with the views of Drexel, Bolton, and Furniss, as quoted above, he was tame. Although he insisted that our actions have consequences here and hereafter, he didn't harp on the undying worm or the unquenchable fire.

Even in more conservative churches, the idea of hell as an eternal torture chamber has, of late, floundered. The prominent British evangelical John Wenham wrote: "Unending torment speaks to me of sadism, not justice. It is a doctrine which I do not know how to preach without negating the loveliness and glory of God."[23] John Stott, the famous Anglican cleric, confessed: "Emotionally, I find the concept [of eternal torment] intolerable and do not understand how people can live with it without either cauterizing their feelings or cracking under the strain."[24] Stott—falling in line with the Doctrine Commission of the Church of England, whose members in 1995 construed hell as "total non-being"—became an annihilationist. Another evangelical, Rob Bell, made it to the cover of *Time Magazine* in 2011 for his book *Love Wins*, wherein he surrenders to hopeful universalism.

Bell isn't only a sign of the times but, surely, a harbinger of things to come. I've been teaching future pastors for almost two decades now, and even when they've been on the evangelical side of the great theological divide, few have sounded like Father Furniss. Indeed, only one, of dozens assigned to write on damnation, has zealously defended literal hellfire. He compared being hurled into hell to being thrown into the molten stream of an old Pittsburgh foundry.

It's amazing how far the discomfort with hell has spread. Several years ago I happened upon a book entitled *In the Hands of a Happy God: The No-hellers of Appalachia*.[25] It's an absorbing study of a group of Primitive Baptists in Central Appalachia. They too have decided that the old hell doesn't exist. Rather, hell assails people in this life. Jesus, they teach, died for all, so all will be saved in the end. These people are fundamentalists and universalists at the same time.

································

One can document hell's waning even in other religions.

Hell is the main theme of *The Book of the Righteous Virazi*, a Zoroastrian best-seller for centuries.[26] This tells the tale of a man leaving his body and visiting, with the help of two angelic beings, the Zoroastrian inferno. The place turns out to be inside the earth and full of demons and deceitful souls. Those souls suffer terribly and cry out in agony. Unaware of the miserable multitudes all about them, they grieve from loneliness.

The Book of the Righteous Verazi recalls, in many respects, Dante's hell, and like that hell, it's not doing well. A recent survey of the Parsi laity in India indicated that almost nobody fears perdition. Another survey, this one of Zoroastrians in the worldwide diaspora, found more belief. Yet even here, half or more of Zoroastrians appear to have said good-bye to hell. In Sydney, the percentage of believers in hell is down to 38. In Hong Kong, the number is 33; in Canada, 31.

································

So far I've been wholly one-sided, and although hell has, without doubt, fallen upon hard times, it'd be premature to declare it extinct. When Bell published his book, many in his mega-church left. They didn't want a hell-less pastor. Members of another church, this one in North Carolina, fired their Methodist pastor after his Facebook page endorsed Bell. The Southern Baptist convention also responded, officially declaring that hell is "eternal, conscious punishment."

If you doubt that the menacing doctrine is alive and well in some places, get hold of the 2001 documentary "Hell House." This tells the story of the annual, money-making haunted house run by Trinity Church in Cedar Hill, Texas. The various rooms—around a dozen, all told—depict sinners doing evil acts and sinners getting their hellish deserts. There's the rave room, the suicide room, the abortion room, and so on. Before the gawkers walk through, they must agree to listen, when done, to an abridged presentation of the turn-or-burn gospel. The aim is to frighten people into accepting Jesus as their personal savior. Some do.

Perhaps it's not out of place here to record a personal anecdote. Several years ago, I had a remarkable conversation with a Christian academic. He insisted that hell is necessary to keep Christians in line, and further that only a hell of interminable duration will do the trick. I was incredulous. "Wouldn't the prospect of a million years of hell fire be sufficient deterrent? Heck," I said, "if to be in hell is to be on fire, I'd move heaven and earth to avoid spending sixty seconds there." I can quote his response word for word because it was not only succinct but also the strangest thing anybody has ever said to me: "If hell is not eternal, I'm going to the orgy tonight."

I forego analysis of this dumbfounding confession, except to observe that it conveys the grip that fear of an everlasting hell still has on some folks. Here was a well-educated man confessing to me that he refrains from sexual promiscuity, not out of love or respect for his wife or for some other noble reason, but in order to avoid eternal damnation.

....

Popular opinion polls sometimes record a surprisingly high percentage of belief in hell. A 2003 Fox News poll, for example, reported that 74 percent of Americans still believe in the place. This matches the data, a few years later, from the Baylor survey of American religion, which put the number at 73 percent. As for my own denomination, the Presbyterian Church USA, the most recent numbers I've run across indicate that 57 percent of the laity, 61 percent of the elders, and 64 percent of the pastors profess belief in hell.

Yet this means that over a third of Presbyterian pastors and elders don't believe, and that more than two out of five of the laity don't either. Furthermore, bare numbers can be misleading. What sort of a hell is it in which so many believe? Hell is a genus with many species. Dante's *Inferno* isn't C. S. Lewis's *Great Divorce*. How many people, moreover, are going to inhabit the place? Imagining that a vast swath of humanity will reside there isn't the same as supposing that it holds only a few over-the-top nasties, such as Hitler and Stalin. Above all, what role does this professed belief play in people's everyday lives? You can assent to things that don't much matter. That Helena is the capital of Montana is a fact without existential import for most of us. Another poll of North Americans, conducted by the Barna Research Group about ten years ago, reported that, of those who do believe in hell, less than one half of one percent seriously thinks he or she may end up there. As the old song has it: "The Bells of hell go ting-a-ling-a-ling, for you but not for me."

Beyond the suggestive statistics, the titles of some recent books are revealing. They include *Four Views on Hell* (1992), *Hell on Trial* (1995), *The Battle for Hell* (1995), *Two Views of Hell* (2000), *Hell Under Fire* (2004), *The Problem of Hell* (2010), *Is Hell for Real or Does Everybody Go to Heaven?* (2011), *Erasing Hell* (2011), and *Heaven and Hell: Are They Real?* (2014).[27] These books chiefly reflect current debates among evangelicals. Even within their circles, hell is "on trial" and "under fire."

Even more telling, however, is this: In recent decades, the most popular and influential book on hell in the English-speaking world has undoubtedly been Lewis's *The Great Divorce*. Written in the mid-1940s, it's remarkable for its distance from so many earlier treatments of its subject. There's no physical torture. All pain is mental: the kingdom of hell is within. Further, the damned damn themselves. In fact, they can at any time hop a bus to heaven and, if they wish, stay. It's just that very few of them like the place.

It's particularly significant that *The Great Divorce* is a novel. Its premise is that hell is best approached through parabolic fiction. In its very form, Lewis's tale rejects the old literalism. The popularity of *The Great Divorce* suggests that many of its readers also reject the old literalism. They're fond of a book in which the citizens of hell aren't physically abused, and in which people aren't thrown into Gehenna against their wills but suffer of their own free choice, a choice they can undo after death. Put otherwise, Lewis's audience must include many who, whether they know it or not, have opted for Origen over Father Furniss. The great church father didn't take the biblical language about Gehenna literally. There was neither material fire nor animate worm in his hell, only mental and spiritual pain. He further maintained that hell is the upshot of freedom, that it's basically the state of a mind without God: "the individual sinner kindles the flame of his personal fire."[28]

That I'm not reading too much into the success of Lewis's novel gains support from the recent philosophical defenses of hell, such as those by Richard Swinburne and Jonathan Kvanvig.[29] These and other sophisticated discussions—which often cite Lewis—by and large agree on three points. First, God doesn't send people to hell against their wills. Rather, people reject God and so reject heaven. Hell is where they choose to be. Second, hell isn't a Hieronymus Bosch painting but rather a state of mind. The chamber of horrors is gone. Third, hell can't be objectively described. We can make theological assertions about it, and we can construct useful parables, but we have no precognitive snapshots.

Even the popes are on board with all this. In 1999, Pope John Paul II explained that hell is self-imposed exile from God, and in 2007, Pope Benedict XVI preached that hell is a "state of eternal separation from God" that should be understood "symbolically rather than physically."

Now none of this is, to be sure, strictly new. Even putting Origen and his admirers to the side, one can, without effort, find theologians who, long before Lewis, understood hell to be the outcome of freedom and who shied away from literalism. Calvin took both worm and fire to be figures, and Swedenborg and F. D. Maurice taught that the human will makes its own hell.[30] Indeed, certain passages in Swedenborg read like *The Great Divorce* in nuce.

Yet one can scarcely deny that things are different today. Hell just isn't what it used to be. Torture is out, metaphor is in, and just about everyone who defends hell does so in terms of human freedom. Not often anymore are we reminded that Matthew's Jesus warns about being "thrown into Gehenna," "thrown into the oven," "thrown into the fire," and "thrown into the outer darkness"—expressions that hardly underline free will.

What explains the revolution in theological attitude? Why has the old hell, in the last three or four centuries, become more problematic than it appears to have been in the past?

The question takes me back to my teenage years, when I ran into promoters of an old-fashioned hell. In hindsight, it appears that I was pre-programmed to reject their idea that vast numbers of human beings will forever suffer torment. But programmed by what?

It wasn't my mainline Presbyterian upbringing. I recall nothing of hell in Sunday school or my first decade of pew-sitting. Nor do I remember my parents ever broaching the subject. I've concluded that I must have absorbed my prejudice from the larger Zeitgeist. What then accounts for the spirit of the age?

....

If you want to explain the chilling of hell, there's a lot to consider. You can wonder about the Protestant denial of purgatory, which made it less likely that your nominally Christian friends and relatives would wind up in the right place, and who'd want that? Or you can contemplate the post-Reformation impact, on certain theological circles, of renewed acquaintance with Origen, whose works became widely available in the West in the 1600s. Or you can track the growing latitude, beginning in the seventeenth century, regarding belief in the devil, and wonder about the effect of demythologizing Satan, who was so closely, in the popular mind, associated with hell.[31] Or you can invoke Norbert Elias's sociological theory of the civilizing process, according to which, in recent centuries, the sight of human suffering has progressively become more repugnant to more people, a violation of heightened sensitivities (which explains why criminal punishment has moved behind walls).[32] Or you can entertain the thesis of the historical criminologist Pieter Spierenburg, who argues that, in the eighteenth and nineteenth centuries, people began to identify more with those outside their social class, so that it became more common to think, when musing on evildoers, There but for the grace of God go I.[33] Or you can ponder the spread of the conviction that we're products of our genes and our environment, and how this has assailed the concept of original sin and diminished our sense of personal responsibility, so that everlasting chastisement seems profoundly unfair. Or you can consider how increasing censure of the corporal punishment of children, whether at home or at school, has problematized the image of God as a punishing father.[34] Parents who put their kids on time-out instead of spanking them are less likely, I've read, to profess belief in hell than are those who don't spare the rod.

....

Here, however, I'd like to reflect on some other factors in the undirected historical process that humbled hell. The first has to do with the growth of modern relativism, which stems from modern pluralism. There's a clear historical progression here. First came the Age of Discovery, when European Christians encountered foreign civilizations across the globe. Then the Industrial Age arrived, when workers moved from countryside to city, pushing different sorts of people into the same place. And then, for the last two hundred years, there's been the age of modern travel—steam boats then trains then cars then airplanes—which has brought unprecedented mobility. More and more of us have been going to more and more places and so meeting more and more people.

Now in theory, running into various sorts of human beings scarcely ensures religious relativism. Yet what in fact happens to many of us when we come to know people who don't confess Jesus as Lord? Don't we discover that they can love their children, prize education, enjoy food, delight in music, laugh at jokes, want to be good, find life a struggle, and grieve when friends die? In other words, don't we find that, in important ways, they're just like us? This can't be good for the old doctrine of hell. For it's not at all relativistic. It's rather us vs. them. The premise is that outside the church, there's no salvation. That is, outside the church, there's only hell. In the words of the Council of Florence (1442): the church "firmly believes, confesses, and proclaims that neither the heathens nor the Jews nor the heretics and schismatics will have a share in eternal life, but will enter the eternal fire that has been prepared for the devil and his angels, if they do not join the church before their death." If, however, you're at all kindly inclined to your non-Christian friends and acquaintances—who may both outnumber and often behave better than your Christian friends and acquaintances—it can be very difficult to map hell's uncompromising antithesis onto your daily life. For many of us, the doctrine's bifurcation of the human race doesn't illuminate our experience but rather collides with it.

When my children were young, we attended a Presbyterian church in Wichita, Kansas. That church had, shortly before we joined, called a babysitting service to request a couple of sitters for Sunday morning. When they showed up, they happened to be Hindus, a mother and her daughter. So every Sunday morning, my wife and I, before going to worship, entrusted our little ones to the care of two non-Christian women with bright red dots on their foreheads.

Now what if I had said or implied to my kids that these two kind, attentive individuals were bound for divinely sanctioned agony? Having been taught that God is love, they would, I'm sure, have been more than nonplussed.

It's much the same for many of us outside the nursery. Even if we might work up some enthusiasm for the post-mortem torments of Pol Pot, we feel quite differently about the Jewish family down the street or the Muslims next door; and our feelings in this matter are unlikely to be much cauterized by theological arguments on behalf of the old hell.

················

If my youthful antipathy for hell was due partly to my pluralistic and so relativistically inclined culture, I'm also sure that my conscience was the product of modern ideas about punishment.

Why do we punish criminals? For at least three reasons. The first is to protect society: execution or imprisonment prevents future crimes by discouraging imitators. Second, we hope that punishment is remedial, that fines inhibit further dishonesty, that penitentiaries lead to penitence. Third, we punish because retributive justice demands it, an eye for an eye and a tooth for a tooth.

What does all this have to do with hell? The old hell with its torments isn't needed to protect us. God could stuff all the damned into a gigantic air-conditioned sports arena and let them watch the Jumbotron for eternity. As long as the doors are locked, they wouldn't trouble the rest of the universe.

The traditional hell also isn't remedial. It's not a justice that restores broken relationships. It's instead a Christian variation of the myth of Sisyphus: The sentence never ends. It's eternal life without parole.

By default, then, the chief goal of punishment in hell must be retribution. W. G. T. Shedd spoke the truth: hell "is righteous retribution, pure and simple, unmodified by considerations either of utility to the criminal, or of safety to the universe."[35] Hell's raison d'être is that sin must, on principle, be punished. The old debates as to how an eternal sentence can be commensurate with the crimes of a finite being confirm the point. The standard rationalization was this: To sin against God is to sin against an infinite dignity and so requires infinite retribution, which in turn demands a punishment of infinite duration.

Now here's the catch. Punishment has a social history, and we live in a culture that, for about three centuries, has laid more and more emphasis upon reforming perpetrators. Thomas Hobbes anticipated many moderns when he urged that punishment is just only when it cures or deters, and the French Legislative Assembly, in 1791, decreed that "penalties should be proportioned to the crimes for which they are inflicted" and "are intended not merely to punish, but to reform the culprit."

The principle of retributive justice, to be sure, hasn't gone away. It necessarily informs judicial decisions, and those who've lost a loved one in a senseless crime regularly give it voice on the news. Nonetheless, most of us now believe that, even if punishment ought to fit the crime, we should care for the welfare of criminals and, whenever possible, hope for and work for their reform. Why else do so many of today's penitentiaries, in stark contrast to yesterday's prisons, allow convicts to study in libraries? Don't we hope that crime is a bit like a disease that can be treated? The traditional hell, however, wasn't a "reformatory" or a "house of correction." It barred effective repentance.

....

There's also the closely related issue of torture in post-industrial Europe. State after state—Sweden, Denmark, Poland, France, Prussia, and Austria, among others—abolished torture in the last part of the eighteenth century; and at that time the United States added to its constitution the eighth amendment, which prohibits "cruel and unusual punishment." By 1851, torture was outlawed everywhere in Europe.

Older historians typically explained the judicial sea change in terms of an optimistic, progressive humanism: people were becoming less barbaric. More recent historians, less sanguine about human progress, often appeal to other things. There was the spread of prisons, which housed many lawbreakers who formerly would've been maimed. There was the protest against the zealotic prosecution of supposed witches, who were

often tortured to get bogus confessions. There was the advent of new judicial standards and evidentiary procedures, which made obtaining criminal confessions, for which torture had often been the chief means, less
important.

Whatever the precise causes, jurisprudence has changed, as have sentiments. Even if our world remains awash in violence, and even if torture
has scarcely been eradicated, as the work of Darius Rejali and others won't
let us forget,[36] it remains true that a larger percentage of people now than
in the past reject torture on principle. This is why modern democracies,
when they resort to the practice, generally favor "clean torture": perpetrators, fearful of public monitoring, don't want to leave visible traces of
what they've done. One recalls the indignation when evidence of torture
in Abu Ghraib surfaced. Torture was a scandal. Some of the culprits were
prosecuted; and even those who defended waterboarding did so by arguing
that it causes no permanent damage and that it shouldn't be categorized as
torture. How many publicly proclaimed that torture is fitting punishment
for a crime?

All this matters for us because the traditional hell flourished when op-
ponents of torture were harder to find. It's true that Augustine made some
critical comments about torture, and also true that, for a thousand years,
church rules prohibited ecclesiastics from personally brutalizing heretics.
The later Augustine, however, came around to the view that "there is a
righteous persecution, which the Church of Christ inflicts upon the im-
pious";[37] and torture—which included the rack and jabbing with red-hot
metal—was allowed in the later empire, in the law codes of Theodosius II
(438) and Justinian (534), both Christian emperors.

When torture did, beginning in the seventh century, go out of fashion,
Christian humanism wasn't the cause. Rather, the Germanic peoples, who
came to dominate the Latin West, preferred for the most part trial through
combat, or the ordeal. They found truth by waiting to see whether or not
God would rescue those thrown into rivers with millstones around their
necks, or help the accused to survive a walk over hot iron, or enable defendants to retrieve a stone from the bottom of a boiling kettle.

With the revival of Roman law in the twelfth century, torture made,
with little difficulty, a comeback among Christians. It wasn't long before
Aquinas conceded that torture can be "in accord with the requirements of
justice,"[38] and not long before Pope Innocent IV authorized torture for the
First Inquisition. In time, prisoners within Christendom were run through
with thumbscrews, and lawbreakers were hung in cages outside town halls

and cathedrals. In the sixteenth century, a one-time Inquisitor General, Gian Pietro Carafa, even managed to become pope (Paul IV). Sadly, we have to wait until 1624 and the Dutch Arminian Joannes Graevius before we get a full-length, thoroughgoing theological rejection of torture in the post-Reformation period.[39]

Legalized torture had its eschatological corollary. If you assumed that everyday courts could justly inflict physical torture, then it wasn't so hard to imagine that the divine court could do the same. Indeed, the eschatological future was prophesied in a figure when, in the castle above, the privileged ate and drank while the brutalized, underfoot in the dungeon below, were suspended by chains and stretched out on the rack.

It's conspicuous that, in the exhibition known as "Inquisition," the collection of torture instruments that toured Europe between 1983 and 1987, the old artistic depictions of punishment consistently remind one of the old artistic renditions of hell.[40] The chains, spikes, axes, forks, wheels, whips, saws, racks, pincers, and skull-splitters of hell were migrants from the human sphere. The truth is obvious in one of Isaac Watts' atrocious hymns, which speaks of hell's "heavy chains," "tormenting racks," and "iron bands."[41] As above, so below. As in this world, so in the next.

The correlation held later also, but to opposite effect: when the West began to have second thoughts about torture, it began to have second thoughts about hell. If God is just, and if torture is unjust, then how can God practice it? Doesn't the old hell have to go? Growing opposition to torture roughly coincided with growing opposition to hell, and as instruments of torture began to retire from the European scene, they also began to disappear from theological accounts of the infernal environs. Lyman Abbott saw the truth long ago: "It was impossible for the community at the same time to abolish torture from punishment in this life and to believe that the Father retained it in the life to come."[42]

It's no coincidence, to revert to the personal level, that I recall being, as a youngster, repulsed not only by hell but also by grisly sixteenth-century watercolors of Spanish soldiers clubbing, mutilating, hanging, and burning Native Americans. My response to the one was exactly my response to the other.

....

The decline of hell correlates not only with the decline of torture but also with the demise of burning as a capital punishment. In Christian tradition, the dominant image of hell is of sinners writhing in flames. This must have been less upsetting when heretics were still burned at the stake. Those who incinerated the Cathars and Jan Hus, Joan of Arc and Michael Servetus, and Thomas Cranmer and Giordano Bruno had the law on their side, and they presumably thought they were acting rightly. That's why they could do what they did in public. It was the same much earlier, with the emperor Justinian, in whose presence certain Manicheans were roasted alive.

Execution by fire belonged to Roman legal tradition. The Law of the Twelve Tables prescribed immolation by fire for those who, with malice aforethought, burned a building; and the Theodosian Code imposed "avenging flames in the sight of all the people" for certain sexual offenses.[43] Some early Christian martyrs, such as Polycarp, were burned at the stake.

That setting fire to criminals could be fair punishment also accorded with Scripture. The Torah decrees burning for certain sexual offenses (Lev. 20:14; 21:9), and Elijah called down fire from heaven to devour over a hundred of king Ahaziah's soldiers (2 Kings 1). God sent fire to consume Nadab and Abihu, two of Aaron's sons (Lev. 10). The hapless citizens of Sodom and Gomorrah met a like fate (Gen. 19). Unsurprisingly, the rabbis delineated the procedures for burning certain criminals, and their instructions weren't, it seems, purely hypothetical.[44]

All this, however, seems barbaric to most of us today. No Western government incinerates lawbreakers, even where capital punishment remains. The practice, along with breaking on the wheel, began to be outlawed in the eighteenth century, when the West decided it was too horrible, even for the worst offenders. Governments eventually resolved that capital punishment should be less painful. The preferred methods of execution became sword, axe, guillotine, and rope.

Dominant public opinion has, since then, been like the Jesus of Luke 9. When James and John want, in imitation of Elijah, to command fire from heaven to cremate unfriendly Samaritan villagers, Jesus rebukes them, as if to say, The prophet's ways aren't our ways; we don't do that anymore (Luke 9:51-56).

For most of us today, burning anyone for any reason is immoral. Our society, when it wants to kill criminals, uses lethal injection. We don't even want books burned. So if hell means incineration, as it does in so much of our theological tradition and in so much of our art, we must find it offensive.

....

But what then, in the light of all this, and to turn to the hermeneutical issue, should we make of the biblical texts about hell?

I can't be objective here. The cultural history that I've introduced has made me who I am. I oppose torture, believe that punishment should, whenever possible, be remedial, and recognize myself in my non-Christian friends. So I can't believe in the old hell, which projects onto God the brutal and callous jurisprudence of the past. I want others to disbelieve, too.

A desire to ameliorate hell, however, isn't an argument. So do we have any decent theological reasons for dismantling the eschatological torture chamber?

....

Some have assayed the task by attempting to isolate Jesus himself from hell. Even if the New Testament has him speak of Gehenna, maybe he didn't. The Jesus Seminar voted to excise from its red-letter edition of *The Five Gospels* (1993) every motif associated with eschatological judgment.[45] They had precursors. In *The Lord of Thought*, published in 1922, Lily Dougall and Cyril W. Emmet contended that, although Jesus abandoned traditional conceptions of divine judgment, early Christians added retribution to his sayings.[46] A few years later, Percy Dearmer, in *The Legend of Hell* (1929), rehearsed the same argument: the passages depicting a punishing God are all secondary.[47]

I'm not sure how far back this claim goes, but I've found it already in the great Romantic poet, Percy Bysshe Shelley. He insisted that, on the topic of hell, we must choose between the God of the historical Jesus and the God of the Gospel writers. Although a self-declared atheist, Shelley wasn't without religious sentiments, and he was much attracted to the figure in the Gospels. At the same time, hell was for him "absurd and execrable," so he urged, long before source criticism or redaction criticism, that the Evangelists attribute to Jesus sentiments he didn't hold.[48]

As I see it, there are at least two problems with Shelley and the Jesus Seminar. The first is that, even if we could detach Jesus from hell, that wouldn't get the doctrine off the pages of the New Testament. It'd still be there for all to read. The second difficulty is that, as a historian, I'm not convinced. It's pretty obvious that Matthew authored some of the relevant verses. Yet eschatological judgment also shows up in Mark, Luke, and John. Transcendent judgment appears, furthermore, in Synoptic parables, prophecies, exhortations, and warnings. So this is a motif that runs across the sources and occurs in various sorts of materials. That it's wholly secondary isn't plausible.[49]

....

Maybe more promising is the claim that, whatever its precise nature, hell can't be eternal, because the relevant Greek expression, *eis ton aiōna,* while habitually translated as "forever," doesn't mean that. Rather, the phrase and its Semitic equivalents, such as the Hebrew, *'ad-'olam*, refer, as often as not, to an indefinite or extended period of time. Consider these texts:

> Exodus 21:6: "and his master shall pierce his ear with an awl; and he shall serve him forever" (*le'olam; eis ton aiōna*).

> Isaiah 32:14–15: "the palace will be forsaken, the populous city deserted; the hill and the watchtower will become dens forever [*'ad-'olam; heōs tou aiōnos*], the joy of wild asses, a pasture for flocks; until a spirit from on high is poured out on us. . . ."

> 1 Macc. 14:41: "And the Jews and their priests decided that Simon should be their leader and high priest forever [*eis ton aiōna*], until a trustworthy prophet should arise."

> *Jubilees* 5:10: "They were bound in the earth forever, until the day of great judgment."

> 2 *Baruch* 40:3: "And his [Messiah's] dominion will last forever, until the world of corruption has ended, and until the times which have been mentioned before have been fulfilled."

The most recent, full-length treatment of the Greek word *aiōnios* has come to this conclusion: "apart from the Platonic philosophical vocabulary, which is specific to few authors, *aiōnios* does *not* mean 'eternal'; it acquires this meaning only when it refers to God. . . . In particular, when it is associated with life or punishment, in the Bible and in Christian authors who keep themselves close to the Biblical usage, it denotes their belonging to the world to come."[50] Maybe, then, we should read less into the biblical sentences about hell than has been our theological wont.

Augustine and Basil the Great thought otherwise. While conceding that *eis ton aiōna* and related expressions don't, in and of themselves, mean "forever," they yet urged that, in the threats about hell, they must mean this. They argued from symmetry. The Greek has to mean "forever" in the parallel promises about "life"; otherwise, the righteous have no guarantee that they won't someday perish.

Although the argument has had a long run, it's problematic. For one thing, the church fathers were inconsistent, because they disallowed the force of symmetry when it didn't suit their purposes. When interpreting Romans 5:18—"just as one man's trespass led to condemnation for all, so one man's act of righteousness leads to justification and life for all"—they denied that "all" in the second half of the sentence means what it does in the first half. So too for Romans 11:32: "God has imprisoned all in disobedience so that he may be merciful to all."

More importantly, the implicit premise, that the texts about hell contain precise, empirical data about the world to come, is problematic. Language can be formal or informal. If you complain, "That speaker's gone on forever," you're not aiming at mathematical exactitude. If you remark, "She has an unquenchable thirst," there's no medical mystery involved. And when Paul says, in the New Revised Standard Version of 2 Corinthians 11:23, that he's suffered "countless" floggings, it would be absurd to retort that the number must in fact have been finite. It can't really be different with "eternal" hell and "unquenchable" fire. Those expressions appear in sentences formulated by a Jewish prophet seeking to exhort, not a scholastic logician concerned with the precise meaning of terms.

Debating the connotations of *eis ton aiōna* is perhaps a bit like fretting over the length of the days in Genesis 1. Once you've decided not to read Genesis literally but instead to see it as something other than sober history, the problem dissipates. In like fashion, the biblical admonitions about hell aren't history written ahead of time, nor do they outline the penalties of a legal code. Rather, they concern what eye has neither seen nor ear heard and so are necessarily parabolic. Attempts to interpret them otherwise post-date the first century. In the New Testament, the hortatory hasn't yet become the descriptive, nor has the hyperbolic morphed into the literal. Soon enough, however, the prosaic did replace the rhetorical, and the sentences about hell suffered the same fate as Jesus' warning that it's easier for a camel to go through the eye of a needle than for a rich person to enter the kingdom. Some Greek manuscripts turned "camel" into the more plausible "rope," and some theologians urged that Jesus must have been talking about a small gate in a city wall known as the "needle's eye," through which a camel could indeed pass, although it'd be tight. Philological precision usurped imaginative exhortation.

....

The New Testament's warnings about hell don't cohere as prosaic propositions. Hell, it says, is a place of fire, yet it's dark. It brings destruction, yet it lasts—at least in the Augustinian tradition—forever. Fire, however, sheds light, and if something's destroyed, it's gone. Furthermore, biologists have yet to discover an immortal worm that makes its home in fire, or even the salamander that, according to Augustine's misinformed apologetics, bathes in flames.

The literal-minded harmonizers have, to be sure, urged that hell's fire gives off a dim light (so Aquinas), or that there's a lot of smoke there (so Thomas Newton). But one might as well worry how, if Jesus gave his life as a ransom for many, only a few will enter the narrow gate to life, or how either circumstance lines up with five bridesmaids being wise and five being foolish, because doesn't this intimate that the ratio of saved to unsaved will be fifty-fifty?

As for the standard line that hell's destruction doesn't destroy because the damned are like the burning bush on Sinai, which was aflame yet not consumed, surely it makes more sense, if you want to be a proof-texting harmonizer, to hold, as did a few rabbis, that there are two regrettable fates: everlasting hell for the most wicked, destruction by fire for the religiously nonchalant. Or you can follow the Seventh-Day Adventists, who contend that the fire, which never goes out, burns up the damned, who cease to be. Early Christians could certainly have thought this. In some old Egyptian texts, the guilty are first punished and then destroyed. This also appears as an option in the Talmud.

....

It's occurred to me, however, that there's yet another solution. One could invoke relativity theory to prove that the wicked will both suffer forever and be annihilated. Here's my end-time prophecy:

At the end of days, Captain Almighty God will build a celestial ark, put the righteous in it, squish the wicked and some tormenting demons into the center of the earth, take off at near light speed, circumnavigate the universe in five minutes, surpass light speed for a few seconds—Captain Almighty can, as the name indicates, do anything—then decelerate and return to earth. According to relativity theory, five minutes and a few seconds of time on the ark are an eternity on earth, so when the ark docks, the wicked have spent forever in hell. What then? Having fulfilled the prophecies about eternal torment and still needing to fulfill those about destruction, Captain Almighty will retrieve a mysterious box from the ark's hold, carefully open the lid, remove from within the holy hand grenade prepared from the foundation of the world, utter a few solemn words, pull the sacred pin, and toss the thing out the window. The wicked and the sin-wracked universe will disappear. Then Captain Almighty will make all things new. (Alternatively, the good Captain might rather want, upon returning to earth, to save the wicked and so fulfill those Pauline texts that speak of all being saved, thus resolving a different conundrum.)

This is, of course, juvenile nonsense. Yet it's unclear how those who profess to "take the Bible literally" could recognize it as such.

It's equally unclear how so many can be literal about one thing, figurative about another. Consider John Wesley's interpretation of Mark 9:43–48, the passage where Jesus exhorts people to cut off a sinning hand, sinning foot, and sinning eye, lest they go to "the unquenchable fire," where the "worm does not die." Wesley doesn't counsel amputation—hand, foot, and eye represent, for him, persons or things that are "dear"—and he, like Augustine, identifies the worm with a guilty conscience. Here, then, we have metaphors. Yet Wesley insists that the fire must be material—an "immaterial fire" would be "absolute nonsense"—and that, since the worm never dies and the fire is unquenchable, punishment will have no end.[51] Mark, however, offers no hint that readers should take some words literally, some figuratively, and wouldn't it make more hermeneutical sense to take everything one way or the other? If cutting off a hand is a figure of speech, and if the worm is metaphorical, what sense does it make to insist on the literal denotation of "unquenchable fire"?

We're free, I believe, to follow Emil Brunner and the like-minded others who've taught that it's wrong-headed to divine, in eschatological admonitions, concrete descriptions of the future. The New Testament's sentences about hell are rather words of alarm and challenge, calls to repentance. On this view, everything coheres just fine. For the point of threatening destruction is the same as the point of threatening long-lived suffering: you don't want either, so watch out. Both are, if I may so put it, the worst possible outcome. Similarly, the point of threatening fire is the same as the point of threatening darkness: you want to avoid both, so take heed. It's like the Talmudic passage which declares that, if you keep one commandment, you will have life in the world to come, and if you fail to keep one commandment, you won't have life in the world to come. Logically, this makes no sense. Construed as exhortation, there's no problem: keep the commandments.

. . . .

So where does all this leave us? Even if we repudiate the sadistic torture chamber and refuse to transmute hyperbolic exhortations into prosaic predictions, we don't thereby do away with hell. The biblical nightmare remains to be deciphered. Like all dreams, it presents itself for interpretation.

Here I can only outline a few points. The first is that hell, despite its defects and abuses, has helpfully served to prevent death from canceling human responsibility. No one knows what has become of either Heinrich Himmler or Mother Teresa of Calcutta. If, however, there's even a tincture of moral rhyme or reason in the universe, not all of us can be equally well off the instant we depart, for we aren't uniformly guilty. It was almost inevitable that the Jewish Sheol divided into heaven and hell, and that the Greek Hades split into Tartarus and the Elysian Fields.

If the world to come were instead morally neutral, if it were instantly to treat all the same, if it were to discern no difference between the Hutu militias and the Tutsis they slaughtered, then good and evil would have the same end, and our behavior would seem to be of no enduring consequence. Hell blocks that possibility. So while its gruesome forms outrage our moral sensibilities, it's paradoxically in accord with those sensibilities. It's a doctrine of the conscience, a postulate that holds us responsible for our deeds and their lasting significance. God, it implies, isn't a sentimental fool, an amicable chap who looks the other way no matter what. Hell presupposes that what we do matters, that the conflict between good and evil is real, that complacency is ruinous. One understands why Nicholas Berdyaev believed that the "modern rejection of hell makes life too easy, superficial and irresponsible."[52]

....

But what about the now popular conceptualization of hell as radical freedom, as God letting us choose what we want, including a godless existence? It's problematic, although it makes for effective apologetics. For if we hate hell, then learn that it's simply the unavoidable consequence of individual liberty and self-actualization—things we prize so highly—then perhaps hell computes after all. We can think of our freedom to reject God as on a par with all those other freedoms that we can't do without—academic freedom and economic freedom, freedom of speech and freedom of association, and so on.

Yet when human freedom is front and center, God moves to the wings. In the modern myth, our names are on the marquee, and our destiny is up to us. What we make of ourselves here determines what we are to become there.

Should we, however, desire starring roles and such Pelagian freedom? Although not an old-fashioned Calvinist, I think it's obvious that all of us are broken creatures, that we're selfish and self-deluded, and that we constantly abuse our freedom, which is so often illusory. Because of this, I find little use for a deity who lets me decide my fate. I don't want to be my own God. Nor do I want the Supreme Being to respect my alleged autonomy no matter what, just as I don't want the police to respect the autonomy of the despondent guy threatening to jump off the top of the high-rise. I rather desire, for myself and for everyone else, rescue. Our decisions need to be undone, not confirmed. We need to be saved despite ourselves. Even if we're allowed, in our freedom, to kindle the fires of hell and to forge its chains, isn't it God's part to break our chains and put out the fire?

················

If the libertarian hell doesn't give God enough to do, it's also, perhaps, simplistic in its binary logic. It posits that people move either toward God and so toward heaven or away from God and so toward hell. But, as the Scarecrow says to Dorothy, "People do go both ways."

Human beings aren't unidirectional vectors but bundles of contradictions. Saints are sinners; sinners are saints. Everyone is Jekyll; everyone is Hyde. And everyone is in between. We advance toward God one moment and sound retreat the next, and most of the time we're stuck in the middle.

We're confused and divided in ourselves, or rather fragmented. Our wills, our desires, our faith are always veering off course. We don't just fail to do the good that we will; we just as often fail to do the bad that we will. Who travels the straight and narrow, whether up or down? The modern hell, however, posits that, in the world to come, we keep moving in the direction we're already headed. Our momentum, so to speak, carries us up to heaven or down to hell. Yet what if, like me, you keep moving in circles?

The problem is that while the modern hell of freedom is a vast improvement upon the old torture chamber, it remains, like its predecessor, too devoted to retributive justice. It presupposes an evenhanded measure: we reap what we sow. It's a Christian version of karma: what you do comes right back on you. But listen to Isaac of Nineveh:

> Do not call God just, for his justice is not manifest in the things concerning you. . . . How can you call God just when you come across the Scriptural passage on the wage given to the workers? "Friend, I do thee no wrong: I choose to give unto this last even as unto thee. Or is thine eye evil because I am good?" How can a person call God just when he comes across the passage on the prodigal son who wasted his wealth with riotous living, how for the compunction alone which he showed, the father ran and fell upon his neck and gave him authority over all his wealth? . . . Where, then, is God's justice?—for while we were sinners Christ died for us![53]

Isaac was confident that just "as a grain of sand cannot counterbalance a great quantity of gold, so in compassion God's use of justice cannot counterbalance His mercy. As a handful of sand thrown into the great sea, so are the sins of all flesh in comparison with the mind of God."[54]

Many Christians would of course dispute this. They imagine that God's left half-brain is love, and God's right half-brain is justice. In the words of John Gerstner, "God is love but he is more than love and other than love."[55]

Such a proposal deeply disturbs me, because I'm of the same mind as Berdyaev: "I can conceive of no more powerful and irrefutable argument in favor of atheism than the eternal torments of hell. If hell is eternal then I am an atheist."[56]

Isaac, however, would have considered Gerstner's sentiment blasphemous, and Isaac was, I'm happy to say, canonized. So I'm cheered when the saint teaches that God always "acts towards us in ways He knows will be advantageous to us, whether by way of things that cause suffering, or by way of things that cause relief." "Among all his action there is none which is not entirely a matter of mercy, love and compassion: this constitutes the beginning and end of his dealings with us." It was inconceivable to Isaac that "the compassionate Maker created rational beings in order to deliver them mercilessly to unending affliction for things of which He knew even before they were fashioned . . . and whom (nonetheless) He created." On the contrary, it must be that God "is going to manifest some wonderful outcome, a matter of immense and ineffable compassion on the part of the glorious Creator, with respect to the ordering of this difficult matter of (Gehenna's) torment: out of it the wealth of His love and power and wisdom will become known all the more."[57]

Now I'm quite aware that God's freedom entails, as do countless other facts, epistemological modesty. Perhaps, then, it would be incautious to endorse, without reservation, Isaac and his fellow universalists—Origen, Gregory of Nyssa, Hans Denck, Jane Leade, J. A. Bengel, Thomas Erskine, George MacDonald, Sergius Bulgakov, Jacques Ellul, John Hick, Marilyn McCord Adams. I nonetheless ardently hope that they're right, and I don't understand anyone who feels differently. Even if, as the New Testament more than suggests, God allows some of us to carry our personal hells into the next life, even if there will be weeping and gnashing of teeth, why should that go on forever? Can't we hope that the Governor of all, the most merciful and philanthropic Lord, will, in the end, show clemency? According to Philo, God "tempers his judgment with the mercy which he shows in doing kindness even to the unworthy. And not only does this mercy follow his judgment but it also precedes it. For mercy with him is older than justice."[58] James is more succinct: mercy triumphs over judgment (2:13).

....

Over and over, the book of Amos prophesies punishment for Israel's sins. It's verse after verse of relentless threat, chapter after chapter of uncompromising judgment. And yet, following all the rebukes and calamitous forecasts, the book, in its canonical form, mercifully concludes with a promise of salvation: Israel's fortunes will be restored. Surely we may hope that human history will turn out to be Amos writ large.

CHAPTER 6

Heaven and Experience

....

Invention is never more lively than when it is stimulated by hope.

JAMES FENIMORE COOPER

At present the Christian mind is in danger of
anticipating too little rather than too much.

H. R. MACKINTOSH

The imagination can both enliven and destroy the plausibility of belief.

DAVID BROWN

....

S OME PASTORS DO their best to dodge the subject of heaven. Although
funerals find them comforting mourners with John 14—"in my Father's
house are many mansions"—Sunday mornings address other topics. These
reverends, unlike Calvin, don't believe that "commendation of the future
and eternal life is a theme which deserves to be sounded in our ears by day
and by night . . . and made the subject of ceaseless meditation."[1]

Reticence about the last things isn't new. A century ago, H. R. Mackintosh observed that "modern feeling makes it more than . . . difficult to
teach or preach with effect about what divines have been accustomed to
call topics of eschatology. . . . An evidence of difficulty is the marked infre-
quency with which the thing is done. Sermons on the joys of heaven . . . are
now tolerably rare."[2]

Today, as when Mackintosh wrote, some ministers are discreetly mum
about heaven because they disbelieve that there is one, or because they're
undecided. Their attention to other matters makes sense. Others, however,
say little despite being optimistic about the world to come. I know this from
conversations with some of them. While they confidently expect God to

escort their congregants to a better world, they're shy of saying so in their weekly sermons.

The triumph of the Marxist critique—hope for heavenly bliss diverts attention from earthly woe—is one cause of their sermonic silence. Another culprit is popular culture. One can hardly converse about "heaven" without conjuring up silly cartoons with Peter at the pearly gates, or calling to mind insipid pictures of winged humans playing harps on puffy clouds, and who wants that? While most understand that such images aren't to be taken seriously, that they're something like juvenile poetry, it's difficult not to call them to mind, and it's difficult to know what to put in their place.

It's the pastor's task, however, to do just that, to put something in their place, something that's truly interesting, that's not "minimalist, meagre, and dry."[3] To be boring is to be irrelevant.

....

The subject of post-mortem felicity didn't bore Socrates. When addressing his Athenian judges, who'd condemned him to death, he said two prospects faced him. Either death is unconsciousness, like a night of dreamless sleep—a rather pleasant prospect, Socrates imagined—or it's a change of habitation, a move to the realm of the dead, where one can meet Hesiod and Homer and converse with Ajax and Odysseus. Socrates declared that he would die many times over if it enabled him to carry on with such people.

This has always sounded wonderful to me, and my imagination has substituted its own names. What wouldn't I give to sit at the feet of Origen, Isaac of Nineveh, and Pascal, or to quiz Plato, William James, and Aldous Huxley? My only point here, however, is that Socrates was able to muster authentic enthusiasm for the other side, and isn't it pitiable that many churchgoers aren't able to match him on that score? Even Mark Twain, who so often lampooned worn-out myths about heaven, thought better of the place when he dreamed that it might enable him to "hear Shakespeare and Milton and Bunyan read from their noble works."[4]

....

Of course there's the objection that it's not just the old pictures that are boring. Some have urged that, if you're philosophically astute, you'll conclude that heaven, by its very nature, entails unbroken monotony. The argument is this: Given an infinite amount of time, everything would repeat itself again and again, with the inevitable result that a world without end would be tedium without end. Eternity would cancel Heraclitus: You'd forever be stepping into the same river twice. Eternal bliss in heaven, on this estimate, can't be achieved, for infinite time means eternal recurrence, and eternal recurrence would be unbearable. Not much to look forward to there. Augustine, in one of his sermons (# 362), already fretted about this, as did Aquinas after him.[5] In more recent times, much discussion has attended philosopher Bernard Williams' version of the claim that the indefinite prolongation of life would eventually become a dreary burden.[6] Maybe the problem with heaven isn't that it's too good to be true but that it's too much of a good thing.

I'm dubious that there's an authentic enigma here. Although some non-terminating sequences involve repetition—the inverse of 11 is .09090909 and so on—other infinities don't: the irrational number pi has no reiterating pattern. Beyond the mathematical point, maybe the conundrum won't apply to heavenly subjects oriented to something other than self-fulfillment. Or maybe it won't hold for transformed individuals who, as some theologians have supposed, will transcend time. Or maybe, as Gregory of Nyssa believed, eternal life will mean always moving from one new beginning to the next, so that one will never arrive at any limit of perfection: fresh possibilities will always come into view. If God is truly an infinite mystery, how could such a mystery ever be exhausted?

Theologians have traditionally taught that God is both eternal and blissful. Maybe what the Eastern Orthodox speak of as our "deification" (*theosis*) will allow the same to be true for us.

....

However one resolves the riddle of boredom, Christians have entertained a variety of ideas about heaven. For some, heaven has meant first of all being with Jesus. As the old hymn has it: "My Savior comes and walks with me,/ And sweet communion here have we;/He gently leads me by His hand,/ for this is heaven's borderland."

For others, the chief hope has been the beatific vision, understood as the distinct, supernaturally bestowed, unmediated knowledge of God. In the words of Pope Benedict XII: in heaven, all the saints "have seen and do see the divine essence by intuitive vision and even face to face, in such a way that nothing created intervenes as an object of vision, but the divine essence plainly reveals itself to their immediate gaze, clearly and openly."[7]

Christians have also pictured heaven as principally a place of worship and participation in the angelic liturgy. When the prophet Isaiah had his vision of heaven, he beheld the seraphim chanting, "Holy, holy, holy is the LORD of hosts; the whole earth is full of his glory" (Isa. 6:1-3); and when the visionary who penned Revelation entered heaven, he saw elders worshiping the One who lives forever and ever and heard them singing: "You are worthy, our Lord and God, to receive glory and honor and power, for you created all things, and by your will they existed and were created" (Rev. 4:1-11).

Then there's the popular—although less popular now than it used to be—idea of heaven as an unending Sabbath, when saints from their labors rest. This hope, known already to Second Temple Jewish literature, appears in Hebrews 4:8-11: "For if Joshua had given them rest, God would not speak later of another day. So then, there remains a sabbath rest for the people of God; for whoever enters God's rest also ceases from his labors as God did from his. Let us therefore strive to enter that rest, that no one fall by the same sort of disobedience." Abelard spoke of "endless Sabbaths,"[8] and in the traditional Catholic Requiem Mass, the priest prays: "Grant them eternal rest, O Lord." Richard Baxter's *The Saints' Everlasting Rest* (1650) was once a bestseller.

....

Despite the popularity of these several expectations, I shall, in what follows, set them aside. I choose instead, for reasons that will appear later, to review three other conceptions of the afterlife—heaven as angelic existence, heaven as reunion with family and friends, and heaven as an incomparably beautiful natural landscape. Before exploring these models, however, a few remarks on the word "heaven" are in order.

The term refers, most commonly in modern English, to the blissful place or blessed state the redeemed enter upon death. This accords with several New Testament texts, or at least with common, conventional readings of them:

> Matthew 6:20-21: "Store up for yourselves treasures in heaven, where neither moth nor rust consumes and where thieves do not break in and steal. For where your treasure is, there your heart will be also."

> 2 Corinthians 5:1-2: "For we know that if the earthly tent we live in is destroyed, we have a building from God, a house not made with hands, eternal in the heavens. For in this tent we groan, longing to be clothed with our heavenly dwelling."

> Hebrews 12:22-23: "You have come to Mount Zion and to the city of the living God, the heavenly Jerusalem, and to innumerable angels in

festal gathering, and to the assembly of the firstborn who are enrolled in heaven, and to God the judge of all, and to the spirits of the righteous made perfect."

1 Peter 1:3–4: "By his great mercy he has given us a new birth . . . into an inheritance that is imperishable, undefiled, and unfading, kept in heaven for you."

Revelation 7:9: "There was [in heaven] a great multitude that no one could count, from every nation, from all tribes and peoples and languages, standing before the throne and before the Lamb, robed in white, with palm branches in their hands."

In addition to such verses, the New Testaments affirms (1) that Jesus was, after his resurrection, taken up into heaven[9] and (2) that his followers will, at death, be "with" him.[10] Christians have naturally inferred (3) that deceased saints are "in heaven," where Jesus is. Didn't he say to Peter, "Where I am going . . . you will follow afterward" (John 13:36)? Doesn't 2 Timothy have Paul declare that the Lord has rescued him from every evil and saved him for the "heavenly kingdom" (4:18)?

Some theologians have refused the inference. Wycliffe and Milton, for instance, rejected the idea of an intermediate state in heaven. They instead endorsed the doctrine of soul sleep. This allowed them to put all the emphasis upon resurrection at the end of time. For multiple reasons, some of them introduced in Chapter 2, I'm not in this camp. Rather, regarding this particular, I side with Calvin: some sort of intermediate state commends itself.[11] Given this, and given the lack of a better word, "heaven" will include, in what follows, whatever felicitous reality one might hope to enter at the point of death.

....

It's worth noting that N. T. Wright has recently adopted a different strategy. Although he doesn't endorse soul sleep, and although he doesn't totally dismiss "going to heaven" as a tag for what happens at death, he prefers not to say much about the place. This is because, in popular parlance, "heaven" is thought of as bodiless and otherworldly, whereas Christian hope, according to Wright, envisions "a renewed body living on a renewed earth." For him, heaven is only a "temporary, intermediate state," and since God's eschatological kingdom will be a permanent kingdom on the earth, "going to heaven" isn't what Christian faith is all about.[12] In other words, if resurrection is what matters most, and if heaven isn't resurrection, then heaven doesn't matter so much.

One sympathizes to some extent with Wright's reticence vis-à-vis "heaven." He's worried about the unwelcome connotations of the word, of which it has been said that "scarcely any other . . . has been so defiled, so abused, so torn to shreds."[13] Wright is further anxious about an otherworldly escapism that might deflate social responsibility. Yet all but the most technical theological terms come with annoying popular associations. In this regard, "heaven" is no different than "God" or "Jesus Christ." It's inevitably part of the theological task to redefine and reclaim ill-used words and phrases. Furthermore, despite the dubious baggage that it undeniably carries, "heaven" remains a word that's still prominent both in English translations of the Bible as well as in liturgies, so it's prudent to do something with it.

There's a second issue here. Wright, like Jürgen Moltmann, insists that the eternal kingdom of God will be a this-worldly kingdom: the meek will inherit the earth. I don't share their geocentric faith. I freely concede that most of the biblical writers with eschatological thoughts supposed that the earth will welcome God's glorious kingdom. Given, however, their utter ignorance of the true size and scope of the universe, why should their supposition be our dogma? Are we any more committed to the Bible's assumption that the kingdom of God will be on the earth than we're committed to its assumption that heaven is over our heads?

I'm not a premillennialist, a postmillennialist, or an amillennialist. My inclination is to suppose that the future is open, and that while divine victory within the arena of eternity is assured, God's triumph within this world isn't. Someday, perhaps, the earth will enjoy, by God's grace, a golden age of universal peace and good will. Alternatively, it's possible that our nuclear or biological weapons will annihilate us all. Or perhaps the earth will disappear when the sun enters its red giant phase and roasts us with ionized plasma. Or maybe a low-energy state bubble from an anomalous quantum fluctuation will spread, engulf, and annihilate the cosmos. Again, perhaps the universe will dissipate in the Big Freeze or be squashed to nothing at the Big Crunch.

Genesis says that the world is good, not that it's the best; and, with the older Lutheran theologians, I see no reason to hold that it will last without end, or that it must be our home for eternity. How can we know that our destiny is always to inhabit our current spatial coordinates, that we'll forever be confined to a minute speck of the cosmos, a cosmos which may in turn be only a minute speck within an unfathomable multiverse? I find it curious that, while sci-fi novelists can envisage humanity traveling to the stars, some theologians are content to leave us earthbound. If the Creator isn't a one-planet deity, why should we be one-planet beings? And why would anyone be troubled if the earth and its environs, or even the entirety of the visible cosmos, turn out to be, in the long run, a cocoon that, after incubating some new reality, ceases to be? According to the Old Testament, although God laid the foundation of the earth, and while the heavens are the work of God's hands, "they will perish" and "wear out like a garment" (Ps. 102:25-27). According to the New Testament, "the heavens will pass away with a loud noise, and the elements will be dissolved with fire" (2 Pet. 3:10), and the sea will be no more (Rev. 21:1).

One last comment about the meaning of "heaven." If the word often refers to the reality between death and the universal finale, it can also signify the final state, when God will be all in all. Now it's sensible to suppose, for various reasons, that whatever happens to us immediately after death isn't the only thing that happens to us forever, so personal eschatology and cosmic eschatology need not be the same thing. Nonetheless, the three conceptions of heaven to be considered below, like those briefly introduced above, have been associated with the intermediate state as well as with the final state, so the following pages won't fret about drawing neat lines between the two.

For precedent I can, incidentally, appeal to the New Testament, which likewise blurs some eschatological distinctions. If it can speak of entering paradise at death (Luke 23:43), it can also speak of entering paradise at the end (Rev. 2:7); and if it can identify death as the moment when the saints go to be "with" Christ (Phil. 1:21-24), it can say the same of the second coming (1 Thess. 4:17); and if it can envision entering into judgment at death (2 Cor. 5:10), it can also associate judgment with the last day (Matt. 12:41). The Bible frames no coherent picture of things to come.

With all this as preface, we may now consider three different ideas of heaven.

. . . .

Everybody over a certain age, as well as many younger people, have seen *It's a Wonderful Life*, the 1946 movie starring Jimmy Stewart and Donna Reed. It's been shown on American TV every Christmas season for decades. One of its main characters is Clarence Odbody, angel second-class. He's a human being who's been dead for two hundred years and has recently become the guardian angel of Stewart's character, George Bailey.

His assignment is to rescue Bailey from despair and suicide. When he succeeds, Clarence finally earns his wings.

That human beings, at death, become angels or guardian angels has been, for decades, a staple of popular literature and the entertainment industry. In Hans Christian Andersen's short story "The Angel," a little boy who's just died learns that the angel escorting him to heaven was once a poor, sick lad who walked with crutches. Charles Tazewell's *The Littlest Angel*, a perennial best-selling children's book since it first appeared in 1946, tells the story of heaven's youngest angel, who is so new to the place that he doesn't yet know how to behave. Then there's "Highway to Heaven," a well-known TV show from the 1980s featuring Michael Landon as an angel named Jonathan Smith. Every week, Smith sought to help human beings in trouble. He too, like Clarence Odbody, wanted to earn his wings.

One may object that all this is pure entertainment and doesn't merit thoughtful attention. But the Mormons and Emanuel Swedenborg's followers teach the angelization of human nature, and some New Age books, such as Andrea Garrison's *In the Presence of Angels* (2013), also sponsor the idea. It even shows up occasionally in serious theology, as in the work of Christian philosopher Geddes MacGregor, for whom angels "represent a stage toward which at least some human beings might be moving, however slowly, in the course of a spiritual evolution."[14]

There's also the Internet, with its multiple sites dedicated to memorializing dead infants and toddlers. Some of these tribute pages bear names such as "Remembering Our Angels" and "Cherished Angels Forever." If you spend time with any of them—which isn't easy, because they're the records of broken hearts—you realize that some of the contributors gain comfort from imagining that their children really have become angels.

The sociologist Tony Walter has observed that, in contemporary Britain, departed loved ones are more often "angels" than "souls."[15] In accounting for this, he speculates about the diminishing cachet of the word "soul." He further observes that, while "souls" traditionally rest in peace and dwell in heaven, "angels" often come and go between there and here. Some of them, moreover, belong to the guardian species, so if your loved one has become one of these, he or she needn't be far away, and perhaps a reunion can be had shortly.

To Walter's observations one may add that angels, in popular entertainment, don't usually appear in formal religious contexts. The celestial beings on TV and in the movies are non-denominational, and they don't insist on a confessional response to their therapeutic ministrations. Indeed, much contemporary literature and film suggests, in the words of Robert Wuthnow, "that angels are rather ill-disposed toward institutional religion, that they transcend religious and theological distinctions, and that they simply appear to good-hearted people who need them."[16] This must make them attractive to the spiritual-but-not-religious crowd.

....

The angelic future of human beings isn't a modern invention.

Jesus, in Luke 20:35–36, says this: "Those who are accounted worthy to attain . . . to the resurrection from the dead neither marry nor are given in marriage, for they cannot die any more, because they are equal to angels and are sons of God, being sons of the resurrection." Exegetes dispute the precise implications of this odd declaration. Many hold that the resemblance between humans and angels extends only to the lack of reproduction: a world without death won't need sex, and a world without sex won't need marriage. This minimalistic reading is, however, far from obvious.

While it's possible that human beings won't marry and for this reason will be like angels, it's a tad more likely that the reasoning is the other way around: human beings will be like angels and therefore won't marry. Origen found here the notion that human bodies will become, like angelic bodies, ethereal and brilliant.[17] He may have been onto something. Angels were, in Jesus' day, known as "sons of God,"[18] so being "equal to angels" and being "sons of God" amount to the same thing: the sons of the resurrection will become, at the end, what the angels are in the present.

Several old Jewish texts teach that redeemed humanity will become angelic. A fragment from the Dead Sea Scrolls envisages saints becoming God's "just people, his army and servants, the angels of his glory."[19] Philo wrote that, when Abraham departed this life, he became "equal to the angels, for angels—those disembodied and blessed souls—are the host of God."[20] The late-first-century Jewish pseudepigraphon, *2 Baruch*, asserts that, after the resurrection, the righteous will be transformed into glory, that their faces will shine with light, and that they will be changed into "the splendor of angels." They will then live in the heights of heaven and be "like angels" (51:1–10). *The Martyrdom and Ascension of Isaiah*, another old pseudepigraphon, promises Isaiah that, when he dies, he will "be equal to the angels who are in the seventh heaven" (8:15). *The Shepherd of Hermas*, a collection of the visions and homilies of a second-century Christian in Rome, imagines that "bishops and hospitable people" already have "their place with the angels."[21] From a much later time, a Jewish midrash on Genesis declares that all the pious, upon death, become angels.[22]

It's possible that Acts assumes the angelization of the dead. When Peter, whom everyone thinks is in prison, knocks at the door of a house and a maid reports hearing his voice, some respond with, "It is his angel" (12:15). Although this could refer to Peter's guardian angel, it's equally possible that "angel" here means his departed spirit. For when Acts 23:8 reports, of the Sadducees, that they say "there is no resurrection, neither angel nor spirit," the likely meaning is either "there is no resurrection or disembodied existence as an angel or spirit" or "there is no resurrection either in the form of an angel or the form of a spirit." Furthermore, some early Christians, when hearing that Stephen's face became, right before his death, like that of an angel (Acts 6:15), might have supposed that he was turning into an angel. *The Martyrdom of Polycarp* (from the second century) claims that, in their hour of martyrdom, certain martyrs "were no longer human but already angels" (2:3).

....

Several factors encouraged identifying glorified or heavenly humans with angels. (1) In some biblical stories, such as that in which Abraham welcomes three strangers, the visiting angels are, at least initially, mistaken for human beings (Gen. 18). As Hebrews 13:2, with an eye on this passage, has it: "some have entertained angels without knowing it." The failure of recognition implies a close resemblance and so a kinship. The same implication is near to hand in Genesis 6, where the Sons of God—widely identified as fallen angels—go into the daughters of men. It's not surprising that, in some sources, angels are the "brothers" and "friends" of human beings,[23] or that people can speak their language (1 Cor. 13:1).

(2) If, like many ancient Jews, one identified angels with stars—in the Old Testament, the set phrase "the host of heaven" can denote both stars and angels—and if one also believed, as did so many in the Hellenistic world, in astral immortality, it followed that humans will be angels. Whether or not this explains Daniel 12:3 (the resurrected righteous will "shine like the splendor of the firmament"), the logic is clear in the extra-canonical *2 Baruch*: the resurrected "will be like the angels and be equal to the stars" (51:10).

(3) Angels were believed to live primarily in heaven. So if you believed that the souls of the righteous ascend to heaven, then the human destination was the angelic residence. This explains the vision in *1 Enoch* 39:4–5 ("There my eyes saw their dwellings with his righteous angels and their resting places with the holy ones") and the statement in Hebrews 12:22–23 (in the heavenly Jerusalem are "innumerable angels in festal gathering" along with "the spirits of the righteous made perfect").

(4) Not only was the Greek word we translate as "angel" (*angelos*) used of human beings, including John the Baptist (Mark 1:2) and Jesus' disciples (Luke 9:52), but some angels in Scripture are called "men." This is true of Abraham's three visitors (Gen. 18:16; 19:10), the angel who appears to Manoah and his wife (Judg. 13:6–11), the angel Gabriel in Daniel (9:21), the two angels at the empty tomb in Luke (24:4), and the angel who tells Cornelius to send for Peter in Joppa (Acts 10:30–33). It's equally relevant that two of the better-known titles for angels—"holy ones"[24] and "sons of God"[25]—were also used of people.[26]

....

After the New Testament period, angelic transmogrification became important especially for many Christian ascetics. They sought to anticipate eschatological existence by living the present tense of Luke 20:36: "they are (*eisin*) equal to angels." This meant imitating angels in the here and now. To fast was to be like the angels, who do without food. To be celibate was to be like the angels (or at least the good angels), who do without intercourse. To stay awake was to be like the angels, who slumber not. To pray constantly was to be like the angels, who ceaselessly worship. Evagrius wrote: "Have heaven for your homeland and live there constantly—not in mere word but in actions that imitate the angels."[27] It may even be that those who stood on pillars, such as Simeon Stylites, were seeking by their peculiar behavior to imitate the angels, for multiple texts speak of angels standing before God,[28] and according to the *Jerusalem Talmud*, there's no sitting in heaven since angels lack knee joints (*Berakoth* 2c).

Whatever one makes of the suggestion about Simeon and his fellows, the notion that humans will, at death or the resurrection, become angels, or at least angel-like, has always had Christian sponsors. The *Acts of Paul and Thekla*, from the second century, contains this beatitude: "Blessed are those who fear God, for they will become angels of God" (3:5). Tertullian taught that, when the saints enter heaven, they will be transformed "in a moment into the substance of angels."[29] According to Clement of Alexandria, the afterlife will be like a classroom, and human souls, after sitting under the tutelage of angels for a thousand years, will become like their teachers.[30] Origen spoke of "the change of saints into angels"[31] and likewise of the resurrection raising saints "to the order of the angels."[32] An inscription from a fourth-century tomb in the Via Latina in Rome declares that the commemorated has taken an angelic body in heaven.[33] Bernard of Clairvaux referred to angels as "our future fellow heirs."[34] Richard of St. Victor spoke of the Christian's spiritual progress as assimilation to the cherubim in their virtue, in their contemplation, and in their nearness to God: "the human soul transforms itself into the symbolic expression of heavenly and winged beings and transfigures itself into their image."[35] Thomas Burnet, the seventeenth-century English divine, wrote that the saints will live above "in the charming Seats and Society of Angels, through endless Ages happy."[36] In Elizabeth Stuart Phelps's nineteenth-century best-selling novel, *The Gates Ajar*, one of the main characters insists that angels are dead believers.[37]

There remain hints of this belief even in today's mainline churches. For example, most Protestants know Charles Wesley's hymn, "Love Divine, All Loves Excelling." This is its third stanza:

Come, Almighty, to deliver,
Let us all Thy life receive;
Suddenly return and never,
Nevermore Thy temples leave.
Thee we would be always blessing,
Serve Thee as Thy hosts above,
Pray and praise Thee without ceasing,
Glory in Thy perfect love.

Those who enter into these words are seeking to be, even now, like the "hosts above," that is, the angels, who never leave the heavenly temple, and who always bless and praise God without ceasing.

....

What might we make of this tradition—or, if you prefer, myth—whether in its ancient or later forms? It would be easy, following post-Enlightenment skepticism, to dismiss it as escapist nonsense. Aren't angels passé, the fictional remnants of an antiquated worldview? Didn't many nineteenth-century theologians rightly quit discoursing about them? I should like to suggest, however, that whatever the ontological status of angels, consideration of how this belief has likely functioned may create some sympathy.

....

Although angels sometimes bear personal names—Michael, Raphael, and Gabriel, for example—they're nowhere remembered as having private, personal lives. They're instead utterly theocentric beings. They are God's obedient messengers. They stand before or around the heavenly throne. And they worship and sing to the One who sits on the throne. Indeed, in popular piety, perhaps the chief attribute of the angels is that they hymn the deity.

Even many who've never entered a church are familiar with Christmas carols in which "the herald angels sing 'Glory to the newborn King!'" and in which the "angels we have heard on high," with their "joyous strains," sing sweetly "o'er the plains . . . 'Gloria, in excelsis Deo.'"

To think of an angel is inevitably to think of God, because it is to think of a creature with no existence or purpose apart from God. It follows that to gain an angelic nature would be to gain a God-centered nature. Put otherwise, a being who wasn't God-centered wouldn't be an angel. Nor would a being who wasn't near God, or a being who didn't perfectly obey God, or a being who didn't worship God. Seen from this point of view, the promise of angelization has suitably served to commend aspiration for a perfected affiliation with God.[38]

. . . .

What else might the notion of a transformation into angels convey? Angels are, in the traditional stories, depicted as being, in multiple respects, superior to humans. They know more, for instance. This is why, in Daniel and Revelation, they deliver and interpret oracles. They're also more powerful, which is why, in Exodus 14, the angel of the Lord protects Israel in the wilderness. They further have the miraculous ability to appear and disappear, as in Luke 1, where John the Baptist's father suddenly sees an angel inside the sanctuary in Jerusalem. On the whole, then, human beings are, as Psalm 8 puts it, "lower" than the angels. Indeed, angels are in some ways so much greater than mortals that these last can be tempted, as in Colossians 2 and Revelation 19 and 22, to worship them.

It follows that acquiring an angelic nature would be akin to making a large evolutionary advance, would involve gaining abilities and attributes which human beings, in their current condition, can only dream of obtaining. This harmonizes with any number of New Testament texts which characterize the eschatological future by setting it over and against present limitations. In 1 Corinthians 15, Paul contrasts the weakness, perishability, and mortality of the current human condition with the power, imperishability, and immortality to be granted at the eschaton. In 1 Corinthians 13, he concedes that, for now, he knows "only in part," but boldly claims that, in the end, he will "know fully," even as he has been known. In short, when the apostle anticipates the eschatological future, he anticipates a new and improved human nature.

It's the same in the Gospel of Matthew, where the parallel between the human future and the angelic present is implicit. In 5:8, Jesus promises that the pure in heart will see God, whereas later, in 18:10, he avows that the an-

gels of the "little ones . . . continually see the face of my Father in heaven."
So the beatific vision the angels enjoy now is what the disciples will later
on experience. Of like import is Matthew 13:43, where the righteous, after
the Last Judgment, "shine like the sun in the kingdom of their Father." This
promise marks another way in which the saints will be like angels, because
angels were traditionally associated with light, as in Matthew's story of the
empty tomb, where the angel appears "like lightning" and with "clothing
white as snow."[39]

The promise of angelization has potentially functioned, then, much as
has the doctrine of the resurrection, to assure people that the eschaton will
mean more, not less. It's been a way of imagining how people might, as
full "participants in the divine nature" (2 Pet. 1:4), transcend some of the
spiritual and bodily limitations that now constrict us.[40]

So much for the angelic conception of heaven.

....

In their engrossing book *Heaven: A History*, Bernhard Lang and Colleen
McDannell seek to show that, over the last three centuries, the afterlife
has become, in the Western world, less theocentric and more anthropocentric, that Christian hope has focused less and less on the vision of God,
more and more on the continuance of human bonds.[41] Heaven will mean
"homes restored, families regathered and friends reunited."[42]

Their general thesis isn't without evidence. "We shall meet on that
beautiful shore" is repeated twice in one of the more popular Protestant
hymns from the nineteenth century, "In the Sweet Bye and Bye." Another
old standby, "Blest Be the Tie That Binds," winds down with these famous
stanzas:

> When we asunder part,
> It gives us inward pain;
> But we shall still be joined in heart,
> And hope to meet again.
>
> This glorious hope revives
> Our courage by the way;
> While each in expectation lives,
> And longs to see the day.
>
> From sorrow, toil, and pain,
> And sin, we shall be free,

And perfect love and friendship reign
Through all eternity.

Yet while hymns such as these undoubtedly tell us a lot about their times, reunion in the afterlife didn't first appear after the Industrial Revolution, when home became the romanticized haven from work, and heaven more of the same. Tertullian taught that the saints in heaven will retain their memories and so will recognize each other, and even that marriages will endure, albeit without sexual intercourse.[43] Cyprian imagined that, in paradise, "a great number of our dear ones await us, and a dense crowd of parents, brothers, children long for us, already assured of their own safety, and still solicitous for our salvation."[44] In line with this, there's a picture on the second floor in the Roman Catacomb of Priscilla featuring a woman and her five small children in a bucolic heaven.[45]

Some Gothic cathedrals feature a very maternal Abraham cradling miniature people against his chest, and the same touching motif appears on Greek and Russian icons, sometimes with Isaac and Jacob also embracing little ones in their laps. These visual depictions of "Abraham's bosom" communicate that, in the world to come, the saints will be gathered together as the children of one family.

One of Luther's last remarks was reportedly this: we "shall know our Parents, Wives, Children, and everything else, much more perfectly than Adam knew Eve."[46] Thomas Becon, Luther's contemporary, wrote that "if your friends live in the fear of God, and depart in the Christian faith, they may be sure to come thither, where you shall be; even unto the glorious kingdom of God, where you shall both see them, know them, talk with them, and be much more merry with them (than) ever you were in this world."[47] In the ensuing century, William Ford preached that "an infinite number of acquaintance expect us there: our parents, our brethren and sisters, our children, our kindred, our friends, that are already secure of their own immortalities, but yet sollictious for our safetie, what ioy, what comfort will it be to see, to imbrace them."[48] John Donne opined: "we are not bound to think that souls departed have divested all affections towards them whom they left here."[49]

The Old Testament may already presuppose something similar. In the Pentateuch, the notices of the deaths of Abraham, Ishmael, Isaac, Jacob, Aaron, and Moses are accompanied by the remark that they were "gathered" to their "people." The idiom intrigues because it isn't a way of saying they were laid in the family tomb, beside their ancestors. Abraham was buried in a cave on property he'd purchased from the Hittites, and Moses was buried in an undisclosed location in the land of Moab. Such texts might, then, envisage a reunion in the afterlife.

When we come to the New Testament, we find Jesus looking forward to eating in the kingdom with his disciples and with Abraham, Isaac, and Jacob;[50] and to envision the eschatological celebration as a banquet with friends and patriarchs is inevitably to conjure something like a very large family get-together.

Paul must have imagined something similar. He sought to comfort his Thessalonian converts with these words: "The dead in Christ will rise first; then we who are alive, who are left, shall be caught up together with them in the clouds to meet the Lord in the air; and so we shall always be with the Lord" (1 Thess. 4:16–17). The apostle was writing to people who'd lost beloved family or friends, and he used communal plurals to instill hope: "we shall always be with the Lord," "we shall be caught up together." So as Philip Esler has remarked, "there will be a reunion between living and once-dead Christ-followers. . . . The communion they enjoyed in life will be restored after death."[51]

. . . .

Although the relevant biblical passages aren't numerous—the lengthiest treatment of this theme known to me, Henry Harbaugh's *The Heavenly Recognition* (1860), makes much of little[52]—most Christians would presumably insist that eternal life would be loss, not gain, if it obliterated all familial and social bonds established in this world. Indeed, surveys suggest that modern people in the West, when they think about a world to come, imagine it first of all as a place where relationships severed by death are reinstated.[53]

I count myself with the majority here, and not just for sentimental reasons. We're all social beings socially formed. We are who we are because of our continual interactions with others. If, then, our individual identities are to be, in some measure, preserved beyond death, then it seems that our social identities will likewise need to be, in some measure, preserved beyond death. Of this circumstance, then, the hope of reunion with family and friends can serve as a fitting symbol. Bunyan wrote: "Since Relatives are our second self, tho that state will be dissolved there, yet why may it not be rationally concluded that we shall be more glad to see them there, then to see they are wanting?"[54]

And yet: to conceive of heaven as an agreeable family assembly rather than a confrontation with a Mystery that re-creates us is to leave us undisturbed. It's to leave our wayward egos with the familiar and so with the comfortable. It's to have God give us what we would otherwise give ourselves—family and friends, but without the everyday ills and irritations that so annoy us now. Freud called this wish fulfillment. Demosthenes, ages ago, anticipated him: "What each one wishes, that he also believes to be true."[55]

The domestic heaven has, understandably, left some theologians uneasy. Aquinas opined: "If we speak of the perfect happiness which will be in our heavenly fatherland, the fellowship of friends is not essential ... since man has the entire fullness of his perfection in God.... That glory which is essential to happiness, is that which man has, not with man but with God.... If there were but one soul enjoying God, it would be happy, even though it had no neighbor to love."[56] William Perkins wrote, in 1600, that "whether men shall knowe one another after this life or no" is "oftener moved by such as are ignorant, than by them that have knowledge ... but whether they shall know one another after an earthly manner, as to say, this man was my father, this was mine uncle, this mine teacher &c. the word of god saith nothing: and therefore I will be silent."[57] A century later, the Jansenist Pierre Nicole fretted about an overemphasis upon this-worldly affections and thought it preferable to posit instead a life of "eternal solitude with God alone."[58] In like manner, the Baptist theologian John Gill cautioned that "all natural and civil connections will cease; and whether it will give any peculiar and superior pleasure, to see a relation or friend in this happy state, more than to see another saint, is a question not now to be resolved."[59] More severe was the old Anglican Bishop Joseph Hall:

> I find much inquiry of curious wits, whether we shall know one another in Heaven. There is no want of arguments, on both parts.... But, O Lord, whether or not we shall know one another, I am sure we shall all, thy glorified Saints, know thee; and in knowing thee, we shall be infinitely happy: and what would be more? Surely, as we find here, that the sun puts out the fire, and the greater light ever extinguisheth the less; so, why may we not think it to be above? When thou art all in all to us, what can the knowledge of any creature add to our blessedness? And if, when we casually meet with a brother or a son before some great prince, we forbear the ceremonies of our mutual respects, as being wholly taken up with the awful regard of a greater presence; how much more may we justly think, that when we meet before the glorious Throne of the God of Heaven, all the respects of our former earthly relations must utterly cease, and be swallowed up of that beatifical

presence, divine love, and infinitely blessed fruition of the Almighty! O God . . . if, upon the dissolution of this earthly tabernacle, I may be admitted to the sight of thy All-glorious Essence . . . I shall neither have need, nor use of enquiring, after my kindred according to the flesh.[60]

This seems unduly harsh to me, and one might wonder whether Hall had issues with his parents, wife, or children. But we shouldn't just dismiss him as an old crank. If Paul claimed no longer to care about others "from a human point of view" (2 Cor. 5:16), why should the denizens of heaven care? The first commandment of the Decalogue is a call for allegiance to God above all else. This dislodges the family from pride of place.

One sees the outcome in the ministry of Jesus. He calls the sons of Zebedee to get out of their boat and leave their father. When someone alerts him that his mother, brothers, and sisters are nearby, he unsentimentally observes: "Whoever does the will of God is my brother and sister and mother" (Mark 3:35). To a would-be follower who wants to bury his father, Jesus responds with "Let the dead bury their own dead" (Luke 9:60). It's not remarkable, then, that when Jesus—who was, we should remember, despite occasional claims to the contrary, almost certainly unmarried— thought of heaven, he didn't think of relocated marital bliss: "in the resurrection they neither marry nor are given in marriage, but are like angels in heaven" (Matt. 22:30). In the light of all this, a hope that fixes firstly upon the restoration of familial relations seems shallow.

This shouldn't, however, wholly negate the popular hope for reunion, for it's not so easy to draw a line between the theocentric and the anthropocentric. In this life we don't perceive God directly but indirectly, through divine effects. This is why we come to know and learn of God above all through the words and deeds of other people. Perhaps it won't be altogether different in the world to come. If our likeness to God is now diminished, and if in the future it will be enhanced, then won't we be able to see God in our redeemed neighbors and in our redeemed selves? Augustine inferred: "Perhaps God will be known to us and visible to us in the sense that he will be spiritually perceived by each one of us in each one of us, perceived in one another, perceived by each in himself."[61]

. . . .

One last point about the popular notion of heaven as reunion. While it's easy for many of us to be romantic about families, it's not easy for everybody. Unhappy and alienated families are all around. Often the alienation can't be repaired, which is why some children run away and why countless adults are divorced. From their point of view, the notion of heaven as a family gathering may not be welcome. In the same way that addressing God as "Father" may unsettle some who've been abused by a father, so too the depiction of heaven as an assembly of near relations might not commend itself to all. Some would no doubt prefer to think of heaven as an escape from family rather than its reinstatement. The presence of such people in congregations should never be forgotten.

....

If one plugs "heaven" into Google Images, one will see mostly clouds, dozens and dozens of images representing heaven as in the clouds or beyond the clouds. A few pictures, however, are more terrestrial. They're of gorgeous green fields, or spectacular mountains, or beautiful trees. These images promulgate the idea that heaven will feature unsurpassed natural landscapes.

This is very much the heaven of C. S. Lewis's *The Great Divorce*—a glorious world with waterfalls and lakes, flowers and grass, with mountain ranges and great valleys, steep forests and groves of trees, as well as romping lions and singing birds. Lewis's vision reflects the modern romanticism of nature, and it's related to the sentimentality made visible in the private rural cemeteries of the nineteenth century that feature lovely gardens and tree-filled parks as previews of the afterlife. Yet it's also true that Lewis's depiction of heaven has precedent in writings from long ago. Shortly before the Reformation, Johannes Brugman preached a sermon which includes these words: "I saw them [deceased monks and nuns] sitting over yonder in a beautiful orchard, in which all kinds of flowers were to be found. There was the loveliest columbine. Words cannot express how they stood there; and the most beautiful things of all were the lilies."[62] From an even earlier time, we have the old life of St. Andrew, the ninth-century Fool for Christ of Constantinople. This biographical text claims that once, when the saint nearly froze to death, he reportedly found himself

> in a beautiful and most marvelous garden. . . . I rejoiced in this beauty, marveled at it with my mind, and rejoiced in my heart at the sweetness of God's Paradise as I walked through it. I saw many gardens with tall trees which moved their tops and were pleasant to look at; their branches emitted a wonderful fragrance. Some of the trees were perpetually in bloom; others were full of golden leaves; still others bore various fruit of unspeakable beauty and sweetness. It is impossible to compare these trees to any that grow on earth, for it was God's hand, and not that of any man, that had planted them. There were countless multitudes of birds in these gardens.

Some were sitting on the branches of the trees and sang beautifully—so beautifully that I did not remember who I was.[63]

Going back further in time, the *Passion of Perpetua*, from the early third century, recounts a vision of the heavenly world that includes these details: there was "a great open space . . . which seemed to be a garden. The trees were as tall as cypresses, and their leaves were constantly falling, song without pause. And in that orchard there were four other angels brighter than those before . . . . We went on foot through the grove through the violet-covered field."[64]

Some pre-Christian Greeks already entertained this sort of hope. The poet Pindar characterized the place where the just dwell after death with these words:

In meadows of roses their suburbs lie,
Roses all tinged with a crimson dye.
They are shaded by trees that incense bear,
And trees with golden fruit so fair.[65]

The Bible assumes something similar. When Revelation looks into the future, it foresees "the river of the water of life, bright as crystal," on both sides of which will be the tree of life, with "its twelve kinds of fruit, yielding its fruit each month," the leaves of which will be "for the healing of the nations" (22:1-2).

This utopian picture unfolds a promise made earlier in Revelation, in the second chapter, where the Spirit says to the churches: "To him who conquers I will grant to eat of the tree of life, which is in the paradise of God." The Greek word *paradeisos* (= "paradise") derives from an old Persian word that literally means "garden." Now in Hellenistic Judaism, including the Greek translation of the Hebrew Bible, this word came to be used of the Garden of Eden. Moreover, while some Jews imagined that the Garden still existed somewhere on earth, others thought that God must have transported it to the upper regions, to heaven. This explains the language of 2 Corinthians 12, where "caught up to the third heaven" stands in synonymous parallelism with "caught up into paradise." Comparable is Luke 23:39-43, where the dying Jesus vows to the so-called good thief: "Truly, I say to you, today you will be with me in paradise." Despite occasional attempts to urge otherwise, this can't be about anything other than the ascent of souls to heaven at death.

Once you call heaven "paradise" or put paradise in heaven, you inescapably envision the afterlife as some sort of nurturing natural landscape, for the original paradise was a luxurious garden: "the LORD God planted a garden in Eden, in the east. . . . Out of the ground the LORD God made to grow every tree that is pleasant to the sight and good for food, the tree of life also in the midst of the garden, and the tree of the knowledge of good and evil. A river flows out of Eden to water the garden, and from there it divides and becomes four branches" (Gen. 2:8-10). This explains what we find in Revelation, as well as in 2 *Enoch*, an old Jewish apocalypse. The latter describes paradise, which it locates in "the third heaven," as follows:

> And that place has an appearance of pleasantness that has never been seen. Every tree was in full flower. Every fruit was ripe, every food was in yield profusely; every fragrance was pleasant. And the four rivers were flowing past with gentle movement, with every kind of garden producing every kind of good food. And the tree of life is in that place, under which the Lord takes a rest when the Lord takes a walk in paradise. And that tree is indescribable for pleasantness of fragrance. (8:3 recension A)

What might we make of this old idea of heaven as an Edenic paradise? It'll appeal to those who find God in nature, those such as my late father, who on his deathbed wanted to hear Edna Saint Vincent Millay's "Renascence." Among its lines are these:

> About the trees my arms I wound;
> Like one gone mad I hugged the ground;
> I raised my quivering arms on high;
> I laughed and laughed into the sky,
> Till at my throat a strangling sob
> Caught fiercely, and a great heart-throb
> Sent instant tears into my eyes;
> O God, I cried, no dark disguise
> Can e'er hereafter hide from me
> Thy radiant identity!
> Thou canst not move across the grass
> But my quick eyes will see Thee pass,
> Nor speak, however silently,
> But my hushed voice will answer Thee.

I know the path that tells Thy way
Through the cool eve of every day;
God, I can push the grass apart
And lay my finger on Thy heart!

If one deems God and the natural world to be as intimately allied as these words convey, then it's hard to envisage heaven without imagining grass and trees.

....

Encounters with the natural world often trigger religious feelings, and reports of people who've sensed the divine in or behind nature are countless. Here are two typical examples, both taken from the archives of the Religious Experience Research Unit now housed at the University of Wales, Lampeter:

"I went for a walk in the field with my dog. My mind suddenly started thinking about the beauty around me, and I considered the marvelous order and timing of the growth of each flower, herb and the abundance of all the visible growth going on around. I remember thinking "Here is mind." Then we had to get over a stile and suddenly I was confronted with a bramble bush which was absolutely laden with black glistening fruit. And the impact of that, linked with my former reasoning, gave me a great feeling of ecstasy. For a few moments I really did feel at one with the Universe or the Creative Power we recognize."

"I was almost to the wood when I paused, turning to look at the cornfield, took two or three steps forward so I was able to touch the ears of corn and watched them swaying in the faint breeze. I looked to the end of the field—it had a hedge then—and beyond that to some tall trees towards the village. The sun was over to my left. . . . Everywhere surrounding me was this white, bright, sparkling light, like sun on frosty snow, like a million diamonds, and there was no cornfield, no trees, no sky, this light was everywhere; my ordinary eyes were open but I was not seeing with them. . . . I have never experienced anything in the years that followed that can compare with the glorious moment; it was blissful, uplifting, I felt open-mouthed wonder. . . . I know Heaven is within us and around us."[66]

One recalls that, in the Bible, God speaks through a burning bush when Moses is on Sinai and from a cloud when Jesus is transfigured on Mount

Tabor. Although these episodes are what theologians call "special revelation," Scripture also knows of a more general revelation that comes through the natural world: "Ever since the creation of the world his eternal power and divine nature, invisible though they are, have been understood and seen through the things he has made" (Rom. 1:20). While some have been uneasy with the idea that God can be known in any way apart from Jesus Christ, Paul seems to say otherwise.

Returning to the subject of heaven with this in mind, some words that Augustine wrote when ruminating upon the world to come merit our attention:

> We will then see the physical bodies of the new heaven and the new earth in such a fashion as to observe God in utter clarity and distinctness, seeing him present everywhere and governing the whole material scheme of things by means of the bodies we will then inhabit and the bodies we will see wherever we turn our eyes. It will not be as it is now, when the invisible realities of God are apprehended and observed through the material things of his creation, and are partially apprehended by means of a puzzling reflection in a mirror. Rather in that new age the faith, by which we believe, will have a greater reality for us than the appearance of material things which we see with our bodily eyes. Now in this present life we are in contact with fellow-beings who are alive and display the motions of life; and as soon as we see them we do not believe them to be alive, we observe the fact. We could not observe their life without their bodies; but we see it in them, without any possibility of doubt, through their bodies. Similarly, in the future life, wherever we turn, the spiritual eyes of our bodies will discern, by means of our bodies, the incorporeal God directing the whole universe. God then will be seen by those eyes in virtue of their possession (in this transformed condition) of something of an intellectual quality, a power to discern things of an immaterial nature.[67]

Augustine appears to be saying that, while nature as we know it can mediate a partial knowledge of God, nature in the world to come will unfailingly mediate a much fuller knowledge of God.

I'm reminded of a lecture I once heard in a college philosophy class. The professor, a confident atheist, was sharing reasons for his unbelief. At one point, however, he interrupted his long string of skeptical observations to confess that once, years before, on a late afternoon, in a sun-drenched glade, he was overwhelmed by beauty and, for a few minutes, was compelled, against his habit, to believe in a creator. Fortunately, from his point of view, he was able, after a bit, to shake off this unwelcome thought and return to normal. I take Augustine to imply that, in the world to come, my former professor won't be able to do such a thing.

....

Having introduced three different models of heaven—heaven as angelic existence, heaven as social reunion, heaven as natural landscape—I'd like to ask, before concluding, From whence do they come? Why have people imagined that, in another world, they will become angelic or see their loved ones or enjoy a perfected natural world?

The teachings of religious texts and inferences from them have obviously been foundational, as has the human proclivity to project our deepest wishes onto the future and hope for the best. It's my conviction, however, that visionary experiences have also likely played their role, both in prompting certain beliefs and in reinforcing them.

....

Modern accounts of near-death experiences (NDEs) are filled with reports such as these:

> "I was just in a wonderful peace and wellness in a beautiful landscape setting of grass, lawns and trees and brilliant light, diffused, not coming from any central source, with a feeling of being surrounded by wonderful love, joy and peace, no illness or pain."

> "I floated upward to a beautiful vivid green field."

> There was "the most beautiful garden, filled with flowers which were beautiful."

> "Inside was the most beautiful garden, no lawn, path, or anything else, but flowers of every kind. Those that attracted me most were Madonna lilies, delphiniums and roses, but there were many, many more."[68]

Such visions aren't reported only by NDErs. I know this not only from my reading but from my experience. One Sunday morning a few years ago, I woke up and unaccountably found myself not in my bed but in some sort of paradise. What occasioned this, I've no idea. What I do know is that I saw a sky-blue land filled with what I can only call—words fail me— "bird souls." They were slowly gliding through the air and singing what

I dubbed, when I soon thereafter wrote it all up, "the song of creation." This was a place of beauty and bliss beyond comprehension, and I could stand the unsurpassed joy for no more than a few seconds, after which I willingly withdrew.

Whatever the explanation may be, visions of exquisite transcendent scenes have come to people in multiple times and various places. I've already cited long-ago examples from Revelation and the *Passion of Perpetua*. One could also quote reports from modern Hindus and from ancient Buddhists.[69] The experience is, I submit, sufficiently well-attested cross-culturally to encourage the inference that firsthand testimony has helped inspire the widely held belief that there's another world which features spectacular landscapes.

. . . .

It's much the same with the belief that people will meet their loved ones on the other side. The conviction isn't just Christian but is far-flung, appearing already in old texts from Mesopotamia, Egypt, Iran, India, and China.[70] And once again, visionary experiences have surely buttressed the belief. Reports of people encountering the dead come from almost all times and places. Reports of the dying seeing dead relatives are particularly common. The Zohar says: "For we have learned: When a person is about to depart the world, his father and relatives are present with him, and he sees and recognizes them. And all those with whom he shared the same run in that world, they all gather around him and accompany his soul to the place where she will abide."[71] "We have learned" is the voice of experience.

Why people so often seemingly see the dead is up for discussion, but the phenomenological fact isn't: the reports are everywhere.[72] So it's only to be expected that, before the modern dismissal of all visions as hallucinations, many gathered that, upon death, they were going to be with their ancestors. If the dead seemingly show themselves to their relatives and friends, then death doesn't terminate earthly bonds.

. . . .

There's even a good chance that visions of the dead have reinforced the idea of an angelic destiny. Most ghosts tend to be either ethereal—the stereotypical see-through ghost—or they're perfectly realistic, so much so that their nature often isn't recognized at first. Once in a while, however, a deceased individual will appear self-illumined and glorious.

In an earlier chapter, I shared that I once ostensibly saw, shortly after her death, my dear friend Barbara. She was a beautiful, luminous presence, reminiscent of some artistic representations of Jesus' transfiguration. I could've thought her an angel. My experience doesn't stand alone:

> "I suddenly became aware of a very bright blue and gold light of tremendous brilliance. There are no words in our language to describe these colors. A sense of the magnitude and beauty of this being was impressed on me as this light. It became very clear that this was Joshua [a nine-year-old boy who'd died three days earlier] and that he wished to send a message to his mother."[73]

> "I was sitting in a chair in my living room when I suddenly realized Gladys was coming down the stairway. I was just dumbfounded when I saw her! Her appearance was not the same as when she was sick—she was beautiful. The brilliant lighting and the intensity of her was next door to unbelievable! It's impossible to describe the brilliance, absolutely impossible."

> "She was bright, sort of glowing, and was dressed in a sparkling, dazzling white gown."

The word "angel" sometimes actually appears in reports from those who've had visions like these. Here's an example:

> "My mother passed away last February 17, a little after midnight. She was in California while I was in Wichita, Kansas. At 9:40 am, February 17, I was sitting in my bedroom at my mirror setting my hair when the room was suddenly lighted with the strangest light. One I can't fully describe. I felt a rustle of wind across my shoulders and a faint sound as the brushing of bird's wings. Then I looked in the mirror. My mother was standing behind my chair, the most beautiful angel you can imagine. She just stood and smiled at me for 30 seconds. I said, "Mother," and rushed for her and she, light and all, disappeared. . . . About 1 pm that same day, the call came that my mother was gone."[74]

The Jungian therapist Aniela Jaffé, who analyzed a collection of 1,500 visions reported mostly by Europeans in 1954 and 1955, offered this generalization: "the great or even supernatural beauty of the ghosts" is sometimes "recorded as a kind of transfiguration. The light that accompanies the transfiguration usually appears in cases involving the manifestations of

deceased relatives or beloved persons."[75] When one adds that these transfigured figures typically appear suddenly out of nowhere, convey a brief
message, then inexplicably disappear in the blink of an eye, the parallel
with the angels of Western religious tradition is undeniable.

....

I here forego discussion of the nature of NDEs or the other visionary experiences just introduced. Many would reflexively discard them all by invoking
the discussion-halting term "hallucination," or by protesting that anteced-
ently held religious ideas must have generated the contents of the various
sorts of visions. While I deem such anathematizing deficient, lazy ways
of dogmatically dismissing and marginalizing reports that, if approached
with an open mind, provoke perplexing questions,[76] all that's needed for
our immediate purpose is the recognition that, in different cultures and
epochs, many have reported seeing otherworldly landscapes, just as many
have reported seeing dead relatives and friends, some of them luminous
and glorious. That's enough for us to surmise that our eschatological ideas
owe something, and maybe a great deal, to relatively common visionary
experiences.

....

In bringing this book to an end, I'd like to observe that, if one doesn't dis-
dain its main topic as an intellectual anachronism, on the ground that modern knowledge has obliterated the possibility of life beyond brain death,
several tactics are possible. One is to uphold hope for more without saying
more. As one theologian put it, "I believe that personal consciousness sur-
vives the shock of that physical episode we call death. As to the conditions
or employments of that future life, I have no conception whatever."[77] Here
we have hope without content.

A second approach is to mine the Bible for information about the future,
on the supposition that its true author, God, knows what's coming and has,
in the interest of warning and encouraging us, considerably revealed a
few details. Some thus minded find within Scripture the proof texts for
purgatory. Others deduce the duration of hell or the circumstances of the
millennium.

A third approach is to explore what human experience has to say. Maybe
not all mediums are frauds, and maybe, as William James thought, the
rare exception is on occasion in touch with more than their subconscious
selves. Or perhaps some NDErs have caught glimpses of a reality beyond
our restricted space and time. If so, maybe we're less in the dark than generally supposed.

Difficulties beset each strategy. While saying next to nothing might appear prudent, such Kantian reticence may, within a religious context, leave puzzled or even dispirited those, such as myself, who don't appreciate eschatological hopes being ignored or reduced to ciphers for something else. Those for whom death and what might lie beyond are vital concerns may not feel much allegiance to a church or pastor with an exclusively or almost exclusively imminent deity, a deity who, in sermon after sermon, remains nebulous about the future, uncommitted as to where the story might be headed. James Moorhead is right: "a religious movement must provide its adherents with a satisfying vision of the end; when it fails to do so, many people will be drawn elsewhere."[78]

As for mapping the future with the Bible, that's even more problematic. Scripture offers no consistent teaching about life after death or the world to come. The Old Testament's Sheol isn't the New Testament's paradise, and the skepticism of Ecclesiastes isn't the eschatological optimism of Paul. It's not even clear whether we can harmonize 1 Corinthians 15, the topic of which is resurrection, with 2 Corinthians 5, the topic of which is life after death. Beyond all that, Christians who believe in a concretely prophesied future invariably believe in a concretely prophesied past; that is, they hold that the Old Testament foretold, in some detail, the first advent. Yet they have to concede that, before he appeared, no one came close to sketching Jesus' ministry and its outcome. All the matching of text to episode was done *ex eventu*, in retrospect. Is it sensible to hold that the prophecies of the Second Advent are essentially different?

What then of seeking knowledge by listening to those who claim that, one way or another, they've been in contact with the other side? Although some will deem me naive, I don't believe that we should be either contemptuous of or indifferent to all the relevant testimony, especially when patterns repeat across sundry times and diverse places. Nonetheless, the task of assaying the huge mass of conflicting claims is Herculean given the interpretive nature of all perception, the reconstructive character of memory, the magnitude of human gullibility, and the widespread—and typically ill-informed—prejudice which so many, both within and beyond religious circles, hold against meta-normal experiences. I've understandably eschewed that chore for another occasion. Herein I've traveled down other roads.

....

One of my major goals has been to consider, against their larger cultural contexts, the waxing and waning of certain eschatological expectations and their interpretation and reinterpretation. We can't rightly understand doctrines without understanding the people who've promoted and demoted them, and we can't do that without understanding broad historical trends and social tendencies.

A second task has been to show that, even if great circumspection is required at every turn, the last things needn't muzzle us. There's much to ponder, much to explain, much to criticize, and much to imagine.

Nonetheless, while foundational theological convictions may encourage some large generalizations about the human *telos*, a third task has been to insist that the Bible and the interpretive traditions parasitic upon it, when scrutinized critically, don't offer details.

Paul, although an apostle, confessed that the future remained dim to his sight. The author of 1 John agreed: "what we will be has not yet been revealed" (3:2). Our tradition has been at its best when it's gone along, when it's conceded how little we know. In this connection I recall some words of Luther, or at least words that my imperfect memory attributes to him: "We know no more about heaven than a child in its mother's womb knows of the world into which it is about to be born." Some Eastern icons offer a visual parallel: souls exiting the mouths of the dying are depicted as infants. Here death is birth, or as in the catacomb inscriptions, the day of one's death is *dies natalis*, one's birthday.

....

Although some may find this a tad morbid, part of me, with a sort of reverent curiosity, now looks forward to it. Most of the time, to be sure, life is full, and I'm all for staying with the familiar as long as possible. On the usual morning I eagerly anticipate the coming day, and on the usual evening I return thanks for most of what's happened.

On occasion, however, the adventure seems stale, and it's not so easy to feel grateful. The world, which is ever full of wonder, isn't the problem. It's rather me. I repeatedly resolve to do better, and I fail. I set out to pursue the good, the true, and the beautiful, and my attention wanders. I aspire to love God with all my heart and soul and mind, and my neighbor as myself, but I get distracted.

My incessant failures are more than frustrating, and sometimes I grow weary of myself. My fatigue can become such that I long to quit this stage for some other stage, to wake up in a new and different world, to swap my current self for something better, to undergo whatever will turn Romans 7—"I can will what is right, but I cannot do it"—into nothing but a bad memory. As it became evident long ago that this isn't going to happen in this world, I don't always mind the aches and pains and the memory glitches that attend aging. They remind me that night comes. My hope is that light shines in the darkness.

Notes

Notes to Chapter 1

1. The classic examination of the different reasons people fear death is Jacques Choron, *Death and Western Thought* (New York: Macmillan, 1963).

2. John Bunyan, *Grace Abounding to the Chief of Sinners*, in *The Complete Works of John Bunyan* (Philadelphia: Bradley, Garretson & Co., 1873), p. 49.

3. Plutarch, *Moralia* 1105A.

4. Francis Bacon, *Bacon's Essays: With Annotations by Richard Whatley* (London: John W. Parker, 1856), p. 13.

5. C. A. Phillips, "Rendel Harris," *Expository Times* 52 (1941): 352.

6. Michael S. Gazzaniga, *Who's in Charge? Free Will and the Science of the Brain* (New York: HarperCollins, 2011).

7. See Larry R. Squire, *The History of Neuroscience in Autobiography*, vol. 7 (Oxford: Oxford University Press, 2012), pp. 118–19.

8. Philippe Ariès, *The Hour of Our Death* (New York: Knopf, 1981).

9. Pieter W. van der Horst, *Ancient Jewish Epitaphs: An Introductory Survey of a Millennium of Jewish Funerary Epigraphy (300 BCE–700 CE)* (Kampen: Kok Pharos, 1991), p. 73.

10. Aubrey de Grey and Michael Rae, *Ending Aging: The Rejuvenation Breakthroughs That Could Reverse Human Aging in Our Lifetime* (New York: St. Martin's, 2007).

11. Paul Ramsey, "Death's Pedagogy," *Commonweal* 20 (1974): 501.

12. Bertrand Russell, *Why I Am Not a Christian* (New York: Simon & Schuster, 1957), p. 51.

13. As quoted in a letter from Adam Smith to William Strahan, reprinted in David Hume, *Dialogues Concerning Natural Religion*, ed. Norman Kemp Smith (Indianapolis: Bobbs-Merrill, 1947), p. 245.

14. See esp. Stephen E. Braude, *Immortal Remains: The Evidence for Life after Death* (Lanham/Boulder/New York/Oxford: Rowman & Littlefield, 2003). For a more popular introduction to the subject, see Patricia Pearson, *Opening Heaven's Door: Investigating Stories of Life, Death, and What Comes After* (New York: Atria Books, 2014).

15. John Dominic Crossan, "The Historical Jesus and Contemporary Faith," in *The Apocalyptic Jesus: A Debate*, ed. Robert Miller (Santa Rosa, CA: Polebridge Press, 2001), p. 158.

16. John Donne, *Devotions upon Emergent Occasions and Death's Duel* (New York: Vintage Books, 1999), p. 103.

17. J. R. R. Tolkien, *The Lord of the Rings, Part Three: The Return of the King* (New York: Ballantine Books, 1965), pp. 281, 283.

Notes to Chapter 2

1. Augustine, *City of God* 22.20.

2. Edward Stillingfleet, *A Sermon Preached before the King and Queen of England* (London: Henry Mortlock, 1670).

3. George Hodgson, *The Human Body at the Resurrection of the Dead* (London: John Mason, 1853).

4. Humphrey Hody, *The Resurrection of the (Same) Body Asserted: from the Traditions of the Heathens, the Ancient Jews, and the Primitive Church, with An Answer to the Objections brought against It* (London: Awnsham and John Churchill, 1694).

5. Calvin, *Institutes* 3.25.11.

6. *Genesis Rabbah* 28.3. Cf. *Leviticus Rabbah* 18.1; *Ecclesiastes Rabbah* 12.5. I have read that some Jews instead contended that teeth never dissolve and so become the core for resurrection, but I have never run across this in a rabbinic text. Tertullian at one point, however, says something like this (*On the Resurrection of the Flesh* 34).

7. George S. Mott, *The Resurrection of the Dead* (New York: Anson D. F. Randolph, 1867), pp. 112–14.

8. Peter van Inwagen, "The Possibility of Resurrection," *International Journal for the Philosophy of Religion* 9 (1978): 121.

9. Thomas Burnet, *A Treatise concerning the State of Departed Souls, Before, and At, and After the Resurrection* (2nd ed.: London: A. Bettesworth and C. Hitch, 1739), already made this argument effectively.

10. Calvin, *Institutes* 3.25.11; Samuel Johnson, *The Resurrection of the Same Body, as Asserted and Illustrated by St. Paul. A Sermon preach'd in the Parish-Church of Great Torrington, Devon, on Easter-Sunday in the Afternoon, March 25, 1733* (London: Lawton Gilliver, 1733), pp. 32–33.

11. Tertullian, *On the Resurrection of the Flesh* 60.

12. Matthias Earbery, *De Statu Mortuorum & Refugentium Tractatus*, vol. 1 (London: E. Curll, 1728), p. 214.

13. Earbery, *De Statu Mortuorum*, 217.

14. Wolfhart Pannenberg, *What Is Man? Contemporary Anthropology in Contemporary Perspective* (Philadelphia: Fortress, 1970).

15. William Rounseville Alger, *A Critical History of the Doctrine of a Future Life* (Philadelphia: George W. Childs, 1864), p. 494.

16. Mott, *Resurrection*, p. 5.

17. D. A. Dryden, *Suggestive Inquiries Concerning the Resurrection of the Dead, as Taught in the New Testament* (Cincinnati: Hitchcock and Walden, 1872), p. 177.

18. For this miserable bit of history see Ruth Richardson, *Death, Dissection and the Destitute* (2nd ed.: Chicago/London: University of Chicago Press, 2000).

19. John Michael Perry, *Exploring the Identity and Mission of Jesus* (Kansas City, KS: Sheed & Ward, 1996), pp. 176–213.

20. Jerome, *Apology against Rufinus* 2.5.

21. Augustine, *City of God* 22.20.

22. Sir Thomas Browne, *Religio Medici*, ed. F. L. Huntley (New York: Appleton-Century-Crofts, 1966), p. 59.

23. See Julian of Toledo, *Prognosticum Futuri Saeculi* 3.31, with quotations from Augustine on the subject.

24. Already in the early seventeenth century, John Moore, *A Mappe of Mans Mortalitie* (London: T. S. for George Edwards, 1617), p. 246, refers to "natural incredulitie" respecting the resurrection, and Paul's apology in 1 Corinthians 15 show that such incredulity goes back to earliest Christianity.

25. John Locke, *An Essay Concerning Human Understanding*, 2 vols. (New York: Dover, 1959), 2:439–70; idem, *Paraphrase and Notes of the Epistles of St. Paul*, ed. A. W. Wainwright, 2 vols. (Oxford: Oxford University Press, 1987), pp. 668–86.

26. For Hartley's views, see Richard C. Allen, *David Hartley on Human Nature* (Albany, NY: SUNY, 1999).

27. Charles Bonnet, *Contemplation de la Nature*, vol. 2 (2nd ed.: Amsterdam: Rey, 1769), pp. 87–88; idem, *Essai analytique sur les faculties de l'âme* (1760), pp. 451–93.

28. For Aquinas see his *Summa Theologica* supplement to the third part, question 88, article 4. On Leibniz, see Lloyd Strickland, "Taking Scripture Seriously: Leibniz and the Jehoshaphat Problem," *Heythrop Journal* 52 (2011): 40–51.

29. Edward Hitchcock, *Religious Lectures on Peculiar Phenomena in the Four Seasons* (Amherst, MA.: J. S. & C. Adams, 1850), p. 17.

30. Charles Gore, *The Creed of the Christian* (4th ed.: New York: Harper and Brothers, 1898), p. 92.

31. See J. H. Kellogg, *Harmony of Science and the Bible on the Nature of the Soul and the Doctrine of the Resurrection* (Battle Creek, MI: Review and Herald, 1879).

32. W. J. Sparrow Simpson, *The Resurrection and Modern Thought* (London/New York: Longmans, Green, and Co., 1911), pp. 378–401.

33. H. D. A. Major, Letter to the Lord Bishop of Oxford, in *The Doctrine of the Resurrection of the Body: Documents Relating to the Question of Heresy raised against the Rev. H. D. A. Major, Ripon Hall, Oxford*, ed. H. H. Burge (London/Milwaukee: A. R. Mowbray & Co., 1922), p. 48.

34. Hubert M. Oxon, Letter to the Rev. C. E. Douglas, in Burge, *Doctrine*, p. 61.

35. *Doctrine in the Church of England: The Report of the Commission on Christian Doctrine appointed by the Archbishops of Canterbury and York in 1922* (London: SPCK, 1938), p. 209.

36. Emil Brunner, *Eternal Hope* (London: Lutterworth, 1954), p. 149.

37. B. H. Streeter, "The Resurrection of the Dead," in B. H. Streeter et al., *Immortality: An Essay in Discovery co-ordinating Scientific, Physical, and Biblical Research* (New York: Macmillan, 1917), pp. 120–21; Ladislaus Boros, *Living in Hope* (New York: Herder & Herder, 1970); Gisbert Greshake and Gerhard Lohfink, *Naherwartung, Auferstehung, Unsterblichkeit: Untersuchungen zur christlichen Eschatologie* (Quaestiones Disputatae 71; Freiburg: Herder, 1975); Gerhard Lohfink, *Death Is Not the Final Word* (Chicago: Franciscan Herald Press, 1977), pp. 21–43. Historically this has also been the view of most Spiritualists.

38. Dean Zimmerman, "The Compatibility of Materialism and Survival: The 'Falling Elevator' Model," *Faith and Philosophy* 16 (1999): 194–212.

39. J. H. Kellogg, *The Living Temple* (Battle Creek, MI: Good Health Publishing, 1903), pp. 467–74. Kellogg speaks of God's memory holding a person's "organization," that is, form and structure, for the day of resurrection. Polkinghorne has presented his

view in several places, one of them being "Eschatological Credibility: Emergent and Theological Processes," in *Resurrection: Theological and Scientific Assessments*, ed. Ted Peters, Robert John Russell, and Michael Welker (Grand Rapids, MI/Cambridge, UK: Eerdmans, 2002), pp. 443–55.

40. Ray Kurzweil, *The Singularity Is Near: When Humans Transcend Biology* (New York: Viking, 2005).

41. Robert Boyle, "Some Phyisco-Theological Considerations about the Possibility of the Resurrection," in *Selected Philosophical Papers of Robert Boyle*, ed. M. A. Stewart (Manchester: Manchester University Press, 1979), p. 192.

42. For all of this, see Peter C. Jupp, *From Dust to Ashes: Cremation and the British Way of Death* (Houndmills, Basingstoke, Hampshire/New York: Palgrave Macmillan, 2006).

43. Tony Walter, *The Eclipse of Eternity: A Sociology of the Afterlife* (London/New York: Macmillan/St. Martin's Press, 1996), p. 111. Cf. Stephen Prothero, *Purified by Fire: The History of Cremation in America* (Berkeley/Los Angeles/London: University of California Press, 2001), p. 75: cremation rendered "less convincing the popular beliefs, behaviors, attitudes, and metaphors that created and sustained the credibility of the resurrection of the body."

44. Some sociologists have offered an analogous argument: the killing fields of WWI, which turned bodies into scraps, made attachment to and the memorialization of corpses impossible in countless cases, and in that situation resurrection of the body made less sense to many.

45. Oscar Cullmann, *Immortality of the Soul or Resurrection of the Dead? The Witness of the New Testament* (New York: Macmillan, 1958).

46. Nancey C. Murphy, *Bodies and Souls, or Spirited Bodies?* (Cambridge, UK/New York: Cambridge University Press, 2006); Joel Green, *Body, Soul, and Human Life: The Nature of Humanity in the Bible* (Grand Rapids, MI: Baker Academic, 2008).

47. Owen Flanagan, *The Problem of the Soul: Two Visions of Mind and How to Reconcile Them* (New York: Basic Books, 2002), p. 167.

48. Interview with *The Guardian*, May 15, 2011; available online at: http://www.theguardian.com/science/2011/may/15/stephen-hawking-interview-there-is-no-heaven (accessed June 6, 2014).

49. James Barr, *The Garden of Eden and the Hope of Immortality* (Minneapolis: Fortress, 1993), p. 99: "Much in the turn against immortality of the soul was not a return to the fountain-head of biblical evidence but a climbing on the bandwagon of modern progress—the very thing that was at the same time being excoriated when it had been done in liberal theology."

50. Benedikt Paul Göcke, ed., *After Physicalism* (Notre Dame, IN: University of Notre Dame Press, 2012); Howard Robinson, ed., *Objections to Physicalism* (Oxford: Clarendon, 1993); Robert C. Koons and George Bealer, *The Waning of Materialism* (Oxford: Oxford University Press, 2010); Edward F. Kelly et al., *Irreducible Mind: Toward a Psychology for the 21st Century* (Lanham, MD: Rowman & Littlefield, 2007).

51. Wilder Penfield, *The Mystery of the Mind* (Princeton: Princeton University Press, 1973); Karl R. Popper and John C. Eccles, *The Self and Its Brain: An Argument for Interactionism* (Berlin: Springer Verlag, 1985); Thomas Nagel, *Mind and Cosmos: Why the Materialist Neo-Darwinian Conception of Nature Is Almost Certainly False* (Oxford: Oxford University Press, 2012); Alvin Plantinga, *Where the Conflict Really Lies: Science, Religion,*

and Naturalism (Oxford: Oxford University Press, 2011); Raymond Tallis, *Aping Mankind: Neuromania, Darwinitis, and Misrepresentation of Humanity* (Durham, UK: Acumen, 2011).

52. William James, *Human Immortality: Two Supposed Objections to the Doctrine* (2nd ed.: Boston/New York: Houghton Mifflin, 1900); Mario Beauregard and Denyse O'Leary, *The Spiritual Brain: A Neuroscientist's Case for the Existence of the Soul* (New York: HarperOne, 2007).

53. Edwin A. Abbott, *Flatland: A Romance of Many Dimensions* (New York: Dover, 1952).

54. John R. Smythies, *The Walls of Plato's Cave: The Science and Philosophy of Brain, Consciousness, and Perception* (Aldershot, UK: Avebury, 1994).

55. Henry Margenau, *The Miracle of Existence* (Boston/London: Shambhala, 1987).

56. Roger Penrose and Stuart Hameroff, "Consciousness in the Universe: Neuroscience, Quantum Space-Time Geometry, and Orch OR Theory," in *Quantum Physics of Consciousness*, ed. Subhash Kak et al. (Cambridge, MA: Cosmology Science Publishers, 2011), pp. 223–62; Stuart Hameroff and Deepak Chopra, "The 'Quantum Soul': A Scientific Hypothesis," in *Exploring Frontiers of the Mind-Brain Relationship*, ed. A. Moreira-Almeida and F. Santana Santos (New York: Springer, 2012), pp. 79–93.

57. C. J. Ducasse, *Nature, Mind, and Death* (The Paul Carus Lectures Eighth Series 1949; La Salle, IL: Open Court, 1951).

58. Colin McGinn, *The Problem of Consciousness: Essays toward a Resolution* (Oxford/Cambridge, UK: Basil Blackwell, 1993).

59. See further Mark Johnston, *Surviving Death* (Princeton/Oxford: Princeton University Press, 2010), pp. 1–125. His conclusion is that "Christian eschatology does stand or fall with the legacy of Plato, namely the immaterial soul, which could carry the identity of the deceased to the Last Judgment. The removal of the Platonic and Aristotelian legacy from Christianity . . . looks to be an operation the patient cannot survive."

60. Nathan A. Heflick, "Why and How Afterlife Belief Occurs," *Psychology Today*, published online Sept. 27, 2009, at: http://www.psychologytoday.com/blog/the-big-questions/200909/why-and-how-afterlife-belief-occurs; accessed June 7, 2014.

61. Thomas Aquinas, *Summa Theologica* supplement to the third part, question 78, article 2, answer to objection 1.

62. For discussion, see further below, pp. 144–47.

63. A. E. Taylor, *The Christian Hope of Immortality* (New York: Macmillan, 1947), pp. 69–70.

64. Origen, *Hom. Lev.* 7.2.

Notes to Chapter 3

1. Daniel L. Migliore, "From There He Will Come to Judge the Living and the Dead," in *Exploring and Proclaiming the Apostles' Creed*, ed. Roger E. Van Harn (Grand Rapids, MI/Cambridge, UK: Eerdmans, 2004), p. 178.

2. For additional and complementary reasons for changing attitudes toward divine judgment, the interested reader can consult James P. Martin, *The Last Judgment in Protestant Theology from Orthodoxy to Ritschl* (Grand Rapids, MI: Eerdmans, 1963).

3. John A. T. Robinson, *On Being the Church in the World* (Philadelphia: Westminster, 1960), p. 135.

4. John Gill, *A Body of Doctrinal and Practical Divinity; or, A System of Practical Truths* (London: Button and Son, and Whittingham and Arliss, 1815), p. 487.

5. See *The Commentary on the Seven Catholic Epistles of Bede the Venerable*, ed. David Hurst, Cistercian Studies 82 (Kalamazoo, MI: Cistercian Publications, 1985), pp. 30–32.

6. William Ames, *The Marrow of Theology* (Boston/Philadelphia: Pilgrim Press, 1968), p. 216.

7. Heinrich Heppe, *Reformed Dogmatics Set Out and Illustrated by the Sources* (London: George Allen & Unwin, 1950), p. 705.

8. As quoted in Ewald M. Plass, *What Luther Says,* volume II: *Glory-Prayer* (St. Louis: Concordia, 1958), p. 700 (number 2180).

9. Jerome, *Homily on Psalm* 1 ad v. 5.

10. Zeno, *Tractate* 2.21.3. The view never caught on, probably because Augustine opposed it. See his *Tractates on the Gospel of John* 22:5, where he urges that John 5:24 can't contradict Paul's assertion that all will appear before the judgment seat of Christ. He finds concord by arguing that "does not come into judgment" means "does not come into condemnation."

11. Gregory the Great, *Moralia* 26.27.50; Maximus the Confessor, as quoted in the *Philokalia tōn hierōn Nēptikōn,* vol. 1 (Athens: A. & E. Papademetriou, 1957), p. 273; Julian of Toledo, *Prognosticum Futuri Saeculi* 3.33; Peter Lombard, *The Sentences* 4.47.3 (272).

12. Paul M. Churchland, *Matter and Consciousness,* 3rd ed. (Cambridge, MA: MIT Press, 2013); Patricia S. Churchland, *Touching a Nerve: The Self as Brain* (New York: W. W. Norton & Co., 2013).

13. Benjamin Libet, C. A. Gleason, E. W. Wright, and D. K. Pearl, "Time of Conscious Intention to Act in Relation to Onset of Cerebral Activity (Readiness-Potential): The Unconscious Initiation of a Freely Voluntary Act," *Brain* 106 (1983): 623–42.

14. C. S. Soon, A. H. He, S. Bode, and J.-D. Haynes, "Predicting Free Choices for Abstract Intentions," *Proceedings of the National Academy of Sciences U.S.A.* 110 (2013): 6217–22.

15. Interested readers might consult Peter G. H. Clarke, "Neuroscientific and Psychological Attacks on the Efficacy of Conscious Will," *Science and Christian Belief* 26 (2014): 5–23; Alfred R. Mele, *Free: Why Science Hasn't Disproved Free Will* (Oxford: Oxford University Press, 2014); Jeffrey M. Schwarz and Sharon Begley, *The Mind and the Brain: Neuroplasticity and the Power of Mental Force* (New York/London/Toronto/Sydney: Harper Perennial, 2002).

16. Basil the Great, *Homily on the Psalms* 33; 48.

17. Dorotheos of Gaza, *Discourses* 3.

18. Augustine, *City of God,* ed. David Knowles (London: Penguin, 1972), pp. 924–25.

19. "The souls of the dead remember everything that happened here—thoughts, words, desires—and nothing can be forgotten. . . . What he did against virtue or against his evil passions, he remembers, and nothing of this is lost. And if a man helped someone or was helped by someone else, this is remembered as are the persons concerned, or if he injured someone, or was injured by someone, all this is remembered. In fact, the soul loses nothing that it did in this world but remembers everything at its exit from this body more clearly and distinctly." See Dorotheos of Gaza, *Discourses and Sayings,* Cister-

cian Studies Series 93 (Kalamazoo, MI: Cistercian Publications, 1977), p. 185 (Discourse 12). Note also Claude Judde, *Oeuvres spirituelles*, 3 vols., ed. Jacques Lenoir Duparc, 3rd ed. (Paris: Méquignon junior, 1825-26), 1:163: "In God, as in a great mirror, we see the whole history of our lives in the twinkling of an eye, and at the same time we become conscious of every little detail."

20. As quoted in Pim van Lommel, "Non-local Consciousness: A Concept Based on Scientific Research on Near-Death Experiences during Cardiac Arrest," *Journal of Consciousness Studies* 20 (2013): 20-21.

21. Jeffrey Long, *Evidence of the Afterlife: The Science of Near-Death Experiences* (New York: HarperOne, 2010), p. 112.

22. Joel L. Whitton and Joe Fisher, *Life between Life* (New York: Warner, 1986), p. 39.

23. Huston Smith, "Intimations of Mortality: Three Case Studies," *Harvard Divinity Bulletin* 30 (2001): 14-15.

24. See Feng Zhi-ying and Liu Jian-xun, "Near-Death Experiences among Survivors of the 1976 Tangshan Earthquake," *Journal of Near-Death Studies* 11 (1992): 39-48; Allan Kellehear, "Census of Non-Western Near-Death Experiences to 2005: Observations and Critical Reflections," in *The Handbook of Near-Death Experiences: Thirty Years of Investigation*, ed. Janice Miner Holden, Bruce Greyson, and Debbie James (Santa Barbara, CA: ABC-Clio, 2009), pp. 135-58; Long, *Evidence of the Afterlife*, pp. 149-71; Ornella Corazza, "Dealing with Diversity: Cross-Cultural Aspects of Near Death Experiences," in *Making Sense of Near-Death Experiences*, ed. Mahendra Perera, Karuppiah Jagadheesan, and Anthony Peake (London/Philadelphia: Jessica Kingsley, 2012), pp. 51-62. The online data base of the Near Death Association Research Foundation (http://www.nderf .org) contains a large selection of NDEs in multiple languages from all over the world.

25. Albert von St. Gallen Heim, "Notizen über den Tod durch Absturz," *Yearbook of the Swiss Alpine Club* 28 (1892): 327-37.

26. Harriet Martineau, *Biographical Sketches 1852-1875*, new ed. (London/New York: Macmillan and Co., 1888), pp. 219-20.

27. E. Schuré, *Pythagoras and the Delphic Mysteries*, rev. ed. (London: William Rider & Son, Ltd., 1923), p. 119.

28. Jan Assmann, *Death and Salvation in Ancient Egypt* (Ithaca, NY/London: Cornell University Press, 2005), p. 74.

29. Richard Whately, *A View of the Scriptural Revelations concerning a Future State* (Philadelphia: Smith, English & Co., 1873), p. 126.

30. Whately, *View of the Scriptural Revelations*, p. 127.

31. Alexander Macleod, *Our Own Lives the Books of Judgment* (Edinburgh: Andrew Elliot, 1869).

32. Samuel Taylor Coleridge, *Biographia Literaria or Biographical Sketches of My Literary Life and Opinions I*, ed. James Engell and W. Jackson Bate (Princeton, NJ/London: Princeton University Press/Routledge & Kegan Paul, 1983), p. 114.

33. Thomas de Quincey, *Confessions of an English Opium-Eater and Kindred Papers* (New York/Cambridge, UK: Hurd and Houghton/The Riverdale Press, 1876), pp. 111-12. Samuel Warren, "A Few Personal Recollections of Christopher North," *Blackwood's Edinburgh Magazine* 76 (Dec. 1854): 733, quotes de Quincey as once saying in conversation: "Possibly a suddenly developed power of recollecting every act of a man's life may constitute the Great Book to be opened before him on the judgment day."

34. Martin Buber, *Tales of the Hasidim: The Later Masters* (New York: Schocken, 1948), p. 311.

35. *Babylonian Talmud Ta'anith* 11a.

36. Long, *Evidence of the Afterlife*, p. 157.

37. Martineau, *Biographical Sketches*, 220. Cf. Catherin Crowe, *The Night Side of Nature, or Ghosts and Ghost Seers* (London/New York: George Routledge & Sons; E. P. Dutton & Co., 1904), p. 133: in 1733, a certain Johann Schwerzeger "said he has seen his whole life, and every sin he had committed, even those he had quite forgotten."

38. Penfield, *Mystery of the Mind*.

39. Long, *Evidence of the Afterlife*, pp. 115–16.

40. As quoted in Herbert Thurston, "Memory and Imminent Death," *The Month* 165 (1935): 53.

41. Robert Crookall, *The Supreme Adventure: Analyses of Psychic Communications* (Cambridge, UK: James Clarke & Co., 1961), p. 88.

42. Long, *Evidence of the Afterlife*, p. 114.

43. As quoted in Thurston, "Memory and Imminent Death," p. 51.

44. Elnathan Parr, *The Grounds of Diuinitie: Plainely discouering the Mysteries of Christian Religion, propounded Familiarly in Diuers Questions and Answeres* (London: N. Okes for Samuel Man, 1614), p. 237.

45. Personal conversation, May 1990. Cf. Hans Urs von Balthasar, "The Judgment of the Son of Man," in *The Von Balthasar Reader*, ed. Medard Kehl and Werner Lösert (New York: Crossroad, 1982), p. 415.

46. In Pseudo Ghazali, *The Precious Pearl*, two angels interrogate the dead as soon as they've been buried. If they return the right answers, they already enjoy a taste of paradise; see Jane Idleman Smith, *The Precious Pearl: A Translation from the Arabic,* Studies in World Religions 1 (Missoula, MT: Scholars Press, 1979), pp. 33–34.

47. S. G. F. Brandon, *The Judgment of the Dead: The Idea of Life after Death in the Major Religions* (New York: Charles Scribner's Sons, 1967), pp. 182–84.

48. *Kierkegaard's Journals and Notebooks,* vol. 2: *Journals EE-KK,* ed. Neils Jørgen Cappelørn et al. (Princeton, NJ/Oxford: Princeton University Press, 2008), p. 179.

49. I attempted this in my first book, *The End of the Ages Has Come: An Early Interpretation of the Passion and Resurrection of Jesus* (Philadelphia: Fortress, 1985); reprint edition by Wipf and Stock, 2013.

50. Calvin, *Institutes* 2.16.18.

51. Father Martin von Cochem, *The Four Last Things: Death. Judgment. Hell. Heaven* (New York/Cincinnati/Chicago: Benziger Brothers, 1899), pp. 27–18.

52. John Pearson, *An Exposition of the Creed*, vol. 2, new ed. (London: Baynes and Son/ Priestley and Weale, 1821), p. 180.

Notes to Chapter 4

1. George Orwell, *Animal Farm* (New York: Harcourt, Brace, 1946), p. 27.

2. Bertrand Russell, *Why I Am Not a Christian: And Other Essays on Religion and Related Subjects* (New York: Simon & Schuster, 1957), p. 90.

3. Mark Johnston, *Surviving Death* (Princeton/Oxford: Princeton University Press, 2010), p. 2.

4. See Chapter 2 above. Note also the books of Braude and Pearson: see Notes to Chapter 1, note 14.

5. Francis Newman, *Phases of Faith* (New York: Humanities Press, 1970; reprint of 1850 edition), p. 136 (italics deleted).

6. Nicholas Lash, "Eternal Life: Life 'after Death'?," *The Heythrop Journal* 19 (1978): 282.

7. Martin Heidegger, *Being and Time* (New York: Harper & Row, 1962), p. 435.

8. Philip José Farmer, "Religion and Myths," in *The Visual Encyclopedia of Science Fiction*, ed. Brian Ash (New York: Harmony Books, 1977), p. 223.

9. Josephus, *Jewish War* 2.157.

10. Johann Gerhard, *Loci theologici: cum pro adstruenda veritate tum pro destruenda quorumvis contradicentium falsitate per theses nervose solide et copiose explicati*, 22 vols. (Tübingen: I. G. Cottae, 1763–89), 19:302.

11. Albert Einstein, *The World as I See It* (New York: Philosophical Library, 1949), p. 27.

12. Gregory Nazianzen, *Oratio* 42.12.

13. Azim F. Shariff and Ara Norenzayan, "Mean Gods Make Good People: Different Views," *The International Journal for the Psychology of Religion* 21 (2011): 85–96.

14. The quotations are from William Booth, "Salvation for Both Worlds," *All the World* 5 (January 1889): 1–6.

15. Robert D. Putnam and David E. Campbell, *American Grace: How Religion Divides and Unites Us* (New York: Simon & Schuster, 2010), pp. 443–92.

16. Russell Noyes Jr., Peter Fenwick, Janice Miner Holden, and Sandra Rozan Christian, "Aftereffects of Pleasurable Western Adult Near-Death Experiences," in *The Handbook of Near-Death Experiences: Thirty Years of Investigation*, ed. Janice Miner Holden, Bruce Greyson, and Debbie James (Santa Barbara, CA: ABC-Clio, 2009), pp. 41–62.

17. Krister Stendahl, "Immortality Is Too Much and Too Little," in *End of Life*, ed. J. D. Roslansky (Amsterdam/London: North-Holland Publishing Company, 1973), pp. 73–83.

18. Herman Pleij, *Dreaming of Cockaigne: Medieval Fantasies of the Perfect Life* (New York: Columbia University Press, 1997).

19. Ludwig Feuerbach, *The Essence of Christianity* (New York: Harper & Brothers Publishers, 1957), p. 184.

20. Plato, *Phaedo* 63.

21. William Whitaker, *An Answere to the Ten Reasons of Edmund Campian the Iesuit: In Confidence wherof he offered Disputation to the Ministers of the Church of England, in the Controversie of Faith* (London: Felix Kyngston, 1606), p. 106.

22. Francis Turretin, *Institutes of Elenctic Theology*, vol. 3: *Eighteenth through Twentieth Topics* (Phillipsburg, NJ: P&R Publishing, 1997), p. 617.

23. John Rogers, *A Discourse of Christian Watchfulnesse: Preparing how to Liue, how to Die, and to be Discharged at the Day of Iudgement, and so Enioy Life Eternall* (London: William Jones, 1620), p. 356.

24. Peter Berger, "New York City 1976: A Signal of Transcendence," in *Facing Up to Modernity: Excursions in Society, Politics, and Religion* (New York: Basic Books, 1977), pp. 211–20.

25. The statistic is from Robert Wuthnow, *The God Problem: Expressing Faith and*

Being Reasonable (Berkeley, CA/Los Angeles/London: University of California Press, 2012), p. 155. Cf. p. 182 and the literature to which he refers there. Wuthnow's interviews with Americans (see *The God Problem*, pp. 154–212) reveal how thoughtful and reflective many are regarding this subject. On p. 169 he remarks: "among adults in the United States, a majority says they have spent a lot of time thinking about what heaven is like and another third have spent some time thinking about it."

26. John B. Cobb, "The Resurrection of the Soul," *Harvard Theological Review* 80 (1987): 213–27.

27. Grace M. Jantzen, "Do We Need Immorality?," *Modern Theology* 1 (1984): 38.

28. G. K. Chesterton, *Charles Dickens: A Critical Study* (New York: Dodd Mead & Co., 1906), p. 89.

29. Johannes Weiss, *Jesus' Proclamation of the Kingdom of God* (Philadelphia: Fortress, 1971); Albert Schweitzer, *The Quest of the Historical Jesus: A Critical Study of Its Progress from Reimarus to Wrede*, 2nd ed. (London: A. & C. Black, 1931).

30. For interested readers, I have made the case for this in Dale C. Allison Jr., *Constructing Jesus: Memory, Imagination, and History* (Grand Rapids, MI: Baker Academic, 2010).

31. Schweitzer, *Quest*, p. 400.

32. Gustavo Gutiérrez, *The God of Life* (Maryknoll, NY: Orbis Books, 1991), p. 120.

33. Johann Baptist Metz, "Thesen zum theologischen Ort der Befreiungstheologie," in *Die Theologie der Befreiung: Hoffnung oder Gefahr für die Kirche*, ed. Johann Baptist Metz (Düsseldorf: Patmos, 1986), p. 152.

34. Peter Brown, "The Rise and Function of the Holy Man in Late Antiquity," *Journal of Roman Studies* 61 (1971): 80–101.

35. Roderick Firth, "Ethical Absolutism and the Ideal Observer," *Philosophy and Phenomenological Research* 12 (1952): 317–45.

36. John Rawls, *A Theory of Justice* (Cambridge, MA: Harvard University Press, 1971).

Notes to Chapter 5

1. Jeremiah Drexelius, [Jeremias Drexel], *The Reflections on Eternity*, ed. Henry Peter Dunster (London: James Burns, 1844), p. 184.

2. Robert Bolton, *Mr. Boltons Last and Learned Worke of the Foure Last Things: Death, Judgement, Hell, and Heauen* (London: George Miller, 1633), pp. 99–100.

3. J. Furniss, *The Sight of Hell*, Books for Children and Young Readers, Book X (Dublin: James Duffy and Co., n.d.), p. 21.

4. https://archive.org/details/sightofhell661furn; accessed June 9, 2014. This Web site includes an 1855 endorsement from the Vicar General of Dublin, William Meagher: "I have carefully read over this Little Volume for Children and have found nothing whatsoever in it contrary to the doctrine of the Holy Faith; but, on the contrary, a great deal to charm, instruct and edify our youthful classes."

5. Henry James Coleridge, *The Life and Letters of Saint Francis Xavier*, 2 vols., 3rd ed. (London: Burns & Oates, 1876), 2:347.

6. Coleridge, *Life and Letters of Saint Francis Xavier*, 2:337.

7. Incidentally, when generous, consoling answers appeared, as they sometimes did,

in a sermon or theological treatise, Roman apologists were quick to pounce; see Peter Marshall, *Beliefs and the Dead in Reformation England* (Oxford: Oxford University Press, 2004), pp. 205–10. Marshall refers among other things to William Wright, *A Briefe Treatise in which, Is made playne, that Catholikes liuing and dying in their Profession, may be saued, by the Iudgment of the most famous and Learned Protestants that euer were. Against a Minister [N.E.] who in his Epistle exhorteth an Honourable Person, to forsake her ancient Catholike Roman Religion, & to become one of his new-found-out Protestant Congregation* (St Omer: English College Press, 1623; reprint ed.: Menston, Yorkshire: The Scholar Press, 1973).

8. Albert Barnes, *Practical Sermons Designed for Vacant Congregations and Families* (Philadelphia: Henry Perkins, 1841), pp. 123–25.

9. Charles Hodge, *Systematic Theology*, 3 vols. (New York: Scribner, Armstrong, 1874), 3:870.

10. Augustine, *City of God* 21.12.

11. Oecumenius, *Commentary on Revelation* on 9:5–6.

12. John Henry Newman, *An Essay in Aid of a Grammar of Assent* (London: Burns & Oates, 1881), pp. 422, 502–3.

13. Kallistos Ware, "One Body in Christ: Death and the Communion of Saints," *Sobornost* n.s. 3/2 (1981): 179–91.

14. So already Samuel Richardson, *A Discourse of the Torments of Hell: The Foundation and Pillars thereof Discovered, Searched, Shaken and Removed. With Many Infallible Proofs, that there is Not to be a Punishment after this Life for Any to Endure that Shall Never End* (London: n.p., 1658); see the reprint edition, *The Doctrine of Eternal Hell Torments Overthrown* (Boston: James B. Dow, 1833), esp. pp. 14–16.

15. John Tillotson, *A Sermon Preach'd before the Queen at White-Hall, March 7th, 1689–90* (London: Brabazon Aylmer, 1690).

16. See *A Jonathan Edwards Reader*, ed. John E. Smith, Harry S. Stout, and Kenneth P. Minkema (New Haven, CT/London: Yale University Press, 1995), p. 283.

17. George Howard Sabine, ed., *The Works of Gerrard Winstanley* (Ithaca, NY: Cornell University Press, 1941), p. 83.

18. Thomas Newton, "Dissertation LX. On the Final State and Condition of Men," in *The Works of the Right Reverend Thomas Newton* (London: John, Francis, and Charles Rivington, 1782), p. 729.

19. Charles Darwin, *The Autobiography of Charles Darwin, 1809-1882: With Original Omissions Restored* (New York: Harcourt, Brace, 1959), p. 87.

20. As quoted in *Voices of Unbelief: Documents from Atheists and Agnostics*, ed. Dale McGowan (Santa Barbara, CA: Greenwood, 2012), p. 108, n.2.

21. W. E. Gladstone, *Studies Subsidiary to the Works of Bishop Butler* (New York: Macmillan & Co., 1896), p. 206.

22. Thomas J. Sawyer, *Endless Punishment: In the Very Words of Its Advocates* (Boston: Universalist Publishing House, 1891), p. 23.

23. J. W. Wenham, *Facing Hell: The Story of a Nobody. An Autobiography, 1913-1996* (Carlisle: Paternoster, 1998), p. 254.

24. David L. Edwards and John Stott, *Essentials: A Liberal-Evangelical Dialogue* (London: Hodder & Stoughton, 1988), p. 314.

25. Howard Dorgan, *In the Hands of a Happy God: The "No-hellers" of Central Appalachia* (Knoxville: University of Tennessee Press, 1997).

26. For selections, see Mary Boyce, *Textual Sources for the Study of Zoroastrianism* (Chicago: University of Chicago Press, 1990), pp. 84–89.

27. William Crockett, ed., *Four Views on Hell* (Grand Rapids, MI: Zondervan, 1992); Robert A. Peterson, *Hell on Trial: The Case for Eternal Punishment* (Phillipsburg, NJ: P&R Publishing, 1995); David George Moore, *The Battle for Hell: A Survey and Evaluation of Evangelicals' Growing Attraction to the Doctrine of Annihilationism* (Lanham, MD: University Press of America, 1995); Edward William Fudge and Robert A. Peterson, *Two Views of Hell: A Biblical and Theological Dialogue* (Downers Grove, IL: InterVarsity Press, 2000); Christopher W. Morgan and Robert A. Peterson, eds., *Hell Under Fire* (Grand Rapids, MI: Zondervan, 2004); Joel Bunting, ed., *The Problem of Hell: A Philosophical Anthology* (Farnham, Surrey, UK/Burlington, VT: Ashgate, 2010); Christopher W. Morgan and Robert A. Peterson, eds., *Is Hell for Real or Does Everyone Go to Heaven?* (Grand Rapids, MI: Zondervan, 2011); Francis Chan and Preston Sprinkle, *Erasing Hell: What God Said about Eternity, and the Things We've Made Up* (Colorado Springs, CO: David C. Cook, 2011); Christopher Hudson, *Heaven and Hell: Are They Real?* (Nashville: Thomas Nelson, 2014).

28. Origen, *On First Principles* 2.10.4.

29. Richard Swineburne, "A Theodicy of Heaven and Hell," in *The Existence and Nature of God*, ed. Alfred J. Freddoso (Notre Dame, IN: University of Notre Dame Press, 1983), pp. 37–54; Jonathan L. Kvanvig, *The Problem of Hell* (New York/Oxford: Oxford University Press, 1993).

30. Emanuel Swedenborg, *Concerning Heaven and Its Wonders and Concerning Hell: From Things Heard and Seen* (Boston: Carter, 1844). For Swedenborg, neither God nor the devil is in charge of hell; rather, human beings there torment themselves and one another.

31. The poet Shelley certainly associated the two; see his "Essay on the Devil and Devils," in *Shelley's Prose*, ed. David Lee Clark (Albuquerque: University of Mexico Press, 1954), p. 268.

32. Norbert Elias, *The History of Manners: The Civilising Process*, 2 vols. (Oxford: Basil Blackwell, 1982).

33. Pieter Spierenburg, *The Spectacle of Suffering: Executions and the Evolution of Repression* (Cambridge: Cambridge University Press, 1984).

34. Representative here is the educational philosophy of the nineteenth-century Roman Catholic Don Bosco. He sought to exclude from education "every violent punishment" and "even mild punishments" through a system "based on reason, religion and loving-kindness." See his essay "The Preventive System in the Education of the Young," available online at www.sdb.org.hk/cp/p01/p01c05/p01c05012.doc (accessed 7/11/14).

35. William G. T. Shedd, *The Doctrine of Endless Punishment* (New York: Charles Scribner's Sons, 1886), p. 135.

36. Darius Rejali, *Torture and Democracy* (Princeton: Princeton University Press, 2007).

37. Augustine, *The Correction of the Donatists* 2.11.

38. Aquinas, *Exposition of Job* on 10:4, 7.

39. Joannes Graevius, *Tribunal Reformatum: in quo sanioris et tutioris iustitiae via iu-*

dici Christiano in processu criminali commonstratur, reiecta et fugata torture, Sumptibus I (Wolfenbüttel: Chrisophori Meisneri, 1737).

40. Robert Held, *Inquisition: A Bilingual Guide to the Exhibition of Torture Instruments from the Middle Ages to the Industrial Revolution, Presented in Various European Cities in 1983–1987* (Florence: Qua d'Arno, 1985).

41. *The Psalms and Hymns of Rev. Isaac Watts* (new ed.: London: Henry G. Bohn, 1845), p. 466 (Hymn 44).

42. Lyman Abbott, *Reminiscences* (Boston/New York: Houghton Mifflin Company, 1915), p. 469.

43. *Collatio legum mosaicarum et romanarum* 5.3.1.

44. Note *Mishnah Terumoth* 7.2; *Sanhedrin* 7.2; 9.1; *Babylonian Talmud 'Abodah Zarah* 17b–18a.

45. Robert W. Funk, Roy W. Hoover, and the Jesus Seminar, *The Five Gospels: The Search for the Authentic Words of Jesus* (New York: Macmillan, 1993).

46. Lily Dougall and Cyril W. Emmet, *The Lord of Thought: A Study of the Problems Which Confronted Jesus and the Solution He Offered* (London: SCM, 1922).

47. Percy Dearmer, *The Legend of Hell: An Examination of the Idea of Everlasting Punishment, with a Chapter on Apocalyptic* (London: Cassell, 1929).

48. On Shelley's ideas about hell, see my book *Resurrecting Jesus: The Earliest Christian Tradition and Its Interpreters* (New York/London: T&T Clark, 2005), pp. 100–110.

49. See further Allison, *Resurrecting Jesus,* pp. 56–90.

50. Ilaria Ramelli and David Konstan, *Terms for Eternity: Aionios and Aidios in Classical and Christian Texts* (Piscataway, NJ: Gorgias Press, 2007), p. 238.

51. John Wesley, "Of Hell," sermon 73 in the 1872 collection of Wesley's sermons edited by Thomas Jackson; available online at: http://www.umcmission.org/Find-Resources/John-Wesley-Sermons/Sermon-73-Of-Hell (accessed June 10, 2014).

52. Nicolas Berdyaev, *The Destiny of Man* (New York: Harper & Row, 1960), p. 266.

53. Isaac of Nineveh, *The Ascetical Homilies of Saint Isaac the Syrian,* rev. 2nd ed. (Boston: Holy Transfiguration Monastery, 2011), p. 387.

54. Isaac, *Homilies,* p. 379.

55. John H. Gerstner, *Jonathan Edwards on Heaven and Hell* (Grand Rapids, MI: Baker, 1980), p. 93.

56. Nicolas Berdyaev, *Dream and Reality: An Essay in Autobiography* (New York: Macmillan, 1951), p. 293.

57. Isaac of Nineveh, *"The Second Part," Chapters IV–XLI,* ed. Sebastian Brock, Corpus Scriptorum Christianorum Orientalium 555, Scriptores Syri 225 (Louvain: Peeters, 1995), pp. 163, 172, 165.

58. Philo, *The Unchangeableness of God* 76.

Notes to Chapter 6

1. John Calvin, "Reply by Calvin to Cardinal Sadoleto's Letter," in *Tracts and Treatises on the Reformation of the Church,* vol. 1 (Grand Rapids, MI: Eerdmans, 1958), p. 33.

2. H. R. Mackintosh, *Immortality and the Future: The Christian Doctrine of Eternal Life,* 2nd ed. (London/New York/Toronto: Hodder & Stoughton, 1917), p. 100.

3. Colleen McDannell and Bernhard Lang, *Heaven: A History* (New Haven, CT/London: Yale University Press, 1988), p. 352.

4. Mark Twain, from an unpublished book review of Geo W. Warder, *The Cities of the Sun* (New York: G. W. Dillingham, 1901).

5. Aquinas, *Summa Contra Gentiles* 3.62.

6. Bernard Williams, "The Makropoulos Case: Reflections on the Tedium of Immortality," in *Problems of the Self* (Cambridge, UK: Cambridge University Press, 1973), pp. 82-100. For an effective response, see John Martin Fischer, "Immortality," in *The Oxford Handbook of Philosophy of Death*, ed. Ben Bradley, Fred Feldman, and Jens Johannson (Oxford: Oxford University Press, 2013), pp. 336-54.

7. Heinrich Denzinger, *Kompendium der Glaubenskenntnisse und kirchlichen Lehrentscheidungen*, ed. Peter Hünermann (Freiburg im Breisgau: Herder, 2001), p. 406.

8. The quoted words are from the first stanza of his hymn, "O Quanta Qualia," known in English as "O What Their Joy and Their Glory Must Be."

9. Mark 16:19; Luke 24:51; Acts 1:11.

10. John 17:24; 2 Cor. 5:8; Phil. 1:23.

11. See the discussion in Chapter 2.

12. N. T. Wright, "Response to Markus Bockmuehl," in Nicholas Perrin and Richard Hays, eds., *Jesus, Paul, and the People of God: A Theological Dialogue with N. T. Wright* (Downers Grove, IL: IVP Academic, 2011), pp. 231-32.

13. Hans Küng, *Eternal Life? Life after Death as a Medical, Philosophical, and Theological Problem* (New York: Doubleday & Co., 1984), p. 143.

14. Geddes MacGregor, *Angels: Ministers of Grace* (New York: Paragon House, 1988), p. 140.

15. Tony Walter, "Angels not Souls: Popular Religion in the Online Mourning for British Celebrity Jade Goody," *Religion* 41 (2011): 29-51.

16. Robert Wuthnow, *After Heaven: Spirituality in America since the 1950s* (Berkeley/Los Angeles/London: University of California Press, 1998), p. 128.

17. Origen, *Commentary on Matthew* 17.30.

18. Cf. Deut. 32:8; Job 1:6; 2:1; 38:7; Ps. 89:7.

19. 4QSongs of the Sage[b] (4Q511) frag. 35.

20. Philo, *Sacrifices of Cain and Abel* 5.

21. *The Shepherd of Hermas, Similitudes* 9.27.3.

22. Solomon Schechter, ed., *Midrash Ha-gadol* (Cambridge, UK: Cambridge University Press, 1902), p. 123, as cited in Louis Ginzberg, *Legends of the Jews,* 2 vols. (Philadelphia: Jewish Publication Society, 2003), vol. 1, p. 122.

23. E.g., *3 Baruch* 11:7; *Testament of Isaac* 4:27.

24. E.g., Job 5:1; Dan. 4:17; Zech. 14:5; Mark 8:38.

25. See the references in Notes to Chapter 6, note 18.

26. E.g., Ps. 31:23; 34:9; Matt. 5:9; Gal. 3:26; Heb. 6:10.

27. Evagrius Ponticus, *The Praktikos and Chapters on Prayer* (Kalamazoo, MI: Cistercian Publications, 1972), p. 78.

28. Note 1 Kings 22:21; Tob. 12:13-15; Luke 1:19.

29. Tertullian, *Against Marcion* 3.24.

30. Clement of Alexandria, *Eklogai Prophetikai* 57.

31. Origen, *Commentary on John* 10:18 (30).

32. Origen, *Homilies on Leviticus* 9.11.

33. A. Ferrua, "Questioni di epigrafia Eretica Romana," *Rivista di archeologia cristiana* 21 (1945): 165–67.

34. As quoted in Steven Chase, *Angelic Spirituality: Medieval Perspectives on the Ways of Angels* (New York: Paulist Press, 2002), p. 55.

35. As quoted in Steven Chase, *Angelic Wisdom: The Cherubim and the Grace of Contemplation in Richard of St. Victor* (Notre Dame, IN/London: University of Notre Dame Press, 1995), p. 115.

36. Thomas Burnet, *A Treatise concerning the State of Departed Souls, Before, and At, and After the Resurrection*, 2nd ed. (London: A. Bettesworth and C. Hitch, 1739), p. 182.

37. Elizabeth Stuart Phelps, *The Gates Ajar*, 51st ed. (Boston: Houghton, Mifflin and Company, 1882). In a slightly earlier work by Eunice Hale Cobb, *Memoir of James Arthur Cobb* (Boston: Sylvanus Cobb, 1852), p. 88, a dying nine-year-old boy is reported to have said, on his deathbed, "When I am an angel, I shall not suffer as I now do."

38. The line of thought developed in the previous paragraphs has a close parallel in Richard Saunder, *Angelographia, sive, Pneumata leityrgika, Pneumatologia: or, A Discourse of Angels: Their Nature and Office, or Ministry* (London: Thomas Parkhurst, 1701), pp. 271–316. The complete subtitle includes the phrase "especially for the promoting of an angelical life."

39. Matt. 28:3; cf. Dan. 10:6; Acts 12:7; 2 Cor. 11:14; Rev. 10:1.

40. See further the reflections of MacGregor, *Angels*, pp. 195–202.

41. McDannell and Lang, *Heaven.*

42. Ann Douglas, "Heaven Our Home: Consolation Literature in the Northern United States, 1830–1880," *American Quarterly* 26 (1974): 512.

43. Tertullian, *Monogamy* 10.

44. Cyprian, *De mortalitate* 26.

45. F. Bisconti, "'Sulla concezione figurativa dell' 'habitat' paradisiaco: A propositio di un affresco romano poco noto," *Rivista di Archeologia Christiana* 66 (1990): 25–80.

46. As quoted in Johannes Sledianus, *The General History of the Reformation of the Church, from the Errors and Corruptions of the Church of Rome* (London: Edw. Jones, 1689), p. 362.

47. Thomas Becon, "Selections from The Sick Man's Salve," in *Writings of the Rev. Thomas Becon, Chaplain to Archbishop Cranmer, and Prebendary of Canterbury* (London: The Religious Tract Society, n.d.), p. 358. The quoted words are from a tract first published in 1560.

48. William Ford, *A Sermon Preached at Constantinople: In the Vines of Perah, at the Funerall of the Vertuous and Admired Lady Anne Glouer, Sometime Wife to the Honourable Knight Sir Thomas Glouer, and then Ambassadour Ordinary for his Maiesty of Great Britaine* (London: Edvyard Griffin, 1616), p. 61.

49. John Donne, *Selected Prose* (London: Penguin, 1967), p. 158.

50. Matt. 8:11–12; Mark 14:25; Luke 13:28–29.

51. Philip F. Esler, *New Testament Theology: Communion and Community* (Minneapolis: Fortress, 2005), p. 198.

52. H. Harbaugh, *The Heavenly Recognition; or, An Earnest and Scripture Discussion of the Question, Will we know our Friends in Heaven?*, 2nd ed. (Philadelphia: Lindsay & Blakiston, 1860).

53. See, e.g., David Lester et al., "What Is the Afterlife Like? Undergraduate Beliefs about the Afterlife," *Omega* 44 (2001–2002): 113–26; see also Robert Wuthnow, *The God Problem: Expressing Faith and Being Reasonable* (Berkeley, CA/Los Angeles/London: University of California Press, 2012), pp. 189–94, who records a lot of popular uncertainty about the prospect.

54. John Bunyan, *The Pilgrim's Progress from this World to that Which is to Come*, ed. James Blanton Wharey; rev. by Roger Sharrock, 2nd ed. (Oxford: Clarendon, 1960), p. 292.

55. Demosthenes, *Third Olynthiac* 19.

56. Aquinas, *Summa Theologica,* first part of the second part, question 4, article 8.

57. William Perkins, *A Golden Chaine, or The description of Theologie: Containing the Order of the Causes of Saluation and Damnation, according to Gods Woord* (Cambridge: John Legat, 1592), p. 518.

58. See John McManners, *Death and the Enlightenment: Changing Attitudes to Death among Christians and Unbelievers in Eighteenth-Century France* (Oxford/New York: Clarendon Press, 1981), p. 131.

59. John Gill, *A Body of Divinity* (Grand Rapids, MI: Sovereign Grace, 1971), p. 692.

60. Joseph Hall, *Susurrium cum Deo. Soliloquies: or, Holy Self-Conferences of the Devout Soul,* in *The Works of the Right Reverend Joseph Hall,* ed. Josiah Pratt, vol. 6 (London: C. Whittingham, 1808), p. 364.

61. Augustine, *City of God* 29.30.

62. As quoted in Herman Pleij, *Dreaming of Cockaigne: Medieval Fantasies of the Perfect Life* (New York: Columbia University Press, 1997), p. 195.

63. As quoted in Archimandrite Panteleimon, *Eternal Mysteries beyond the Grave: Orthodox Teachings on the Existence of God, the Immortality of the Soul, and Life beyond the Grave* (Jordanville, NY: Holy Trinity Publications, 2012), pp. 129–30 (from *Lives of the Saints,* October 2).

64. See Herbert Musurillo, *The Acts of the Christian Martyrs* (Oxford: Clarendon Press, 1972), p. 121.

65. As preserved in Plutarch, *Moralia* 120C.

66. These two quotations are from Meg Maxwell and Verena Tschudin, *Seeing the Invisible: Modern Religious and Other Transcendent Experiences* (London: ARKANA, 1990), pp. 52–53.

67. Augustine, *City of God* 22.29.

68. I take the following from Peter Fenwick and Elizabeth Fenwick, *The Truth in the Light: An Investigation of Over 300 Near-Death Experiences* (New York: Berkeley Books, 1997), pp. 75–77.

69. Carl B. Becker, "The Pure Land Revisited: Sino-Japanese Meditations and Near-Death Experiences of the Next World," *Journal of Near-Death Studies* 4 (1984): 51–68; Karlis Osis and Erlendur Haraldsson, *At the Hour of Death* (New York: Avon, 1977), pp. 60–82.

70. See Farnaz Masumian, "World Religions and Near Death Experiences," in *The Handbook of Near-Death Experiences: Thirty Years of Investigation,* ed. Janice Miner Holden, Bruce Greyson, and Debbie James (Santa Barbara, CA: ABC-Clio, 2009), p. 167; Gregory Shushan, *Conceptions of the Afterlife in Early Civilizations: Universalism, Constructivism and Near-Death Experience* (London/New York: Continuum, 2009), p. 158.

71. *The Zohar Pritzker Edition,* vol. 3, *Va-Yḥi* 1:218a (translation and commentary by Daniel C. Matt; Stanford, CA: Stanford University Press, 2006), p. 315.

72. The interested reader might wish to consult my review of the literature: Dale C. Allison Jr., *Resurrecting Jesus: The Earliest Christian Tradition and Its Interpreters* (New York/London: T&T Clark, 2005), pp. 269–99.

73. This and the following two accounts are from Bill Guggenheim and Judy Guggenheim, *Hello from Heaven* (New York: Bantam, 1995), pp. 77, 98, 104.

74. Aniela Jaffé, *Apparitions and Precognition: A Study from the Point of View of C. G. Jung's Analytical Psychology* (New Hyde Park, NY: University Books, 1963), p. 63.

75. Jaffé, *Apparitions,* pp. 56–57.

76. The point is of course much too large to receive attention here, but I may appeal to the brilliant essay of David J. Hufford, "Beings without Bodies: An Experience-Centered Theory of the Belief in Spirits," in *Out of the Ordinary: Folklore and the Supernatural,* ed. Barbara Walker (Logan, UT: Utah State University Press, 1995), pp. 11–45; also now Heiner Schwenke, *Transzendente Begegnungen: Phänomenologie und Metakritik* (Basel: Schwabe, 2014).

77. Charles R. Brown, "Immortality," in *We Believe in Immortality: Affirmations by One Hundred Men and Women,* ed. Sydney Strong (New York: Coward-McCann, 1929), p. 105.

78. James H. Moorhead, "Apocalypticism in Mainstream Protestantism, 1800 to the Present," in *The Encyclopedia of Apocalypticism, Volume 3: Apocalypticism in the Modern Period and the Contemporary Age,* ed. Stephen J. Stein (New York: Continuum, 1998), pp. 103–4.

Index of Names and Subjects